ALSO BY ISRAEL FINKELSTEIN AND
NEIL ASHER SILBERMAN

———

*The Bible Unearthed: Archaeology's New Vision of Ancient
Israel and the Origin of Its Sacred Texts*

DAVID AND SOLOMON

*In Search of the Bible's Sacred Kings
and the Roots of the Western Tradition*

Israel Finkelstein

and

Neil Asher Silberman

FREE PRESS

NEW YORK   LONDON   TORONTO   SYDNEY

FREE PRESS
A Division of Simon & Schuster, Inc.
1230 Avenue of the Americas
New York, NY 10020

FREE PRESS and colophon are trademarks
of Simon & Schuster, Inc.

First Free Press trade paperback edition 2007

For information about special discounts for bulk purchases,
please contact Simon & Schuster Special Sales at
1-800-456-6798 or business@simonandschuster.com

Manufactured in the United States of America

1   3   5   7   9   10   8   6   4   2

The Library of Congress has cataloged the hardcover edition as follows:
Finkelstein, Israel.
David and Solomon : in search of the Bible's sacred kings and the roots of
the western tradition / Israel Finkelstein and Neil Asher Silberman.
p.   cm.
Includes bibliographic references (p.   ) and index.
1. Bible—Antiquities. 2. Excavations (Archaeology)—Palestine—History.
3. Christianity—Influence. 4. Palestine—Antiquities.
BS621.F56 2006
222/.067 21   2005049490
ISBN-13: 978-0-7432-4362-9
ISBN-10: 0-7432-4362-5
ISBN-13: 978-0-7432-4363-6 (Pbk)
ISBN-10: 0-7432-4363-3 (Pbk)

CONTENTS

Prologue: The Shepherd and the Slingstone   1

Introduction: David, Solomon, and the
    Western Tradition   5

PART I   RECOVERING HISTORY

1. Tales of the Bandit   31

2. The Madness of Saul   61

3. Murder, Lust, and Betrayal   91

PART II   THE EVOLUTION OF A LEGEND

4. Temple and Dynasty   121

5. Solomon's Wisdom?   151

6. Challenging Goliath   179

PART III   HOW THE LEGEND SHAPED HISTORY

7. Patron Saints of the Temple   211

8. Messianic Visions   233

   Epilogue: Symbols of Authority   253

Appendixes

1. DID DAVID EXIST?   261

2. THE SEARCH FOR DAVID
   AND SOLOMON'S JERUSALEM   267

3. SOLOMON'S FABLED KINGDOM   275

4. KING SOLOMON'S COPPER
   INDUSTRY?   282

5. DISMANTLING THE SHRINES   285

6. TYRANTS, CITY LEAGUES, AND
   MERCENARY BODYGUARDS   289

7. DEPORTEES, RETURNEES, AND THE
   BORDERS OF YEHUD   293

Bibliography and Suggested Reading   297

Acknowledgments   325

Index   327

DAVID AND
SOLOMON

The Shepherd and the Slingstone

THE SMALL, REMOTE ELAH VALLEY IN SOUTHERN ISRAEL is a place of unique biblical inspiration. According to the famous account in 1 Samuel 17, its harsh, treeless landscape of open fields and low hills was the site of a dramatic confrontation that has remained vivid in the consciousness of the western world.

Even today, in the silence of the valley, one can still imagine the epic scene. On one side were the massed Philistine armies, heavily armored, confident, and ready for battle. On the other side was a volunteer force of Israelite peasants hastily mustered from their villages and sheepfolds, determined to defend their land and their faith.

The fearsome Philistine giant Goliath strode forward. Armed with a sword, javelin, and heavy spear and wearing a coat of mail and bronze helmet, he cursed his lightly armed Israelite opponents and challenged them to choose a single warrior to fight him: "If he is able to fight with me and kill me," Goliath thundered, "then we will be your servants; but if I prevail against him and kill him, then you shall be our servants and serve us."

For forty days, the Philistine giant emerged from the ranks of his waiting army and shouted out his challenge. The Israelites were "dismayed and greatly afraid" and none dared to take it up. Yet a handsome young shepherd named David, who had been sent to the battlefield by his father to bring provisions to his older brothers, suddenly arose as an unlikely savior. Armed only with a shepherd's staff and a bag of slingstones, he approached the mighty Goliath. The arrogant Philistine laughed in scorn at his puny opponent, but David held his ground and boldly proclaimed: "You come to me with a sword and with a spear and with a javelin; but I come to you in the name of the LORD of hosts, the God of the armies of Israel, whom you have defied." David then took a stone from his pouch and slung it. The stone struck the towering giant squarely in the forehead, and Goliath fell to the ground with a thud.

When the Philistines saw that their great champion had been killed by the young shepherd, they fled in panic. David snatched Goliath's sword and used it to take the giant's head as a trophy of Israel's great victory. The men of Israel and Judah "rose with a shout" and pursued the retreating Philistines all the way back to their own territory. The threat to the independence of Israel had been decisively answered, and David's divinely guided career as defender, leader, and ultimately king of all Israel had begun.

The victory of David over Goliath is one of the most memorable scenes in the Bible, yet it arouses many intriguing questions: Did it really happen? Can we consider it to be a reliable historical account? Was the story written in the time of David or many years later? Is there any way of determining when it was composed? Can we detect hidden layers in the story? Why does the Bible, in an often-overlooked passage, credit *another* hero with the killing of Goliath? Why does the story so strongly resemble Homeric descriptions of mythic duels between Greek and Trojan heroes? Is it just a simple tale or does it conceal the circumstances and motivation for its composition? What is its wider significance for understanding the evolution of Judeo-Christian theology?

This book seeks to answer all these questions, not only for David and Goliath, but for the entire story of David and his son Solomon and their fabled careers. For the biblical tale of David and Solomon has been read for many centuries as a lesson about how courage, faith, and wisdom can redeem a people from oppression and establish their independence and prosperity. These are the twin goals that every people longs for and that every just leader strives to attain. The story of David and Solomon's establishment of a powerful, prosperous United Monarchy of Israel has provided a model of righteous leadership enshrined in the Judeo-Christian tradition and in every society that has drawn its moral authority from it. The value of examining this biblical saga is thus twofold. It can reveal the stages of the authorship of the Hebrew Bible (and the use of its images in the New Testament) over a span of almost a thousand years. It can also help to explain why the images of David and Solomon have been—and remain—so powerful in the western tradition by uncovering the historical reasons why the story developed as it did.

Our challenge will be to provide a new perspective on the David and Solomon story by presenting the flood of new archaeological information about the rise and development of the ancient society in which the biblical tale was formed. We will attempt to separate history from myth; old memories from later elaboration; facts from royal propaganda to trace the evolution of the David and Solomon narrative from its ancient origins to the final compilation of the biblical accounts. By following this path, our search for David and Solomon will reveal the fascinating tension between historical fact and sanctified tradition; in this case, between the reality of Iron Age Judah and the West's still-living legend of ancient Israel's sacred kings.

INTRODUCTION

David, Solomon, and the Western Tradition

Ancient Legends, the Bible, and Archaeology

FROM THE SOARING CATHEDRALS AND ELEGANT PALACES of medieval Europe, to the hushed galleries of world famous art museums, to America's backwoods pulpits and Hollywood epics, the story of ancient Israel's sacred kings, David and Solomon, is one of western civilization's most enduring legacies. The figures of David—shepherd, warrior, and divinely protected king—and of his son Solomon—great builder, wise judge, and serene ruler of a vast empire—have become timeless models of righteous leadership under God's sanction. They have shaped western images of kingship and served as models of royal piety, messianic expectation, and national destiny.

Thanks to archaeology, we now—for the first time—can dissect the main elements of the biblical story to see when and how each one emerged. The results of our search may be surprising, for the archaeological discoveries of recent decades have clearly shown how far from the glamorous scriptural portraits the actual world of

David and Solomon was. Yet the legend was not merely a romantic fiction of imaginary personalities and events. It evolved over centuries from a core of authentic memories into a complex and timeless literary creation. In its unforgettable images and dramatic scenes—the battle against Goliath, the rise of David from outlaw to king, the splendor of Solomon's court—the legend of David and Solomon expresses a universal message of national independence and transcendent religious values that people all over the world have come to regard as their own. Yet as we will see, its origins are traceable in the archaeology and history of a single small Iron Age kingdom as it grew from a village society into a complex state.

THE BIBLICAL STORY IN BRIEF

The most elaborate version of the David and Solomon story, contained in a narrative that extends from 1 Samuel to 1 Kings, describes how the people of Israel achieved independence and enjoyed a period of unprecedented prosperity. Attacked and oppressed in their highland villages by the brutal Philistine conquerors from the lowlands, the elders of Israel cried out for a leader who could protect them against their enemies. Until then, the Israelites had been governed in their separate tribes by spirit-filled "judges." At this time of crisis, the venerable prophet Samuel, following God's instructions despite his own misgivings, anointed Saul, a handsome youth of the tribe of Benjamin, to be the first king over all Israel. Saul was a daring military leader, yet he proved to be unstable, subject to deep bouts of depression, impetuous violence, and repeated violations of religious law. God's second choice thus secretly fell to David, son of Jesse, a young shepherd from Judah, who had been summoned to soothe Saul's fits of madness with the music of his lyre.

As the narrative develops, David's grand destiny unfolds, even as Saul continues to reign. On the field of battle against the massed

Philistine armies, David topples the mighty Goliath and earns the acclaim of the nation, enraging King Saul. In a desperate flight into the wilderness to escape from Saul's murderous jealousy, David further proves his leadership, bravery, and skill. As the chief of a roaming band of mighty men, he settles scores, fends off enemy attacks, exacts God's vengeance, and distributes captured booty to the oppressed and poor. When Saul dies on the battlefield, David is proclaimed king of Judah and eventually of all Israel as God's true anointed one, or "messiah." It is a classic tale of the rise of the young hero, a warrior for the true faith and a man of extraordinary charisma, who assumes the mantle of a failed leader and becomes the embodiment of his people's hopes and dreams.

David's subsequent exploits as king of Israel have served as a model for visions of territorial expansion and divine inheritance, over many centuries. In fulfillment of God's promise that Israel would be a great nation, David conquers Jerusalem and makes it his capital, providing a permanent place of honor there for the Ark of the Covenant, which had accompanied Israel in its long wanderings. David and his armies then sweep all of Israel's enemies to defeat and destruction, establishing a vast kingdom that stretches from the Euphrates to the very border of Egypt. Upon his death, David is succeeded by Solomon, his son by the beautiful Bathsheba, who rules the kingdom wisely and ushers in an era of peace and prosperity. It is a stirring narrative of power and divine favor enjoyed by a nation whose rulers have been specially selected by God.

Solomon goes on to build a magnificent Temple in Jerusalem and reigns with justice and intelligence, over a vast bureaucracy, a mighty army, and a great people. Through his international connections and skill in trade and diplomacy, Solomon is celebrated throughout the world as the richest and wisest of kings. He marries a pharaoh's daughter and gains renown as an insightful judge, author of proverbs, and master of knowledge about all the riches of creation—trees, beasts, birds, reptiles, and fish. When the queen of Sheba journeys all the way to Jerusalem from her distant kingdom in Arabia to meet him, "Solomon answered all her questions; there was nothing hidden from the king which he could not explain to her" (1 Kings 10:3). Solomon's image is the ideal convergence of wisdom, opulence, and power in the person of a king. Indeed, Solomon's rule in Jerusalem is a moment when the divine promise comes to its most tangible fulfillment; his reign is a golden age of prosperity, knowledge, and power for all the people of Israel. Forever after, Solomon's rule would be nostalgically recalled as a golden age of spiritual and material fulfillment that might, one day, be experienced again.

Yet in the Bible, both David and Solomon also have great human flaws, as profound as their God-given gifts. During his flight from Saul, David collaborates with the Philistine enemy and undermines Saul's authority by his own great popularity. Immediately after Saul's death, David unconvincingly disavows responsibility for the targeted assassination of Saul's closest supporters and heirs. Later, his marriage to the beautiful Bathsheba comes as the result of an adulterous seduction—and a heartless maneuver to ensure the death of Bathsheba's husband, Uriah, on the battlefield. As the years pass, David seems powerless to control the violent rivalry of his princely sons Amnon and Absalom. When Absalom attempts to oust David from power, the aging king is vulnerable and uncertain—even crying out, when he receives word of Absalom's execution, "Would I had died instead of you, O Absalom, my son, my son!" (2 Samuel 18:33). At various stages in his life, David is a ruthless leader, a greedy lover, a vacillating and sorrowful father. In a word, he is profoundly human, trapped between his destiny and his sins.

In the same way, the biblical Solomon also reveals a darker, weaker side. Solomon eventually betrays his reputation as the pious founder of the Temple, succumbing to the lure of foreign women and gods. His vast harem of Moabite, Ammonite, Edomite, Sidonian, and Hittite wives introduces pagan worship into the holy city. God becomes angry. Once-defeated peoples rise up in rebellion. After Solomon's death, the ten northern tribes of Israel break free and establish a separate kingdom. It is a vivid lesson about how the religious faithlessness of a luxury-loving leader can destroy a golden age.

Yet God had given an eternal, unconditional promise that David's "throne shall be established for ever" (2 Samuel 7:16) and that the Davidic dynasty would never fade away. Even after Solomon's moral collapse and the disintegration of his great kingdom, God assures the people of Israel that he would preserve an eternal inheritance for the descendants of David. One day their affliction would come to an end (1 Kings 11:39). What greater assurance could there be for any people that despite their rulers' human error and weakness, the nation's well-being remained secure?

The biblical portraits of David and Solomon are oversized and unforgettable, painted in bright colors. They are filled with human and theological contradictions, yet God's promise of eternal protection to David and to all his descendants offers the hope that someday a new David or Solomon will arise to usher in a new and even more breathtaking golden age.

THE WEST'S ONCE AND FUTURE KINGS

In the eyes of ancient Israel, David and Solomon were local founding fathers; in the eyes of the Judeo-Christian tradition as it evolved and expanded over centuries, David and Solomon came to represent much more. Embedded in the biblical canon and the traditions of Judaism and Christianity, they are revered as the greatest leaders of God's chosen kingdom of Israel, and as the spiritual forerunners of leaders, princes, and potentates throughout the western world. After the destruction of the Iron Age kingdom of Judah in 586 BCE, the legendary fame of David and Solomon was elaborated and uniquely cherished. Abraham, the great patriarch, slept peacefully in his tomb in Hebron. Moses, the great lawgiver, would never return. But David and Solomon had been the recipients of a divine promise that ensured the people's survival and eventual redemption. The lineage of David, son of Jesse, offered a promise for the future, no matter how grim the present might seem. As expressed in the book of Isaiah:

> *There shall come forth a shoot from the stump of Jesse, and a branch shall grow out of his roots. And the Spirit of the LORD shall rest upon him, the spirit of wisdom and understanding, the spirit of counsel and might, the spirit of knowledge and the fear of the LORD. And his delight shall be in the fear of the LORD. He shall not judge by what his eyes see, or decide by what his ears hear; but with righteousness he shall judge the poor, and decide with equity for the meek of the earth; and he shall smite the earth with the rod of his mouth, and with the breath of his lips he shall slay the wicked. Righteousness shall be the girdle of his waist, and faithfulness the girdle of his loins. (Isaiah 11:1–5)*

That hope fueled Jewish expectations for centuries. But not only Jewish: when the Hebrew scriptures were embraced as the Old Testament of Christianity, the biblical prominence of David and Solomon was adopted to serve a new metaphysical scheme. For Christians, the messianic promise David accepted was inherited by Jesus and, through him, by the kings of Christendom. For Muslims, Daoud and Suleiman were afforded a place in Islamic tradition as great kings and wise judges who carried out Allah's will. Thus, the legend of David and Solomon became a central parable about kingship and divine favor from the deserts of Arabia to the rain-swept coasts of Scandinavia and the British Isles.

Over the centuries, the vivid scenes, symbols, and images of the biblical stories of David and Solomon have been expressed in nearly every artistic medium: the image of the youthful Judahite shepherd with his bag of sling stones, standing over the lifeless body of Goliath; the young man with the lyre who could still evil spirits; the lusty king who stole another man's wife and brought about the death of her husband; and the wise kingly son and successor who hosted the exotic queen of Sheba with great pomp and who ruled in unimaginable splendor and prosperity. The portraits of David and Solomon's divine anointment, majesty on the throne, and world-conquering power articulate a universal vision of divine guidance and national destiny.

The biblical images of the David and Solomon story offered essential tools in the crafting of a wide range of later local and universal kingdoms. The Roman emperor Constantine pantomimed the role of a new Solomon as he assumed control of a Christianized Roman Empire. Justinian boasted how he had outdone even Solomon at the dedication of the massive Hagia Sophia church in Constantinople. Clovis, the king of the Franks, donned a more rustic Davidic persona; and Charlemagne, crowned Holy Roman Emperor on Christmas Day 800, styled himself as a new David who would make a united monarchy of Europe not a biblical fable but a medieval reality. He was followed in his devotion to the image of King David by French, German, and English rulers in the following centuries.

By the thirteenth century, the elaborate Trees of Jesse carved on the façades of great European cathedrals reminded all worshipers of the sacred continuity of the Davidic line. Rising from the reclining figure of David's father, Jesse, the spidery tendrils of these ever-ascending vines of stone, paint, or stained glass extended upward in a great organic chain of divine authority, from David with his lyre, Solomon and his crown, to the later kings of Judah, to Jesus, the saints, and then to the crowned kings of the medieval world. Likewise, the great Ottoman conqueror and lawgiver Suleiman, nicknamed "the Magnificent," consciously cultivated his public image as a second Solomon, to sanctify the historical and religious authority of his empire. In the Renaissance, the famous sculptural depictions of David by Michelangelo, Donatello, and Verrocchio universalized David's embodiment of individual action and confident awareness of personal destiny.

Later, in the paintings of Rembrandt in the golden age of Holland, in the poetry of John Dryden in Restoration England, and in the battle songs of the early American colonists, new depictions of David rose to oust mad Sauls and defeat boastful Goliaths. New Absaloms were condemned and mourned for treacherous acts of rebellion. New Solomons watched over grand empires. The stories of ancient Israel's kings David and Solomon were no longer solely biblical heroes or mystical precursors of Christ's incarnation; they were now also the role models destined to be followed by the earthly rulers of new peoples of the Book.

Even today, an age when western monarchy has passed away in all but its ceremonial trappings, the power of David and Solomon endures. Whether believed literally as history or appreciated for its mythic power, the biblical narrative of the founding kings of a united Israel has remained an important part of western culture. However little most people may know the contents of the Bible, few need to ask what a "David and Goliath" battle is about or what "the judgment of Solomon" means. Put simply, without David and Solomon our world would be different. The biblical stories of David and Solomon offer a template for western leadership and an archetype of kingly power that influences each of us, consciously or not.

ANATOMY OF A BIBLICAL EPIC

To understand the development of this archetype, we first need to examine its written source, the Bible. Before turning to archaeology, it is important to consider the painstaking work of biblical scholars who have attempted to account for when and why the Bible was written. To these scholars, the life and works of David and Solomon are contained in well-defined literary units, whose history and date of composition can be identified through stylistic, terminological, and linguistic clues.

In analyzing the contents of the various parts of the Hebrew

Bible, many biblical scholars have concluded that the long David and Solomon narrative contained in the books of Samuel and 1 Kings is a part of a distinct literary work, known as the Deuteronomistic History, that spans the books of Joshua, Judges, 1 and 2 Samuel, and 1 and 2 Kings. This work—which we will have occasion to refer to again and again—is the main biblical source for the history of Israel, describing the stormy, miraculous, and momentous events that occurred from the crossing of the Jordan River, through the conquest of Canaan, to the establishment of the Israelite kingdoms, ending with the tragic destruction of Jerusalem and the Babylonian exile.

It is called the Deuteronomistic History because scholars have recognized how much it has in common—theologically and linguistically—with the unique and last of the Five Books of Moses, the book of Deuteronomy. Alone of all the books of the Torah, only Deuteronomy imposes a strictly centralized worship on the people of Israel and prescribes a detailed code of legislation about everything from religious ceremonies to dietary habits, to lending practices, to the process of legal divorce. These laws are all conveyed as unambiguous divine commandments. If they are observed, the people of Israel will prosper and inherit divine blessings. If they are violated, the people of Israel will pay dearly for their sins. While Deuteronomy provides the law, the Deuteronomistic History is a long tale of how that divine principle played out in human history. It not only describes events and introduces biblical personalities, but uses them to explain why the conquest of the Promised Land was carried out with such violence, why the Israelites later suffered at the hands of their gentile neighbors, and why Kings David and Solomon, their successors, and the people of Israel either prospered or were punished according to their observance or violation of the laws of Deuteronomy.

According to many scholars, the Deuteronomistic History appeared in substantially its present form in the late seventh century BCE, during the reign of King Josiah of Judah (639–609 BCE), approx-

imately three hundred years *after* the time of David and Solomon.*
But that is not to say that the Deuteronomistic History was an
entirely new or completely imaginative composition when it reached
its recognizable form. Beneath its uncompromising and uniform theological message, the Deuteronomistic History is a literary patch-
work. It is clearly the result of the editing together of various earlier
sources—not a single original work written by an individual or group
of authors at one time. The text contains jarring discontinuities,
snatches of poetry, quotations from other works, and geographical
lists interspersed with long passages of narrative.

Within the longer Deuteronomistic History, the story of David
and Solomon—extending throughout the first and second books of
Samuel and the initial eleven chapters of the first book of Kings—is
itself a collection of earlier sources. Linked, and often interrupted,
by poetic passages, long lists of names, summaries of heroic stories,
and detailed geographical or administrative descriptions are three
long compositions that narrate, in sequence, the major events of
David's and Solomon's lives. These hypothesized early works are
called by scholars "The History of David's Rise" (1 Samuel 16:14–
2 Samuel 5), the "Court (*or* Succession) History" (2 Samuel 9–20
and 1 Kings 1–2), and "The Acts of Solomon" (1 Kings 3–11).

"The History of David's Rise" tells the story of David's anointment as a young shepherd in Bethlehem, his arrival at the court of
Saul, his battle with Goliath, his flight from Saul's court, his adventures as a roving warrior chief, the death of Saul, and David's succession to the throne of Israel. It concludes with David's capture of
Jerusalem and final defeat of the Philistines.

The "Succession History," also known as the "Court History,"
has as its overriding concern the question "who shall sit on the
throne of my lord the king [David] after him" (1 Kings 1:20, 27). It
continues David's story with his establishment of Israel's capital in

---

* The circumstances of the initial compilation of the Deuteronomistic History will
  be described in Chapter 6.

Jerusalem and the complex and morally ambiguous sequence of events, actions, and personal turmoil that took place during David's reign. It ends with his choice of Solomon to be his successor and his death as a feeble, impotent old man.

"The Acts of Solomon" is, in contrast, a straightforward record of King Solomon's great achievements, wealth, and wisdom—ending with his moral decline and the rebellions and dissensions that brought the golden age of Israel to a close.

When were these ancient historical works written? The answer to this question is crucial to assessing their historical reliability. Until quite recently, most scholars believed that they were initially composed during or quite close to the lifetimes of David and Solomon. In a highly influential book published in 1926 and titled *Die Über-lieferung von der Thronnachfolge Davids (The Succession to the Throne of David)* the German biblical scholar Leonhard Rost argued that "The History of David's Rise" was a work of ancient political propaganda, written to legitimize the accession of David to the throne of Saul, and to demonstrate that David was the rightful king of all Israel—south and north alike. This narrative depicts David's rise to power as completely lawful, showing how Saul was rejected by his own human failings and religious misbehavior and that David was elected by God. It explains that the transfer of the throne from Saul to David was simply an expression of the will of God, since "the spirit of the Lord departed from Saul" (1 Samuel 16:14), while the Lord was with David (1 Samuel 16:18). Rost and many other scholars after him have theorized that this composition was written by a supporter of the Davidic dynasty late in the reign of David or during the reign of Solomon, when the Israelites of the north challenged the right of the southern Davidides to impose their rule over them.

Subsequently, the American biblical scholar Kyle McCarter described the narrative as a great apologia, intended to demonstrate David's righteousness despite the violent and bloody events that made his rise to power possible. In its skillful portrait of David, it refutes the implication that David was a disloyal deserter and

Philistine mercenary who was to be blamed for the death of Saul. It places the blame on others for the death of Ish-bosheth, Saul's son and successor, and for the assassination of Abner, the commander of Saul's army. In both of these acts, David is cleared of responsibility—though both acts were instrumental in David's consolidation of power. In short, the apologia aimed to demonstrate that David was blameless in all his dealings with Saul and his family, and that he was neither a traitor nor a usurper. He was Saul's legitimate successor, chosen by the God of Israel.

Similarly, the "Succession History" explains why and how Solomon ascended to the throne instead of the elder sons of David—Amnon, Absalom, and Adonijah. This narrative reaches its climax with the anointment of Solomon, which also is seen as a divinely sanctioned act. According to Rost and the scholars who have followed him, the "Succession History" must have been written by a contemporary eyewitness or participant in the events it describes—most likely a scribe in the Jerusalem court, in the early days of Solomon. Both "The History of David's Rise" and the "Succession History," together with "The Acts of Solomon," were believed by these scholars to represent the fruits of a great period of enlightenment in Israel, in a royal court that included the offices of both secretary and scribe (2 Samuel 8:17; 20:25; 1 Kings 4:3). Rost characterized the "Succession History" as "the finest work in Hebrew narrative art." The great German biblical scholar Gerhard von Rad adopted Rost's ideas and described the "Succession History" as the beginning of Israelite historiography and, in fact, the beginning of history writing in western tradition.

When another German biblical scholar, Martin Noth, wrote his groundbreaking book on the Deuteronomistic History in the early 1940s, he too accepted many of Rost's observations. He argued that the Deuteronomistic historian incorporated into his work these early narratives almost verbatim. Most scholars followed suit, accepting the contention that the major narratives about David and Solomon were originally independent sources written in the early days of the Israelite monarchy. We now know, however, that this theory is mistaken. As we will see, it is clearly contradicted by archaeological evidence. The familiar stories about David and Solomon, based on a few early folk traditions, are the result of extensive reworking and editorial expansion during the four centuries that followed David and Solomon's reigns. Although they contain little reliable history, we will show how they provide an astonishing new understanding of the origins of the biblical tradition—and why it remains so powerful even today.

WHEN DID DAVID AND SOLOMON LIVE?

The first obvious challenge in assessing the historical reliability of the David and Solomon stories is to determine the precise date of their reigns. This must be based on evidence within the Bible, for we do not possess any contemporary references to David and Solomon on well-dated inscriptions from archaeological excavations in Israel or from the neighboring civilizations of Egypt and Mesopotamia.* We must rely—with due caution—on the chronological clues preserved in the Deuteronomistic History.

In recounting the lives and reigns of all of the kings of Judah and of the northern kingdom of Israel, the first and second books of Kings in most cases note each king's age at assuming the throne, the length of his reign, and the correspondence in years and duration to the reigning king from the rival kingdom. If we calculate backward from the last reference to a king of the Davidic dynasty—the mention in 2 Kings 25:27 of the release from Babylonian captivity of the last surviving Davidic king, Jehoiachin, in the first year of the Babylonian ruler Amel-Marduk (known in the Bible as Evil-merodach), we have a fairly secure starting point. Amel-Marduk is known from Babylonian sources to have ascended to the throne in 561 BCE. Counting backward from that date, with proper account taken for

* For a basic discussion of the evidence for David's historical existence, see Appendix 1.

conflicting evidence from other ancient Near Eastern sources, obvious scribal errors, suspiciously round numbers, or possible overlaps
in the rule of kings and their successors, scholars have been able to
construct a chronological sequence that stretches all the way back to
David and Solomon.

These dates—fairly accurate for the later kings and much rougher
for the early ones—are obtained by projecting the biblical chronology back through the reigns of the kings (and one queen, Athaliah)
of the Davidic dynasty who succeeded David and Solomon:

KING	YEARS REIGNED	ESTIMATED DATES
Zedekiah	11	596–586 BCE
Jehoiachin	3 months	597 BCE*
Jehoiakim	11	608–598 BCE
Jehoahaz	3 months	609 BCE
Josiah	31	639–609 BCE
Amon	2	641–640 BCE
Manasseh	55	698–642 BCE
Hezekiah	29	727–698 BCE
Ahaz	16	743–727 BCE†
Jotham	16	759–743 BCE†
Uzziah	52	785–733 BCE†
Amaziah	29	798–769 BCE
Jehoash	40	836–798 BCE
Athaliah	7	842–836 BCE
Ahaziah	1	843–842 BCE
Jehoram	8	851–843 BCE†
Jehoshaphat	25	870–846 BCE†
Asa	41	911–870 BCE
Abijam	3	914–911 BCE
Rehoboam	17	931–914 BCE

*RELEASED FROM IMPRISONMENT IN BABYLON IN 561 BCE.
†INCLUDING COREGENCIES

At certain points this list can be checked against contemporary references to the Davidic kings in the chronicles of Assyria and Babylonia. The Babylonian Chronicle, for example, mentions the siege of Jerusalem during King Jehoiachin's brief reign in the seventh year of Nebuchadnezzar, 597 BCE. Manasseh's tribute to Assyria is noted in an inscription of the Assyrian king Esarhaddon in 674 BCE. The Assyrian attack on Jerusalem during the reign of Hezekiah is mentioned in the Annals of Sennacherib for the equivalent of 701 BCE. Ahaz's payment of tribute to Assyria is listed in an inscription of Tiglath-pileser III, dated to 734 BCE. Correspondences to the reigns of the northern kingdom—which go back to the battle of Qarqar in the days of Ahab in 853 BCE—also confirm the reliability of the general framework. (Another generally accepted synchronism is the invasion of the country by the Egyptian pharaoh Shishak in the fifth year of Solomon's son Rehoboam—c. 926, according to the list above—but this poses significant, and far-reaching, problems, as we will see.)

When we proceed backward from Rehoboam, the chronology gets considerably fuzzier. First, as previously noted, David and Solomon are not mentioned in any contemporary extrabiblical text, and hence do not have any reliably direct anchor to ancient Near Eastern chronology. Second, in 1 Kings 11:42 Solomon is given a suspiciously round figure of forty years of kingship, recalling the traditional biblical typological expression of forty years for "a generation," as in the length of the Israelites' wandering in the wilderness, or just for "a very long time." David's reign, begun in Hebron and then continued in Jerusalem, is likewise recorded as forty years. To make matters even more difficult, the passage containing the length of the reign of Saul, the first king of Israel, has been garbled by scribal copyists over the ages, reading: "Saul was . . . years old when he began to reign; and he reigned . . . and two years over Israel" (1 Samuel 13:1). Many biblical scholars have tried their hand at restoring the original number. On the basis of the sheer number of battles he reportedly waged and the prominence of his dynasty in

Israel's historical memory, they have suggested a reign of approximately twenty years.

Unfortunately, scholars have generally taken these round numbers as precise indications for the dates of the early kings:

KING	YEARS REIGNED	ESTIMATED DATES
Solomon	40	*c. 970–931 BCE*
David	40	*c. 1010–970 BCE*
Saul	22 (?)	*c. 1030–1010 BCE*

The truth is that we can take these symbolic biblical descriptions only as a general indication of the time period when David and Solomon would have lived rather than a precise chronological reckoning of the date and extent of each of their reigns. The problem is compounded by the fact that we cannot even presume that Saul and David reigned in a neat chronological sequence, one after the other, rather than having overlapping reigns. To make a long story short, we simply do not know the exact number of years that David and Solomon each ruled. The most we can say with some measure of security is that they probably both reigned sometime in the tenth century BCE.

THE SEARCH FOR DAVID
AND SOLOMON BEGINS

The tenth century BCE must therefore be our starting point for a search for the historical David and Solomon. As we know from the archaeological remains excavated all over Israel during the last hundred years, the tenth century BCE was a time of upheaval. At city sites and villages, there is evidence of a great transformation. The disintegration of the old palace-based civilization of the Late Bronze Age (c. 1550–c. 1150) had given way to the rise of new territorial entities and ethnic groups throughout the eastern Mediterranean region and much of the ancient Near East. The independent Phoenician city-states along the northern coast were growing in commercial power. The Philistines in the southern coastal cities were expanding their territory and maintaining close links with a weakened Egypt. Some of the old Canaanite cities in the valleys, like Megiddo, were experiencing a brief Indian summer of prosperity. And in the highlands long remembered as the birthplace of Israel and home of its royal traditions, a dense network of rustic hilltop farming villages in formerly sparsely inhabited regions marked the emergence of a culture and a society whose members would later identify themselves as "Israelites."

Archaeology is today the most important tool at our disposal for reconstructing the evolution of ancient Israelite society. Elsewhere in the ancient world, archaeological research has also transformed our vision of the past. The early history of Greece can now be told without resort to the mythic biographies of Minos, Theseus, or Agamemnon as primary sources. The rise of the Egyptian and Mesopotamian civilizations can be understood through inscriptions, potsherds, and settlement patterns rather than simply in tales of ancient wonders and semidivine kings. The discrepancies between art and literature, on the one hand, and documented, verifiable history and archaeological evidence, on the other, have made us see the founder myths of antiquity for what they are: shared expressions of ancient communal identity, told with great power and insight, still interesting and worthy of study, but certainly not to be taken as literal, credible records of events.

Such is the case with David and Solomon, who are depicted in the biblical narrative as founding fathers of the ancient Israelite state. Yet we can now say—as we will argue in considerable detail throughout this book—that many of the famous episodes in the biblical story of David and Solomon are fictions, historically questionable, or highly exaggerated. In the following chapters we will present archaeological evidence to show that there was no united monarchy of Israel in the way that the Bible describes it. Although it seems probable that

David and Solomon were actual historical characters, they were very different from their scriptural portraits. We will show that it is highly unlikely that David ever conquered territories of peoples more than a day or two's march from the heartland of Judah. We will suggest that Solomon's Jerusalem was neither extensive nor impressive, but rather the rough hilltop stronghold of a local dynasty of rustic tribal chiefs. Yet the point of this book is not simply to debunk stories from the Bible. Alone among the great legends of Near Eastern and classical antiquity, the Bible retains its power to inspire hopes and dreams for living communities around the world even today. Our goal is to show how the legends of David and Solomon developed, and how they came to guide western thinking and shape western religious and political traditions in important ways.

As we proceed through the following chapters, we will analyze and attempt to date the various layers of the biblical story, describing the main issues in the now-bitter scholarly disagreements about its historical reliability, and presenting new archaeological evidence that is central to that debate.* We will show, step by step, period by period, how the historical reality of ancient Judah—as revealed by archaeological research—gave rise both to a dynasty and to a legend that was transformed and expanded in a process of historical reinterpretation that continues even today.

For the now-familiar biblical story of David and Solomon is neither a straightforward historical record nor a wholly imaginary myth. It evolved from a variety of ancient sources, adding details, garbling contexts, and shifting its meaning as the centuries rolled on. It contains a complex stratigraphy of folktales, ballads, and dramatic narratives, which, taken as a whole, have little to do with the actual lives of the main characters and almost everything to do with the changing concept of the nation and the king. As we will see, the recognition of this complex process of literary and historical evolu-

---

* For a brief history of the early archaeological search for David and Solomon and a review of the early theories, see Appendixes 2 and 3.

tion, backed by archaeological evidence, is the key to understanding the true character of the biblical David and Solomon story—and to appreciating its timeless insights about the nature of kingly power and national identity.

The discovery of the real lives and roles of David and Solomon in the tenth century BCE is therefore just the beginning. The question of how and why their legends survived the vicissitudes of antiquity to become one of the strongest images of western civilization—and what values and dreams they reflected in every successive period—is, as we hope to show, a story no less fascinating than the biblical narrative itself.

PART I

RECOVERING
HISTORY

PERIOD	STAGES IN DEVELOPMENT OF BIBLICAL MATERIAL
10th Century BCE [Chapter 1]	Early memories of David as an outlaw and bandit leader, active in the Judean wilderness and the Shephelah; elaborated through oral tradition into collections of folktales and ballads by his followers.
10th Century BCE [Chapter 2]	Early memories of Saul as leader of an early north Israelite tribal confederacy; elaborated through oral tradition into a tragic saga by north Israelite villagers after Saul's death.
9th Century BCE [Chapter 3]	Stories about David's rule in Jerusalem, transformed into 9th century ballads recited in the court of David's successors; elaboration of oral legends of David's conquests to match the territorial extent of the North Israelite, Omride state.
Late 8th Century BCE [Chapter 4]	First written version of the tales and ballads about Saul, David, and Solomon's succession, combining earlier southern and northern oral traditions; serves as a unifying national epic for Hezekiah's kingdom.
Early 7th Century BCE [Chapter 5]	Written chronicle of the reign of Solomon as a wise, rich monarch in the high Assyrian imperial style; stress on his wise rule, building activities (including the construction of the Temple), and trade expeditions to foreign lands.

HISTORICAL BACKGROUND	ARCHAEOLOGICAL FINDS
Regional power vacuum in the aftermath of the breakdown of Late Bronze Age palace culture; the eclipse of Egypt.	Jerusalem a small village; Judah sparsely inhabited. Continuation of Late Bronze and Early Iron Age settlement conditions. Few permanent settlements in Judah; large pastoralist population.
Emergence of "Israel," the first Iron Age territorial entity in the highlands. It threatens the interests of a revived Egypt and is weakened by the campaign of Pharaoh Shishak.	Dramatic increase in number of settlements in the highlands north of Jerusalem. Subsequent wave of abandonment around Gibeon.
Judah slowly develops from highland chiefdom to kingdom, but lives in the shadow of the Omride state. The Davidic Dynasty survives the rise of Damascus and fall of the Omride Dynasty.	Jerusalem expands, but still limited to the City of David. First administrative centers in Lachish, Beth-shemesh, Beer-sheba, and Arad. Gath the dominant Philistine city until its destruction by Aram Damascus.
Judah becomes an Assyrian vassal. Israel falls. Torrent of refugees from the north. Judah emerges as a full-blown, bureaucratic state, with a mixed population of Judahites and Israelites.	Dramatic growth of Jerusalem: fortifications, elaborate tombs, the Siloam Tunnel. Impressive demographic growth in the entire territory of Judah. Olive-oil industry. Spread of scribal activity and signs of developed administration.
Assyrian domination continues, after Sennacherib's devastating campaign in Judah in 701 BCE. In an attempt to recover, Manasseh fully incorporates Judah into the Assyrian world economy.	Assyrian activity in the southern coastal plain and Edom. In Judah, revival of cities destroyed by Sennacherib. Early return to the Shephelah. Strong activity in the Beer-sheba Valley and the Judean Desert. Signs of developed administration intensify: seals, seal impressions, weights, ostraca, etc. Rise of Ekron the main Philistine center in the Shephelah with evidence for olive-oil industry.

(Continued on following pages)

(*Continued from previous pages*)

PERIOD	STAGES IN DEVELOPMENT OF BIBLICAL MATERIAL
Late 7th Century BCE **[Chapter 6]**	Elaboration of earlier written sources (History of David's Rise, Succession History, Solomonic traditions) and their incorporation into the Deuteronomistic History of Israel; edited to offer a unified theological message to serve aims of Josiah's religious reform; details such as David and Goliath combat and other Greek realities and condemnation of Solomon added.
6th–4th Centuries BCE **[Chapter 7]**	Second, Exilic Deuteronomistic redaction, bringing the story up-to-date and explaining the exile. Exilic-period prophecies (e.g., Haggai and Zechariah). Use of David and Solomon as religious symbols in Chronicles.
3rd Century BCE **to 5th Century** CE **[Chapter 8]**	Greek Translation of Kings and Chronicles; developed versions of Psalms, Proverbs, Song of Songs; Extra and post-Hebrew Bible material with messianic overtones: Psalms of Solomon, Flavius Josephus, Dead Sea Scrolls. New Testament links Jesus to Davidic tradition; Rabbinic literature and Church Fathers expand and elaborate religious associations and metaphors.

HISTORICAL BACKGROUND	ARCHAEOLOGICAL FINDS
Weakening Assyria withdraws from the Levant. Religious reform in Judah; attempts at Judahite territorial expansion. Josiah is killed at Megiddo by the rising Twenty-sixth Dynasty of Egypt.	Judahite expansion in the Shephelah intensifies. Activity continues in the Beer-sheba Valley and the Judean Desert. More ostraca and seal impressions; evidence for increasing literacy. Egyptian presence (with Greek mercenaries) along the coast. Ekron olive-oil industry continues.
Judah and Jerusalem devastated by Nebuchadnezzar. Judahite deportees in Babylonia. King Cyrus of Persia allows some of the deportees return to Yehud. Construction of the Second Temple. End of hopes for political restoration of Davidic Dynasty.	Jerusalem devastated. Mizpah survives. Seal impressions of Yehud. Jerusalem slowly recovers. Construction of Samaritan Temple on Mt. Gerizim.
Hellenistic period: Rule by Ptolemies and Seleucids; Hasmonean Dynasty. Roman period: Herod the Great, the Jewish revolts fueled by messianic ideologies. Early Christianity and its official establishment in the Byzantine period.	Increasing Hellenistic influence in culture and economy; Hasmonean building activity in Jerusalem and desert areas. Destruction of the Samaritan Temple on Mt. Gerizim. Herod the Great expands Jerusalem and builds a new Temple; builds other cities and forts, such as Masada. Dead Sea Scrolls. Jerusalem devastated by the Romans. Roman and Byzantine period synagogues. Byzantine churches.

PERIOD	STAGES IN DEVELOPMENT OF BIBLICAL MATERIAL
10th Century BCE	Early memories of David as an outlaw and bandit leader, active in the Judean wilderness and the Shephelah; elaborated through oral tradition into collections of folktales and ballads by his followers.

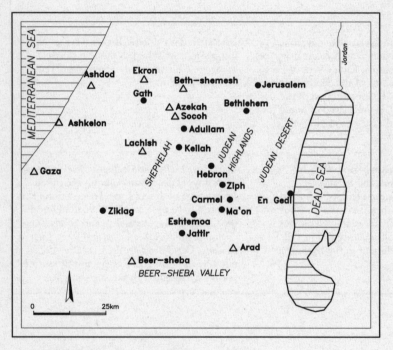

● Sites relevant to this chapter
△ Sites mentioned in other chapters

Area of David's activity as a bandit in southern Judah and the Shephelah.

HISTORICAL BACKGROUND	ARCHAEOLOGICAL FINDS
Regional power vacuum in the aftermath of the breakdown of Late Bronze Age palace culture; the eclipse of Egypt.	Jerusalem a small village; Judah sparsely inhabited. Continuation of Late Bronze and Early Iron Age settlement conditions. Few permanent settlements in Judah; large pastoralist population.

CHAPTER 1

Tales of the Bandit

The Rise of David in the Hill Country of Judah

— TENTH CENTURY BCE —

THE BIBLICAL NARRATIVE OF DAVID'S RISE TO POWER (1 Samuel 16:14–2 Samuel 5)—the vivid drama of the rise of a nobody from Bethlehem to the throne in Jerusalem—has been praised as a masterpiece of western literature and one of the earliest prose epics known. It is filled with acts of daring, bold surprises, bloody violence, and adoring popular acclaim. David enters the stage as a humble young shepherd, sent to the battlefield camp of the Israelites to bring provisions to his three older brothers. There, fired with divine inspiration, he fells the mighty Goliath, and the Philistines are routed. Yet in becoming the new hero of Israel, David must soon flee from the jealous envy and fury of King Saul. During his adventures among the villages and remote wildernesses of Judah, David's story takes on the character of a classical bandit tale—and thereby reveals its earliest threads. In other words, the true, historic David, as far as archaeology and historical sources can reveal, gained his greatest fame as something of a bandit chief.

As the Bible tells it, after fleeing from Saul, David is refused shelter in Philistine territory and escapes to the cave of Adullam, where he gathers around himself a sizable outlaw band. "And every one who was in distress, and every one who was in debt, and every one who was discontented, gathered to him; and he became captain over them. And there were with him about four hundred men" (1 Samuel 22:2).

As a guerrilla force, David's men are quick and mobile. They come to the rescue of beleaguered villagers, humiliate an arrogant local strongman, outsmart the ruler of a powerful neighboring Philistine city, and evade the relentless pursuit of King Saul again and again. Extortion, seduction, deception, and righteous violence are David's methods. His story is filled with larger-than-life ironies, comic episodes, and entertaining events. It is a classical bandit tale of a type known all over the world, then and now, in which popular rebels—like Robin Hood, Jesse James, and Pancho Villa—use bravado and cunning to challenge the corrupt, brutal powers that be. The exploits of some bandits have been gradually forgotten, but the tales of others have grown steadily more vivid over time. Modest events are transformed into astonishing achievements; unique personal traits are exaggerated to a mythic scale. In the case of the biblical narrative, the tales of David's early bandit days merge into the national history of Israel. When King Saul dies on the battlefield, David is proclaimed king of Judah and proceeds to conquer Jerusalem and establish it as his seat of power. His destiny is to become king of all Israel, yet his days of banditry remain an essential part of the legend of the man.

How can we assess the historical reliability of this tale of the rise of a bandit? On literary grounds, many scholars have seen the entire narrative of David's rise as a single composition, written during or soon after David's reign as a kind of royal propaganda to legitimate and celebrate the establishment of the Davidic dynasty. Others, while agreeing that it is a single composition, place its writing centuries later, as a fanciful folktale with virtually no historical value at all. Based on archaeological evidence, and clues within the text, we can now say that the tale could not possibly have been put in writing until more than two hundred years after the death of David. However, the text seems to preserve some uncannily accurate memories of tenth century BCE conditions in the highlands of Judah— and may contain at least the traces of a reliable, original account of the events of the historical David's earliest career.

LIFE ON THE HIGHLAND FRONTIER

Detailed descriptions of environment and settlement patterns are perhaps the most important evidence for dating the Bible's historical texts. The sheer weight of geographical information and long lists of place-names interwoven in its stories testify to a familiarity with the ancient landscape of Judah and Israel. The many biblical geographical descriptions that today appear to us as tedious lists of obscure villages and natural features interrupting the flow of the narrative were once essential components of its tales. They were intended for particular audiences who would *recognize* the names of the various places mentioned and evoke admiration for the achievements of the various biblical characters in a physical setting that they knew well. A reference to a place known to be in the heart of the wilderness would evoke images of freedom from the tedious routines of peasant life. The mention of a city known to be the seat of regional power—or corruption—would make the hero's triumphs or evasions there seem all the more memorable. The mention of villages known to be especially poor or endangered by marauders would heighten admiration for the stories of their rescue or relief.

Thus the frequent appearance of place-names and geographical terms in David's tale in the first book of Samuel should not be seen as a sign of a biblical clerk's insistence for detail. They speak in a coded language of familiarity with contemporary landscapes of power, whose details, once so vivid, might gradually lose their sig-

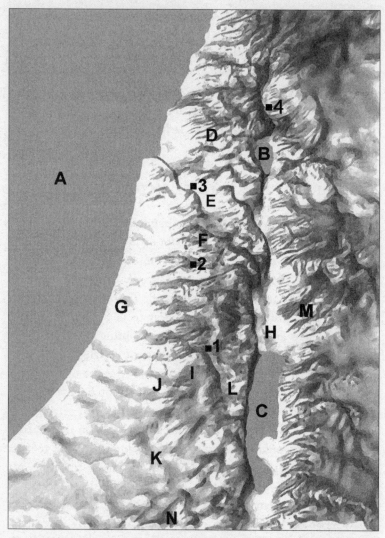

Geographical zones and main archaeological sites in the Land of the Bible:
(A) Mediterranean Sea; (B) Sea of Galilee; (C) Dead Sea; (D) Galilee;
(E) Jezreel Valley; (F) northern highlands (highlands of Samaria);
(G) Coastal Plain; (H) Jordan Valley; (I) southern highlands (Judean hill
country); (J) Shephelah; (K) Beer-sheba Valley; (L) Judean Desert;
(M) highlands of Transjordan; (N) Negev highlands. (1) Jerusalem;
(2) Samaria; (3) Megiddo; (4) Hazor.

nificance as generations succeed one another and new constellations of cities, wilderness, and farmland emerge. Like preserved fossils embedded in the rock of biblical tradition, they are identifiable in their unique patterns and can be placed in quite specific historical periods. They offer us a key to dating some of the story's key elements.

The Judahite hill country where David rose from shepherd to national leader is an isolated highland bloc, largely cut off from the rest of the country, with only a narrow north-south plateau linking its traditional main towns of Jerusalem, Bethlehem, and Hebron. Its topography today as then is rugged, it soils are rocky and poor, its rainfall unpredictable. Its people survived by adopting a difficult, if highly adaptable, way of life. In recent years, archaeologists working in Israel have undertaken wide-ranging surface surveys throughout the country to study the array of settlements in each historical period and to identify archaeological sites with localities mentioned in the Bible and other ancient texts. The general geographical description of Judah in the David story indeed fits the environment, topography, and settlement system of the early phases of the Iron Age, in particular, the tenth century BCE.

Isolation profoundly influenced Judah's history.* Its natural geographical boundaries shaped its relations with the outside world. To the west, the hill country drops steeply through a series of narrow, rocky ridges with steep slopes, separated by deep ravines, to an area of foothills called the Shephelah. It was on those slopes of the eastern Shephelah that David reportedly found shelter in the cave of Adullam (1 Samuel 22:1) and won his first great victory with his band of mighty men in defending the villagers of Keilah from

---

* In this book we will use the geographical terms "Judah" and "Judahite" to refer to the situation beginning in the presumed time of David in the Early Iron Age (tenth century BCE) and ending with the destruction of the kingdom of Judah by the Babylonians in 586 BCE. The more general term "Judean highlands," derived from the Greek and Latin geographical terminology, will be used to describe this highland territory in all other periods.

Philistine attack (1 Samuel 23:5). Communication and travel from the hill country to the more heavily populated Shephelah and the coastal plain beyond is difficult and dangerous. The main routes descend steeply, dropping more than fifteen hundred feet in altitude in the distance of just a few miles. To the west, the Shephelah forms an utterly different landscape—moderate, fertile, and densely settled with villages. David's adventures as the unlikely protégé of the Philistine king Achish of Gath occurred along this border between the hill country, the Shephelah, and the coastal Philistine cities beyond.

In the east, the hill country drops into the Judean Desert. An arid zone starts abruptly as the winter rain clouds from the Mediterranean are emptied of all their moisture on the central plateau of the highland ridge. Within just a few miles to the east, the landscape grows increasingly arid and rugged. Twisting ravines carry torrents of winter runoff eastward into the Dead Sea and the Jordan Valley. In a few places close to the Dead Sea, like En Gedi, they form rough, deep canyons pocked with caves in their sheer cliffs. It was here that the biblical narrative places David's dramatic escapes from a pursuing Saul.

In the south, the Hebron hills slope more gradually down to the Beer-sheba Valley; the transition from the arable land to the arid zone is much less abrupt. Here, still-existing place-names evoke associations with the David stories; many of the villages and ruins preserve the names of the ancient, biblical settlements. Khirbet ("the ruin of " in Arabic) Ma'in is the site of biblical Ma'on. Khirbet Karmil, less than a mile to the north, is the place of biblical Carmel—both are mentioned in the Abigail affair (1 Samuel 25). Khirbet Zif is biblical Ziph—a hideout of David on the run from Saul (1 Samuel 23:14–15). Es-Samu' is the site of biblical Eshtemoa, and Khirbet 'Attir of Jattir—both villages listed among the places that received a share of David's spoils in his great victory over Amalek (1 Samuel 30:26–27).

Thus the biblical geography closely matches the actual landscape of the highlands of Judah. But that fact does not necessarily offer us chronological help. The geographical conditions have existed for millennia and this setting would have been familiar to storytellers and mythmakers throughout all of antiquity. Yet if we are to believe that the David stories are not purely imaginary tales imposed on a familiar landscape, we must look to archaeology to discover if the specific constellation of place-names and geographical conditions reflect a unique tenth century BCE situation—which later generations would not have known and could not have made up.

THE CLUE OF CHANGING SETTLEMENT PATTERNS

In recent decades, intensive archaeological surveys have provided an entirely new perspective on the evolution of society in the Judean highlands over thousands of years. The painstaking work of surface exploration—carefully examining all traces of ancient settlement over large blocs of territory, dating them by the indications of characteristic pottery types, and plotting them on maps arranged according to successive chronological periods—has offered us a dramatic picture of cyclical demographic expansion and retraction. We know when many of the ancient sites in the area were established and we know when certain regions were thickly settled and when they were not. This information offers us an important tool for dating the possible historical background of the biblical narrative.

Since evidence of extensive literacy is lacking in Judah before the end of the eighth century BCE, "The History of David's Rise" is unlikely to have been put into writing less than two hundred years after David's time. Is it possible that the narrative was composed at that time and that the general settlement patterns and population distribution described in the story of David's rise reflect the situation at the *time of writing*—and have no real connection to the situation in the tenth century BCE?

The answer is no. The geographical background behind the earliest David stories simply does not fit the eighth century BCE, when Judah was a fully developed monarchy with the apparatus of literary production and the need for a national history. First and foremost, in the eighth and seventh centuries BCE, the fringe areas of Judah where David is described as fleeing from Saul and conducting his raids and bandit activities were densely settled; they could hardly have been chosen as an appropriate setting for free movement and daring escapes. The area south of Hebron was filled with large villages in easy reach of the central authority in Jerusalem. Even farther south, in the arid zone of the Negev and the Beer-sheba Valley, where David reportedly conducted lightning raids against the neighboring desert peoples (1 Samuel 27:10), a dense network of walled towns, forts, and villages protected the southern borders of the kingdom and offered security for the caravan trade.

As archaeological surveys have shown, this area had begun to be developed as early as the ninth century BCE. Two Judahite forts—at Beer-sheba and Arad—were established in the Beer-sheba Valley to control the roads from Hebron to the desert regions to the south. It was in this period that the Shephelah also came under centralized royal control. Excavations at two important Judahite sites in this region—Lachish and Beth-shemesh—show significant building activities in the ninth century, when they became the most important administrative centers for Judahite rule in the west. It is significant that none of these places is mentioned in the cycle of David stories, not even as a geographical aside.

Thus the description of a "wild south"—of lawlessness and banditry in the fringe areas of Judah, so central to the David story—does not fit the situation in the earliest possible period when "The History of David's Rise" was put into writing. A scribe who lived in Jerusalem in the late eighth century BCE (or later) would not have described such a reality and had no reason to invent it. In fact, there is another important clue that takes us back another century and a half, suggesting that the story must have originated

even before the end of the ninth century BCE—only a few generations after David's time.

That clue is the prominence of the Philistine city of Gath in the
David stories. It is there that David twice seeks refuge from Saul's
vengeance; and its king, Achish, is described as a powerful ruler,
controlling territories and villages well beyond his city. The central
role that Achish plays in the gathering of the Philistine forces before
the climactic battle with Saul (1 Samuel 29) suggests a prominent
role for Gath in a wider coalition, described in the Bible, of five
Philistine cities that extended up the coast, which also included Ashdod, Gaza, Ashkelon, and Ekron. That coalition appears in some
other accounts of the Philistines in the Bible, such as Joshua 13:3
and 1 Samuel 6:17, which refer to the political organization of the
five Philistine cities. Interestingly, in late monarchic and exilic texts
(those parts of the Bible written in the late seventh and sixth century BCE), such as Jeremiah 25:20 and Zephaniah 2:4, only *four*
Philistine cities are mentioned, and Gath is left off the list. Likewise, seventh century Assyrian royal records refer only to Ashdod,
Gaza, Ashkelon, and Ekron in their descriptions of Philistine territory. Gath is not mentioned at all.

What happened? According to 2 Kings 12:17, during the reign of
King Jehoash of Judah (around 830 BCE), Hazael, the king of Damascus, campaigned in the Shephelah and conquered the city of
Gath.* This biblical report has now been confirmed by archaeological excavations at Tell es-Safi, the site of ancient Gath, which show
that the city suffered a major destruction toward the end of the
ninth century BCE. Though it had previously been the most important city in the Shephelah and possibly the largest in the entire
country, Gath dramatically declined in size and importance in the
following centuries. We know from Assyrian records that a century
later it was no more than a small town under the control of the

---

* This event seems to be remembered, as a vivid memory and a sobering lesson, in
an oracle of the prophet Amos (6:2).

coastal city of Ashdod. It is unlikely, therefore, that anyone living after the late ninth century BCE would have chosen Gath to be such an important locale in the stories of David if there had not at least been a memory or a folk tradition of its lost greatness.

Indeed, when we attempt to reconstruct the demographic conditions much closer to the time of the historical David, the general setting of the biblical narrative meshes closely with the archaeological evidence. In the tenth century BCE, Philistine Gath seems to have been the most important regional power. The Judahite hill country, especially to the south of Hebron, was sparsely settled, with only a few small villages in the entire area. It was a wild and untamed fringe area, effectively outside government control. Could this be just a coincidence? Or are there additional indications that at least some parts of the story of David's rise to power reflect a shared communal memory of actual historical events?

IN THE REALM OF ABDI-HEBA

Settlement patterns provide only the physical template. They may offer us a date and spatial distribution of sites in a given period, but they give only indirect evidence of political, social, and economic context. Archaeologists working in various parts of the world, however, have attempted to link certain settlement patterns with particular social formations and modes of existence. In the case of the Judean highlands in the period before the rise of the kingdom of Judah, we can indeed recognize a characteristic way of life. Because of the limitations to agriculture, due to the rocky, wooded terrain and the limited rainfall, the number of sedentary communities was relatively small. Only a handful of permanent sites, including Jerusalem, have been recorded in archaeological surveys of the entire territory throughout the Late Bronze and Early Iron Age (c. 1550–900 BCE). Most were tiny villages. There was no real urban center, and not even a single fortified town. In fact, the small sedentary population of the southern highlands can be estimated, on the basis of settlement size, at no more than a few thousand. This contrasts sharply with the lowland territories to the west; there, the major Canaanite and later Philistine city-states each contained dozens of towns and villages, with a large settled population in the main centers and outlying agricultural lands.

Since the primeval landscape of rocky terrain and a thick cover of woods in the Judean highlands could accommodate only limited cultivation, it appears that the proportion of the nonsedentary groups—shepherds and stock raisers—in the overall population was relatively high. Extensive archaeological surveys in the southern highlands have identified evidence for this mobile population of herders in the form of several Late Bronze Age cemeteries, located far from permanent settlements, that probably served as tribal burial grounds.

The Judean hill country was hospitable to this special mix of settled and pastoral groups because of the variety of landscapes and opportunities it offered. The marginal lands of the Judean Desert and the Beer-sheba Valley could be used for winter pasture and seasonal dry farming, while the central ridge offered land for fields and orchards, and pastureland for the flocks in the summer when the other areas were parched.

Sparsely settled rural societies with a mix of sedentary and pastoral populations are often organized in what anthropologists describe as "dimorphic" chiefdoms, denoting a single community stretching over a significant territory, in which two forms of subsistence, farming and herding, exist side by side. They generally rely on a kin-based political system in which the settled villagers and mobile herders are loosely ruled by a chieftain or a strongman, who resides with his small entourage in a central stronghold.

The characterization of early Judah as a dimorphic chiefdom has some suggestive historical confirmation in an era several centuries before David's time. A collection of almost four hundred cuneiform tablets was discovered by chance in the late nineteenth century by local peasants digging at the site of el-Amarna in Egypt, about 150 miles south of Cairo. Written in cuneiform script in Akkadian, the lingua franca of the ancient Near East, they form part of the diplomatic correspondence between Pharaohs Amenhotep III and Amenhotep IV (the famous Akhenaten), on the one hand, and rulers of Asiatic states and Canaanite city-states, on the other, in the fourteenth century BCE. At this time the Egyptians administered all of Canaan as a province and maintained garrisons in a few major cities, but left most of the country under nominal local control. The lowlands were divided between a number of relatively densely settled territories ruled from city-states, while the highlands comprised much larger but sparsely inhabited territories. The information contained in the Amarna archive conforms quite closely with the archaeological evidence, and its personal and political details offer us a unique glimpse at the structure of society and its inner tensions in the area that would later be called Judah—and that would some centuries later become the scene of David's rise.

In the time of the Amarna archive, Jerusalem was ruled by a certain Abdi-Heba. The six letters he dispatched to Egypt and the letters of his neighbors provide valuable information on his city, his territory, and his subjects. The territory under his control stretched from the area of Bethel, about ten miles to the north of Jerusalem, to the Beer-sheba Valley in the south, and from the Judean Desert in the east to the border between the hill country and the Shephelah in the west—a rough approximation of the core area later controlled by the kingdom of Judah. This area contained a small number of villages and groups of pastoral nomads—called *Shosu*, or "plunderers," in the Egyptian records—who were found in all parts of the country but were especially dominant in the relatively empty regions of the steppe and the highlands. On the basis of the archaeological evidence, we can assume that they formed a relatively large portion of the population of Abdi-Heba's realm.

Abdi-Heba's activities and influence extended over a much larger area—all the way to the Jezreel Valley in the north. A particular flash point of tension was the border with the more populous city-states in the lowlands to the west. In light of possible comparisons to the time of David, it is significant that control of the crops and lands of the border towns located between the hill country and the Shephelah was a matter of constant contention between Abdi-Heba of Jerusalem and his rival Shuwardata, the ruler of the city-state of Gath.

Jerusalem, mentioned in the Amarna letters as Abdi-Heba's seat of power, could not have been more than a small village located on the same ridge that David's Jerusalem later occupied. Over a century of modern archaeological investigations in Jerusalem have revealed no significant remains from Abdi-Heba's era. Only isolated tombs and a few Late Bronze pottery sherds have been found on the ridge of the later City of David—especially in the vicinity of the city's only permanent source of freshwater, the Gihon spring. Abdi-Heba's Jerusalem was probably no more than a highland hamlet, with a modest palace a great deal more rustic than the ornate princely residences in the main lowlands cities. A modest temple may have stood next to it, perhaps surrounded by a few houses for the ruling elite, mainly the family of the regional chief. Certainly it was no more significant than this.

The Amarna letters cover only a short period of time—a few decades in the fourteenth century BCE. Does the situation they describe apply to the centuries that followed, or was it an exception? If we look over the millennia of human settlement in this region, the same pattern emerges time after time. In the marginal southern highlands the proportion of herders and shepherds in the overall population was always significant. Towns and even settled villages were few in number, existing as isolated outposts in an ever-shifting landscape of herding and stock raising in the forests and throughout the desert fringe. Dynasties may have changed; a village may have been abandoned and a new one may have been established; but the general picture of the southern highlands remained that of a sparsely settled dimorphic chiefdom, ruled from one of its main villages as a loose kinship network of herders and villagers. These overall settlement patterns remained quite constant until the rise of the kingdom of Judah in the ninth century BCE, a full century after the time of David. These archaeological and anthropological observations can provide us with a reconstruction of the human landscape in his time—and perhaps an explanation of his rise to power as well.

OUTLAWS AND KINGS

The repeated appeals of Abdi-Heba for help from the Egyptian administration indicate that the political situation in the highlands was turbulent and unstable. With its difficult environment and low population, the highlands provided little agricultural surplus with which a ruler could recruit substantial armed forces or maintain more than a symbolic appearance of authority. Working from a small stronghold with a scribe at his side, Abdi-Heba could do little more than complain to the pharaoh about raids from the lowland city-states on his own already hard-pressed peasantry. And the threats were not only external. There is evidence that even *within* highland regimes like Abdi-Heba's, economic and social pressures were building among the population. A potentially dangerous form of resistance to the established order was on the rise.

The Amarna letters refer repeatedly to two groups that acted outside of the sedentary system of the Egyptian-controlled towns and villages. We have already mentioned the *Shosu*, the mobile communities of herders in the highlands and the steppe. The second group, mentioned more frequently, is more important for our discussion: the Apiru. This term, sometimes transliterated as Habiru, was once thought to be related to the term "Hebrews," but the Egyptian texts make it clear that it does not refer to a specific ethnic group so much as a problematic socioeconomic class. The Apiru were uprooted peasants and herders who sometimes turned bandits, sometimes sold themselves as mercenaries to the highest bidder, and were in both cases a disruptive element in any attempt by either local rulers or the Egyptian administration to maintain the stability of their rule.

In his dispatches to Egypt, Abdi-Heba—like many other contemporary Egyptian vassals—accuses his opponents of joining the Apiru, or giving their land to the Apiru, who were perceived as hostile to Egyptian interests. Many were probably uprooted peasants, displaced or escaping from the brutal feudal system in the towns and villages of the lowlands. There, the peasants formed the lowest level of the social hierarchy, subject to heavy taxation, forced labor, and harassment by the local authorities. Married peasants with families had little to do except try to survive on their land. But when the pressures built and desperation became widespread, young peasants, especially those who had not yet established families, could seek freedom by escaping to areas where the power of the local and foreign rulers was weak. There they could join bandit gangs or live by their wits as roving soldiers for hire. For this way of life, the Judean highlands provided an almost ideal locale.

The British social historian Eric Hobsbawm, in his examination of the worldwide phenomenon of social banditry, showed that bandits and rebels have always been attracted to marginal mountainous environments, and that mountain villages and pastoral communities have often been the scene of their most famous exploits. Hobsbawm also demonstrated that the characteristic bandit unit in a highland area is likely to consist of young herdsmen, landless laborers, and sometimes ex-soldiers. Tracing the phenomenon in the Balkans, Mexico, Italy, Brazil, Hungary, and China, he noted that mountainous regions are most susceptible to this type of activity, since governments are always hesitant to act in these rugged and remote regions and the bandit groups can become a law unto themselves. This was certainly the case in Canaan, where the Apiru operated outside the system, unwilling to be docile peasants and shepherds. To the local rulers, they were a turbulent underclass who had to be bought off, killed off, or somehow controlled.

The Apiru continue to be mentioned as late as 1000 BCE. They help explain David's rise to power in a quite down-to-earth way.

DAVID AS APIRU?

Put simply, the description of the rise of David in the first book of Samuel contains many distinctive parallels to the activity of a typical Apiru chieftain and his rebel gang. David and his "mighty men" make their own rules and cynically form shifting political alliances for the interest of survival alone. They live and act in remote villages and on the fringe of the desert—in the rugged Judean wilderness and across the arid steppe land in the south—far from the easy reach of the central authority. Forced by expedience to find shelter with a neighboring Philistine ruler, they become his willing agents and mercenaries. Yet they are always conscious of their base of support and protection among the villagers and herders from whom they originated—making great demonstrations of protection against outside invaders and sharing their booty with them in order to gain more support. Such social bandits are always viewed with a mixture of contempt and admiration. While the Amarna letters depict the Apiru as treasonous, dangerous cutthroats, the Bible depicts David as a daring, sometimes mercurial figure who wins adulation from the people of the highlands as a protector and leader they can call their own.

On closer comparison, some details of the biblical narrative are almost identical to descriptions of the Apiru bands in the Amarna letters. One of the most revealing is the description, quoted at the beginning of this chapter, of how a wide range of marginal elements in Judahite society flocked to David's band:

> *David departed from there and escaped to the cave of Adullam; and when his brothers and all his father's house heard it, they went down there to him. And every one who was in distress, and every one who was in debt, and every one who was discontented, gathered to him;*

*and he became captain over them. And there were with him about
four hundred men. (1 Samuel 22:1–2)*

The same holds true for the description of David's tactics as he res-
cued the villagers of Keilah from the hands of the Philistines. David
and his private army—fast, maneuverable, and deadly—smash an
outside threat to the rural population, which the central administration was either too fearful or too weak to confront. David takes matters into his own hands and emerges as a local savior. Once the
lightning victory is achieved and the booty carried off, the bandit
gang withdraws to the safety of its wilderness hideouts again.

*And David and his men went to Keilah, and fought with the
Philistines, and brought away their cattle, and made a great slaugh-
ter among them. So David delivered the inhabitants of Keilah. (1
Samuel 23:5)*

*Then David and his men, who were about six hundred, arose and
departed from Keilah, and they went wherever they could go . . . (1
Samuel 23:13)*

*And David remained in the strongholds in the wilderness, in the hill
country of the Wilderness of Ziph . . . (1 Samuel 23:14)*

In fact, we possess a direct geographical correspondence to this situation in the Amarna age. The village of Keilah, identified with the
site of Khirbet Qeila, is located at the very eastern edge of the upper
Shephelah—isolated and vulnerable to attacks from the rulers of the
lower Shephelah and the coastal plain below. The Philistines had
assumed control of this area after the retreat of the Egyptian regime
from Canaan. Attacks by the powerful Philistine city-states upon
the border of the hill country—to loot crops or terrorize the sparse
rural population—could therefore have been expected in this
period. But the biblical Keilah story also seems to reflect a long pat-

tern of raids and counterattacks that had been going in this area at least since the Late Bronze Age.

Indeed, it is significant that Keilah is explicitly mentioned in the Amarna archive as a town whose possession was hotly disputed, in this case between Shuwardata of Gath and Abdi-Heba of Jerusalem. Shuwardata attacked the village (called Qiltu or Qeltu in the Amarna letters), which he considered as belonging to him. A sentence in one of the Shuwardata letters, stating that "I must go fo[rt]h to Qeltu [again]st the t[raitors]," may hint that local Apiru forces were also involved, this time on the side of Abdi-Heba. The David story, taking place in the same region under the same conditions some four hundred years later, is reported by the Bible in a similar way: the defense of Keilah is accomplished by a gang of armed men who repel the invaders, acting independently in place of an impotent central government.

The frequent employment of Apiru as mercenaries underlined their rejection of conventional political loyalty. In the case of David, this could hardly be clearer. The Philistine city of Gath was a powerful, aggressive threat to the people of the highlands; its ruler, Achish, was a deadly enemy. Nonetheless, on two occasions David is described as taking shelter in Philistine territory. On the first (1 Samuel 21:10–15), he appeared alone in Gath and unsuccessfully sought asylum. But on the second occasion, David became a Philistine ally and was given a territorial fiefdom, from which he was free to raid non-Philistine territories:

> *So David arose and went over, he and the six hundred men who were with him, to Achish the son of Maoch, king of Gath. And David dwelt with Achish of Gath, he and his men. . . . Then David said to Achish, "If I have found favour in your eyes, let a place be given to me in one of the country towns, that I may dwell there; for why should your servant dwell in the royal city with you?" So that day Achish gave him Ziklag. . . . Now David and his men went up, and made raids upon the Geshurites, the Girzites, and the Amalekites;*

for these were the inhabitants of the land from of old. . . . And David smote the land, and left neither man nor woman alive, but took away the sheep, the oxen, the asses, the camels, and the garments, and came back to Achish. (1 Samuel 27:2–9)

In other circumstances, David and his gang do not shrink from an occasional attempt at extortion among their own people. David sends ten of his men to Nabal, a rich Judahite sheep owner in the village of Carmel, to "remind" him of the protection that his men had provided to Nabal's shepherds and shearers, and to demand in return "whatever you have at hand." Nabal's angry retort to David could hardly have been more dismissive—or more revealing of the parallel to the Apiru phenomenon.

Who is David? Who is the son of Jesse? There are many servants nowadays who are breaking away from their masters. Shall I take my bread and my water and my meat that I have killed for my shearers, and give it to men who come from I do not know where? (1 Samuel 25:10–11)

Nabal's answer may have been heartfelt, but it was certainly not effective.

And David said to his men, "Every man gird on his sword!" And every man of them girded on his sword; David also girded on his sword; and about four hundred men went up after David, while two hundred remained with the baggage. (1 Samuel 25:13)

According to the Bible, David received his tribute, Nabal dropped dead, and David claimed his widow—the beautiful Abigail—as a new wife for himself. These events may have actually happened as described in the Bible, or they may express in a vivid and colorful way a familiar situation in the southern highlands between village nobles and bandits. Either way, the situation is illuminating.

So too is the hint that David had a larger strategy than just isolated acts of violence and plunder. After Keilah, he was recognized by the local population as a welcome protector and avenger. After his great victory over the Amalekites, he offered a generous share of his booty to all the local elders of the highlands of Judah who had supported or sheltered him (1 Samuel 30: 26–31).* It is not surprising that a short while later the same elders pronounce David "king" of Judah in their assembly at Hebron. From a nobody and a bandit, David rose to be recognized as a popular leader over the sparsely settled southern hills. But Hebron had always been only the second most important town in Judah. No wonder the biblical narrative describes David soon setting his sights on Jerusalem—the key to control over the entire southern highlands.

FROM BANDIT TO CHIEFTAIN

The rise of an Apiru leader to political power was not unprecedented. The Amarna letters provide many indications that local rulers—especially in the highlands—may have come from Apiru backgrounds themselves. Although Abdi-Heba's letters used the term "Apiru" in angry denunciation, it is likely that he himself cooperated with these groups against the lowland cities when it served his interests. It is not out of the question that Abdi-Heba may have risen to power from an Apiru background himself.

That is certainly what occurred in neighboring regions. In the northern part of Mount Lebanon, near the present-day border between Lebanon and Syria, two chiefs, named Abdi-ashirta and Aziru—a father and a son—expanded their influence from their small and remote highland village down to the hilly area at the foot of the mountains and then into the coastal plain in the vicinity of

---

* The original text is apparently 1 Samuel 30:26. As we will see in a subsequent chapter, the list of towns which follow was apparently added much later, to serve the kingdom of Judah's expanded territorial goals.

the modern city of Tripoli in northern Lebanon. They first conquered a local city-state and then took over an Egyptian administrative center. They established the influential state of Amurru, which stretched over a large territory, including both coastal and mountainous areas. A few generations later, in the thirteenth century BCE, this state was strong enough to shift the balance of power between the Egyptian and Hittite empires.

Another example—closer to Judah—is that of Labayu, the ruler of the northern highland city of Shechem. The conspiracies and maneuvers of Labayu, originating in the hill country, eventually expanded to cover large parts of the country—from Gezer and Jerusalem in the south to the Jezreel Valley and beyond in the north. The Amarna letters describe his attempts—possibly in cooperation with groups of Apiru—to expand into the Jezreel Valley and to gain territories from the city-states of that region, including Megiddo. His strategy failed. Condemned as a criminal, he was captured and killed by his neighbors, who acted in the service of the Egyptian authorities.

Unfortunately, we cannot closely follow the political situation in the southern highlands over the four hundred years, between the time of Abdi-Heba in the fourteenth century BCE and David's presumed activities in the tenth century BCE. Egyptian texts are few and highly fragmentary. The biblical narrative indicates that a people called Jebusites were the rulers of Jerusalem at the time of David's conquest. We have no information about them and their time, or how they came to power, but from the archaeological indications, the general settlement patterns of the Amarna age seem to have persisted.

In Jerusalem, remains from the Early Iron Age (the late twelfth century to about 900 BCE) are a bit more substantial than those of the Late Bronze Age, probably indicating that the small hamlet of Abdi-Heba gradually grew in size. Excavations on the eastern slope of the City of David, above the Gihon spring, exposed a system of stone terraces that were probably built to support a fort or even a palace, but we cannot tell if this occurred under the rule of Abdi-Heba's dynasty, or if new leaders emerged to wrest power from his heirs. Nor do we know what relation the Early Iron Age rulers of Jerusalem might have to the biblical descriptions of the Jebusites.

Outside Jerusalem in any case, little was changed. The hill country to the south was still sparsely inhabited, even though the number of settled sites grew modestly. All in all, surveys recorded the remains of only about twenty permanent Early Iron Age settlements in the southern highlands. Their population can be estimated at a few thousand people, to which must be added the roving bandit groups and the large herding communities.

What can we say about the role of David in all this?

The traditional system of banditry was a makeshift way of life, dealing in a haphazard and brutal way with the society's inner stresses and inequalities. But sometimes the growing power and support for Apiru leaders resulted in a permanent change of regime—with some influential or successful bandit chieftains taking the reins of highland rule themselves. Whether we can perceive a historical kernel in the biblical account of David's conquest of Jebusite Jerusalem through a daring assault, we can recognize a familiar pattern of ancient regime change. Throughout the centuries Jerusalem was not merely the southern highlands' most prominent stronghold; it was the ceremonial focus and political anchor for the traditional form of dimorphic chiefdom that encompassed the entire southern highlands area.

The modest expansion of building activities in Early Iron Age Jerusalem is extremely difficult to link to the Bible's events. Whether the terraces and other structures on the eastern slope of the City of David were meant to support a citadel, we cannot say for sure.* We do not even know when, exactly, within the first few centuries of the Iron

---

* For a more detailed description of the debate over the Early Iron Age remains in Jerusalem, see Appendix 2.

Age these construction works took place. We know only that at some point, the followers and descendants of David acknowledged Jerusalem as their capital. The official trappings of David's new regime would have been modest. Business would have been conducted with the highland clans through face-to-face encounters and social interaction. Storytelling would have been a key to his maintaining the continued support of the people of the southern highlands, now that he had been transformed from their occasional protector to their permanent chief.

THE STRATIGRAPHY OF HEROIC TALES

Though the demographic, social, and political realities behind the David-as-Apiru stories all seem to reflect the memories of an early period—possibly memories of the actual realities if not events in the tenth century BCE—it is clear that these stories were not put in writing at that time. The cycle of David-as-Apiru stories, containing some fairly reliable memories about conditions in the highlands at the very start of his career, were probably orally transmitted for some two centuries, until the eighth century BCE, when the first signs of widespread literacy appear in Judah. For two hundred years, David would have been the hero of tall tales and folktales that celebrated his extraordinary career. Yet oral transmission is quite fluid. There can hardly be a doubt that the form in which we have these stories today—incorporated first into the coherent "Rise of David" narrative and then into the larger Deuteronomistic History—is quite different from that of the original tales. Centuries of exaggeration and storytelling surely transformed some of the elements, deleted others, and added successive layers of political and theological interpolation that reflected the concerns and realities of the tellers.

So how can we begin to separate the layers? The American biblical scholar Stanley Isser suggests that we look at the process of folktale creation itself. He examined the narrative of "David's Rise to Power" and identified the common mythic themes it shares with bandit tales and hero myths in different historical periods and in different parts of the world. Particularly intriguing are the literary "fossils" interspersed in the text of David's story. Snatches of ancient heroic tales seem to have been cut and pasted into the narrative at various places. This apparent urge to collect and incorporate all known traditions resulted in two of the most awkward passages in an otherwise well-written text.

Before and after the farewell speech of the dying David—oddly placed in the midst of the narrative of the king's later years of rule— comes a series of colorful yet almost telegraphic summaries of heroic acts (2 Samuel 21:15–22; 23:8–39) of David's followers at the very *beginning* of his career, mainly in the wars against the Philistines. To all appearances, the editor or editors who stitched these passages together had collected additional information about the exploits of some of David's most important followers but failed to integrate these episodes into the free-flowing narrative. So they are placed as something of an appendix containing brief summaries of some stories that must have been well-known folktales themselves.

And Ishbi-benob, one of the descendants of the giants, whose spear weighed three hundred shekels of bronze, and who was girded with a new sword, thought to kill David. But Abishai the son of Zeruiah came to his aid, and attacked the Philistine and killed him. Then David's men adjured him, "You shall no more go out with us to battle, lest you quench the lamp of Israel." (2 Samuel 21:16–17)

And there was again war at Gath, where there was a man of great stature, who had six fingers on each hand, and six toes on each foot, twenty-four in number; and he also was descended from the giants. And when he taunted Israel, Jonathan the son of Shimei, David's brother, slew him. (2 Samuel 21:20–21)

. . . *Josheb-basshebeth a Tahchemonite; he was chief of the three; he wielded his spear against eight hundred whom he slew at one time. (2 Samuel 23:8)*

. . . *Eleazar the son of Dodo, son of Ahohi. He was with David when they defied the Philistines who were gathered there for battle, and the men of Israel withdrew. He rose and struck down the Philistines until his hand was weary, and his hand cleaved to the sword; and the* LORD *wrought a great victory that day. (2 Samuel 23:9–10)*

. . . *Shammah, the son of Agee the Hararite. The Philistines gathered together at Lehi, where there was a plot of ground full of lentils; and the men fled from the Philistines. But he took his stand in the midst of the plot, and defended it, and slew the Philistines; and the* LORD *wrought a great victory. (2 Samuel 23:11–12)*

And three of the thirty chief men went down, and came about harvest time to David at the cave of Adullam, when a band of Philistines was encamped in the valley of Rephaim. David was then in the stronghold; and the garrison of the Philistines was then at Bethlehem. And David said longingly, "O that some one would give me water to drink from the well of Bethlehem which is by the gate!" Then the three mighty men broke through the camp of the Philistines, and drew water out of the well of Bethlehem which was by the gate, and took and brought it to David. But he would not drink of it; he poured it out to the LORD, *and said, "Far be it from me, O* LORD, *that I should do this. Shall I drink the blood of the men who went at the risk of their lives?" (2 Samuel 23:13–17)*

Now Abishai, the brother of Joab, the son of Zeruiah, was chief of the thirty. And he wielded his spear against three hundred men and slew them, and won a name beside the three. (2 Samuel 23:18)

And Benaiah the son of Jehoiada was a valiant man of Kabzeel, a doer of great deeds; he smote two ariels of Moab. He also went down

and slew a lion in a pit on a day when snow had fallen. And he slew
an Egyptian, a handsome man. The Egyptian had a spear in his
hand; but Benaiah went down to him with a staff, and snatched the
spear out of the Egyptian's hand, and slew him with his own spear.
(2 Samuel 23:20–21)

None of these acts of daring are mentioned in the body of the
David story. It is noteworthy that they take place in the same area
as his recorded acts, in the Judean hills and their immediate vicinity. Yet in the form they are presented they strip the stories of all
their drama and beg as many questions as they answer. Why did
Josheb-basshebeth have to battle eight hundred warriors alone?
Where was the battle at which the hand of Eleazar the son of Dodo
cleaved to his sword? Why was Shammah the son of Agee in a field
of lentils? What were the circumstances (and the meaning) of
Benaiah the son of Jehoiada slaying "two ariels of Moab," "a lion in
a pit on a day that the snow had fallen," and an Egyptian with his
own spear?

The content in these summaries is extraordinary (as are some of
their details, like the description of the warrior with twelve fingers
and twelve toes), but they seem intended more to *remind* the reader
of well-known tales, whose details were familiar, rather than provide
an authoritative historical account. Isser pointed out that these literary traces are apparent fragments of an early body of epic ballads
that celebrated the exploits of David and his men. The tales were
popular among the people of Judah, but were not incorporated fully
into the biblical account. As mere summaries, they provide us with
the clear recognition that the compilers of the biblical narrative had
at their disposal a vast body of tradition for inclusion in their work.
Some tales were selected, others were abbreviated, and yet others
were probably rejected altogether. Theirs was a task of collection
and heavy editing, surely not an accurate recording of history.

We have not yet discussed what is surely the most famous folktale
of all about David: his miraculous victory over the Philistine giant

Goliath of Gath, the shaft of whose spear "was like a weaver's beam" (1 Samuel 17:7). One can hardly even think of the young David today without calling it to mind. It is the act that is probably most widely remembered, and it is presumed by many biblical readers to be a historical event. But among the short summaries we have just mentioned is the following, surprising report:

> *And there was again war with the Philistines at Gob; and Elhanan the son of Jaare-oregim, the Bethlehemite, slew Goliath the Gittite, the shaft of whose spear was like a weaver's beam. (2 Samuel 21:19)*

Who killed Goliath? As we will show in a later chapter, the David-and-Goliath story as we now have it shows the clear influence of much later periods. But here, in one of the abbreviated folktales, presumably an early stratum of legend, we hear of Elhanan's achievement. Could this represent an early version of one of the world's most famous biblical tales? Was Elhanan the real name of a hero who toppled a Philistine giant or, as some scholars have suggested, was Elhanan the original name of Judah's future king?

TALES FOR COLD WINTER NIGHTS

The ancient tales of the bandit hero and his mighty men, recited around campfires and at public celebrations, were meant to impress his followers with his extraordinary exploits, and thereby to instill respect for the hero's power. He was a man of the people, a brave rebel who fought fiercely against enemies and injustice. He was a man of strong desires and an equally strong determination to resist the overlords, and the injustices that so many of his contemporaries had learned to accept. In every story of his smashing victories and the astounding acts of bravery of his closest comrades, listeners gained vicarious satisfaction and an enhanced sense of security. As the colorful tales spread from mouth to mouth and from village to village, their details grew more miraculously entertaining and (no doubt) less accurate.

The most plausible historical scenario we can propose—based on the passages of 1 Samuel that match the archaeological and anthropological conditions of the tenth century BCE in the highlands of Judah—is that an Apiru-like leader known as David emerged as a local strongman at a time of political chaos. He eventually gained enough support among the southern highland population that the respected elders of the area proclaimed him chieftain in the old tribal center of Hebron. Before long he established his seat of his power in Jerusalem and ruled over the region's farmers and herders, much as Abdi-Heba had done some centuries before. Since the southern hill country was remote from the main trade routes and centers of lowland power, the rise of the historical David would have been a local matter, of concern at first perhaps only to those Philistine cities that faced Judah's western flank. In that respect, the highly localized stories of David's bandit days in the cave of Adullam, his coming to the rescue of the people of Keilah, his protection of Ziklag, and his dealings with arrogant sheep raisers would have bound the listeners among the villages of the southern highlands and eastern Shephelah into a community of sympathy and support.

It would be a mistake to assume that the people of the southern hill country had a single, uniformly defined national identity at the time of David. The region was fragmented among its farmers and shepherds, and among its many crosscutting clans. Only later would the people of Judah look back and assume that their designation as a single people had always been so clear. That was due in no small measure to the continual transmission and elaboration of the ancient stories about the founder of their dynasty, whose value lay in the sense of local community solidarity they helped to create. In the following chapters we will trace the layers of mythmaking and historical reinterpretation that were gradually added to the earliest stratum of the Davidic bandit tales. Not everything is clearly datable and many questions remain. But we will present archaeological evidence that can show step by step, era by era, how the biblical legend of David and, later, his son Solomon was formed for an ever-wider coalition of communities—eventually for western civilization as a whole.

David was the founder of something new in the Judean hills in the dawning epoch we now call the Iron Age. There may have been—and probably were—other local heroes in the highlands of Canaan. But David was different from all others. His career was not just a meteoric moment of triumph doomed to live on only in the folktales of a famous local bandit king and soon be forgotten. Whether by cunning, intelligence, or extraordinary historical circumstance, he alone, of all the now-forgotten ruffians and freebooters who roamed the rugged country between the Dead Sea and the Judean foothills, established a dynasty that ruled for the next four hundred years. And even after it lost its political power, it was continuously remembered and revered for millennia.

But the question we must now address is how the appeal and influence of this southern chieftain, who rose from the sheep pens and bandits' caves, far transcended his original local role. How did David's memory come to be intertwined with the deepest hopes and national traditions of the vast confederation of hill country villages to the *north* of Judah that would later be identified as Israel?

PERIOD	STAGES IN DEVELOPMENT OF BIBLICAL MATERIAL
10th Century BCE	Early memories of Saul as leader of an early north Israelite tribal confederacy; elaborated through oral tradition into a tragic saga by north Israelite villagers after Saul's death.

HISTORICAL BACKGROUND	ARCHAEOLOGICAL FINDS
Emergence of "Israel," the first Iron Age territorial entity in the highlands. It threatens the interests of a revived Egypt and is weakened by the campaign of Pharaoh Shishak.	Dramatic increase in number of settlements in the highlands north of Jerusalem. Subsequent wave of abandonment around Gibeon.

CHAPTER 2

The Madness of Saul

Egypt, the Philistines, and the Fall of Earliest Israel

—TENTH CENTURY BCE—

DAVID'S CAREER AS A BANDIT IN THE HIGHLANDS OF Judah is only part of the story of his rise to power. His biography, in the biblical narrative, is deeply intertwined with the tragic story of the northern Israelite hero Saul. For Saul—not David—was anointed as the first king of Israel. It is Saul who initially claims the spotlight in the first book of Samuel. David's entrance to the drama comes only after it is apparent that Saul is too humanly flawed and impulsive to deliver the people of Israel from their enemies and to lead them piously. God's favor—and Israel's kingship—shifts from the northerner Saul to David, the man of the south.

Saul was, to all appearances, the greatest of his generation. He was imposing, charismatic, and courageous; "there was not a man among the people of Israel more handsome than he" (1 Samuel 9:2). Born of the tribe of Benjamin, he appeared on the stage of Israel's history at a time of great crisis. At the battle of Ebenezer, the mighty Philistine armies routed the Israelite forces and captured the

Israelites' sacred relic, the Ark of the Covenant (1 Samuel 4). In the wake of this national catastrophe, the elders of Israel traveled to Ramah, the home of Israel's spiritual leader, the aged prophet Samuel, to demand that he appoint for them a king, that "we also may be like all the nations, and that our king may govern us and go out before us and fight our battles" (1 Samuel 8:20). Despite his misgivings, Samuel followed divine instruction and, ceremoniously pouring a vial of oil over Saul's head, announced: "Has not the LORD anointed you to be prince over his people Israel? And you shall reign over the people of the LORD and you will save them from the hand

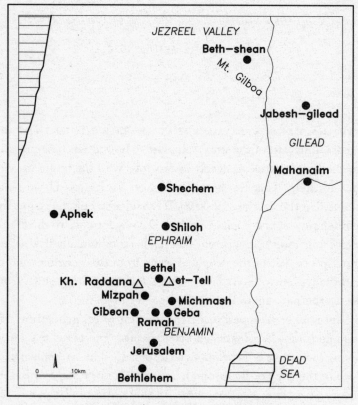

The chiefdom of Saul and Ish-bosheth

of their enemies round about" (1 Samuel 10:1). He thereby declared
Saul to be Israel's first king and "messiah"—in the original sense of
the Hebrew word *mashiach*, "anointed one."

What went wrong in this original selection? How and why did
David, a humble shepherd from Bethlehem, come to inherit the role
of king of Israel? Those are the central questions that the biblical
narrative answers, and as we will see, they are deeply connected to a
basic conflict of later Israelite history—over the relative righteousness and power of the south as against the north. While David is the
preeminent man of Judah and the southern hill country, Saul is the
very personification of the righteous fury of the northern Israelite
highlands. Once anointed, Saul became the greatest of holy warriors,
leading the Israelites to stunning victories over the Ammonites,
Amelekites, and Philistines. Yet even though Saul and his son Jonathan subsequently routed the Philistine invaders and continued to
fight Israel's enemies "on every side," delivering Israel "out of the
hands of those who plundered them" (1 Samuel 14:47, 48), Saul's
cultic missteps and madness grew, ultimately disqualifying him from
his role as the true savior of Israel.

As David gains fame throughout Israel for his heroic toppling of
Goliath and the women of Israel sing his praises—"Saul has slain his
thousands, and David his ten thousands" (1 Samuel 18:7), Saul's
rage against David grows murderous. David has no choice but to
flee for his life.

We have already described David's bandit days in the wilderness,
his growing fame throughout Israel, and his close escapes from the
revenge of the increasingly unstable Israelite king. Yet the sudden
end of Saul's tragic reign comes not in a violent confrontation with
David, but in a showdown with a formidable Philistine force far to
the north. With his madness steadily building and with the Philistines victorious, he takes his own life in a tragic act of desperation
on the battlefield (1 Samuel 31:4).

Saul's tragic fall and David's rise are thus inseparable in the biblical narrative. But is there any way to separate history from legend?

What can archaeology tell us about the very beginnings of kingship in ancient Israel?

WHO, WHEN, AND WHERE?

The biblical story of King Saul raises some difficult questions. Was Saul a historical figure? If so, can archaeology help us determine exactly where and when he ruled? Still more complex is understanding the Bible's contradictory depiction of Saul as hero, sinner, and tragic, tormented figure—being chosen by God as the savior of Israel and then unforgivingly condemned by him. Considering that both Saul and David were, on occasion, sinners, why was Saul singled out and utterly rejected for kingship while David was given an unconditional divine promise of eternal rule?

First, about his historical existence. Saul is not mentioned in any source outside the Bible, that is, in any ancient inscriptions or chronicles of neighboring countries. That absence of contemporary evidence is not surprising and should not lead us to conclude that Saul's life story is entirely fictional. As we have already mentioned, writing was extremely rare in the kingdoms of Judah and Israel and their neighbors until the later Iron Age, and the exploits of an early local highlands ruler were unlikely to be recorded in public inscriptions or in the chronicles of Egypt or Mesopotamia, which are limited and fragmentary during the crucial centuries between the end of the Late Bronze Age and the ninth century BCE. The absence of contemporary confirmation outside the Bible is thus no reason to deny that an early Israelite leader named Saul *could* have existed. Indeed, as we will soon see, there are intriguing archaeological and historical indications that parallel the main points of Saul's biblical biography.

The question of *when* Saul would have ruled is, as we have seen, difficult to answer. It hangs on a single, garbled biblical verse describing Saul's age at the time of his anointment and the length of his reign: "Saul was . . . years old when he began to reign; and he reigned . . . and two years over Israel" (1 Samuel 13:1). Most biblical scholars have come to the reasonable conclusion that the text is defective and he must certainly have ruled for more than just a couple of years. Considering the long sequence of events attributed to Saul's reign, in particular his military exploits across the Jordan, against the Philistines, and against the Amalekites—and taking into account the number two, which does appear in the text—scholars have speculated that the original number might have been twenty-two. Calculating backward from the sequence of later monarchs, for whose reigns we have some external chronological confirmation— and accepting at face value the biblical testimony of a forty-year reign for both Solomon (1 Kings 11:42) and David (2 Samuel 5:4)— most biblical historians have traditionally placed the reign of Saul in the late eleventh century, around 1030–1010 BCE.

But we have already noted that these dates are not as precise as they seem. Generations of historians and biblical scholars have become accustomed to accepting them quite literally; at best they should be taken as only a very rough approximation. The dating of Saul, David, and Solomon is based on the Bible's own chronology, and the numbers of years given for the reigns of David and Solomon—a "generation" of forty years each—seem suspiciously round. The garbled chronological information given about Saul compounds the problem. If the reigns of David and Solomon were shorter (closer to that of most of the later kings of Israel and Judah) and Saul ruled less than the hypothesized twenty or twenty-two years, the century made by the calculation of forty plus forty plus twenty could be considerably reduced. It is also possible that Saul and David's reigns overlapped. If we follow this line of thought, Saul, David, and Solomon would all have lived sometime in the tenth century BCE. We can safely say no more than that. This chronological change might not seem to be so important, but as we will see later in this chapter, the *literal* acceptance of the biblical dates has led generations of archaeologists and historians to misinterpret the evidence about the early history of Judah and Israel.

How large was Saul's kingdom? Despite the biblical claim that Saul was king of all Israel, the text is not completely precise on the extent of the territory that he ruled. Of course we must be extremely careful when we use the terms "king" and "kingdom." For just as Rembrandt depicted Saul as an Oriental despot and medieval artists portrayed David and Solomon as contemporary European monarchs, the biblical authors, living centuries after the time of Saul, David, and Solomon, described them in royal terms appropriate to their own eras. Yet leaving aside for the time being the question of the nature of Saul's kingship, the biblical text clearly localizes the traditions about him.

We are told that Saul was a Benjaminite by birth, and much of the described activity of his reign takes place in his tribal territory and the area immediately to its north. The places most prominent in the Saul stories—Ramah, Mizpah, Geba, Michmash, and Gibeon —are all located in the Benjaminite highlands immediately to the north of Jerusalem. Saul's fateful search for the lost asses of his father (1 Samuel 9) takes him slightly farther north—from Benjamin, to the land of Shalishah, to the land of Sha'alim, and to the land of Zuph in the hill country of Ephraim. It is an area of isolated highland villages, extending north from Judah into the richer and more fertile hill country west of the Jordan.

After his anointment by the prophet Samuel, Saul's activity extends to the hill country *east* of the Jordan, with his rescue of the inhabitants of Jabesh-gilead. This area seems to have become an integral part of the territory associated with Saul and his family. After the death of Saul and his sons at the hands of the Philistines, it is the people of Jabesh who come to rescue their bodies and bury them "under the tamarisk tree in Jabesh" (1 Samuel 31:11–13). Even more significant is the fact that Saul's heir, Ish-bosheth, was brought to the town of Mahanaim in the same region and was proclaimed "king over Gilead and the Ashurites and Jezreel and Ephraim and Benjamin and all Israel" (2 Samuel 2:9). "Gilead" refers to the northern part of the Transjordanian plateau, in which the towns of

Mahanaim and Jabesh-gilead were located. All the other terms refer to the central hill country west of the Jordan, reaching to the Jezreel Valley in the north. This combination of peoples and areas on both sides of the Jordan River does not correspond to any later territorial unit in the history of Israel. Indeed the biblical description of Saul's territorial legacy does not apply the geographic terms used for these regions in late monarchic times.

So how can we summarize the biblical evidence? Although the text declares that Saul was king of "all Israel," his activities were restricted to the northern highlands to the west of the Jordan, with an extension across the Jordan to Gilead to the east. It is important to note that the biblical narrative records no independent actions taken by Saul anywhere in the highlands of Judah. All of the detailed descriptions of the settlements south and southwest of Jerusalem are contained exclusively in the stories connected with Saul's pursuit of David or in the exploits of David alone. Saul, then, apparently did not rule over *all* Israel. The memories embedded in the Bible seem to suggest that he was a tenth-century BCE northern highland leader who claimed a large area on both sides of the Jordan, with a special core in the hill country of Benjamin, *north* of Jerusalem. So, what kind of "kingdom" was that?

THE RISE OF THE NORTHERN HIGHLANDS

If Judah of the tenth century BCE was a remote and isolated chiefdom, the highlands to the north were very different. We get a quite remarkable picture from the large-scale archaeological surveys that have been conducted in the hill country to the north of Jerusalem and from excavations of some important Iron I sites in that area. We now know that in the later phase of Iron I—the late eleventh and tenth century BCE—the territory in which the Bible localizes Saul's territory was relatively *densely* inhabited as the result of a major settlement shift. A dramatic demographic expansion is evident in the number and distribution of settlement sites, and in their growing size. From only about twenty-five recorded sites in the area between Jerusalem and the Jezreel Valley in the preceding Late Bronze Age, the number skyrockets to more than 230 in the late Iron I period. Their estimated population was just over forty thousand, compared to less than five thousand in the entire hill country of Judah.

Environment obviously played a major role in the area's economic difference from rugged, semiarid Judah. Large parts of the highlands north of Jerusalem are well suited for extensive agriculture. The plateau of Benjamin, the small fertile valleys to the south of Shechem, the larger ones between that city and the Jezreel Valley in the north, as well as the less arid eastern flank of the highlands, offered their inhabitants wide areas for the cultivation of grain. Even the more rugged parts of the western side of the northern hill country were extensively terraced for vineyards and olive groves. Indeed, excavations in some of the more important mounds in this area revealed evidence for public construction and clues for significant administrative activity: an elaborate storage facility at Shiloh (reported in the Bible as a central shrine in the later days of the period of the judges) and a possible continuity of activity in the ancient monumental temple of Shechem.

A similarly dramatic settlement expansion took place across the Jordan, in the northern part of the Transjordanian plateau. There, too, the number of settled sites vastly expanded, from about thirty in the Late Bronze Age to about 220 in the Early Iron Age. In the area of Gilead, with its fertile plateau, where agricultural potential was high, surveys have identified the largest single cluster of settlements in this period, indicating a significant settled population there.

Hence, while the number of tenth-century settlements in the Judahite hill country was extremely limited—probably numbering no more than twenty—and the villages were relatively small (most not exceeding an acre in size and inhabited by no more than a hundred people), the highlands to the north were occupied by many more settlements, many of which were larger, representing a much more significant and potentially powerful demographic phenomenon.

In the last chapter we drew some important information from the Tell el-Amarna letters about the society and economy of the highlands in the Late Bronze Age. A south-north division is implicit in their reports of the contemporary situation, since at that time, two main centers—Jerusalem and Shechem—divided the highlands between them, each ruling over extensive areas of approximately six hundred square miles. Yet while the southern territory of Abdi-Heba was beset by strife on its western border and by a shortage of the manpower necessary for territorial expansion, the northern area (ruled from Shechem by a local prince named Labayu) was on the offensive and engaged in repeated attempts to expand its territory. In fact, Labayu seems to have been intent on expanding from his highland base into the lowlands in order to establish a larger, composite political entity. Labayu's aggressive moves were wide-ranging. He threatened Gezer and Jerusalem in the south and attempted to expand his rule into the Jezreel Valley and to gain territories from the city-states of that region, including Megiddo. Yet he was ultimately thwarted by other Canaanite vassals who captured and killed him on the orders of the Egyptian authorities. Nonetheless, his ability to attempt territorial expansion beyond the highlands offers interesting testimony for the military and economic potential of a northern highlands polity.

Archaeological evidence hints that the center of power in the northern highlands shifted southward during the centuries after the Amarna period. Labayu's center was the city of Shechem, but by the tenth century BCE, a significant proportion of the inhabitants of the highlands lived in the plateau just to the north of Jerusalem. This relatively small territory of just over sixty square miles—which, as we have seen, is remembered in the biblical tradition as the core of Saul's kingdom—was dotted with almost fifty settlements, including some elaborate sites, such as Khirbet Seilun (identified as the Israelite cultic center of Shiloh), el-Jib (identified as the biblical Gibeon), and

Tell en-Nasbeh (the location of the biblical Mizpah). Although this settlement phenomenon should be seen as part of the much broader settlement wave that swept over the highlands both west and east of the Jordan, there is something unique in a particular group of sites in the Benjaminite plateau, around Gibeon.

A MYSTERIOUS ABANDONMENT

In marked contrast to the vast majority of Iron I sites in the highlands—over 90 percent of the approximately 250 that have been recorded throughout the entire central hill country—which continued to be inhabited without interruption until the late Iron Age II (eighth and seventh centuries BCE), the area of settlement north of Jerusalem went through a crisis that led to abandonment of a significant number of settlements. New radiocarbon dating and reanalysis of excavated pottery groups suggest that Shiloh was destroyed by fire in the late eleventh century BCE and then abandoned. Et-Tell (biblical Ai), Khirbet Raddana near Ramallah, and Khirbet ed-Dawwara to the northeast of Jerusalem were abandoned in the late tenth century BCE and never reoccupied. Gibeon may also have been abandoned and resettled only after a long occupational gap.

This suggests an intriguing correlation: the area with a dense system of Iron I sites, some of which were destroyed or abandoned in the Early Iron Age, corresponds to the core of Saul's "kingdom" to the north of Jerusalem. Something indeed significant seems to have been developing there, perhaps the emergence of a new highland polity, quite distinct from the isolated bandit chiefdom in Judah. Yet in contrast to the settlement wave in the rest of the highlands, its period of great demographic growth in the twelfth to tenth centuries BCE came to a sudden end.

The redating of the abandonment of sites in this settlement core, placing it in the late tenth century—a time of supposed peace and prosperity under the rule of King Solomon—suggests that the traditional biblical chronology needs to be revised. How does this redating fit into the larger picture of what was happening in the region in this period? What brought about the abandonment of sites in the core of highlands settlement in the plateau of Benjamin? Can a possible answer to that question shed new light on the historical events and developments that underlay the biblical traditions about the rise and fall of Saul? Surprisingly, the answers to these questions come from an entirely unexpected source.

RETURN OF THE PHARAOH

If you mention the name Shishak to close readers of the Bible, a famous passage in the first book of Kings will immediately come to mind. This text has nothing to do with Saul or David, but comes from the time of David's grandson Rehoboam, who, according to the traditional chronology of the Judahite and Israelite kings, reigned at the end of the tenth century BCE. According to the Bible, Rehoboam's reign was one of rampant idolatry, when his Judahite subjects "built for themselves high places, and pillars, and Asherim on every high hill and under every green tree; and there were also male cult prostitutes in the land" (1 Kings 14:23). Misfortune was not long in coming.

In the fifth year of King Rehoboam, Shishak king of Egypt came up against Jerusalem; he took away the treasures of the house of the LORD and the treasures of the king's house; he took away everything. (1 Kings 14:25–26)

Establishing a secure chronology for this earliest phase of Israelite history is, as we have seen, extremely difficult. With a lack of datable inscriptions (presumably due to the decline of Egypt and the other major literate powers in this era), the possibility of confirming or precisely dating the biblical events is virtually nil. But the biblical passage referring to Shishak holds the key to one unique chronological

anchor—or at least it has served as such for many decades. Early in
the modern exploration of Egypt, scholars came upon a huge triumphal relief commissioned by Sheshonq I, a pharaoh of the Twenty-
second Dynasty, who ruled in the tenth century BCE. Reviving the
country after two centuries of decline, in which Egypt lost its leading

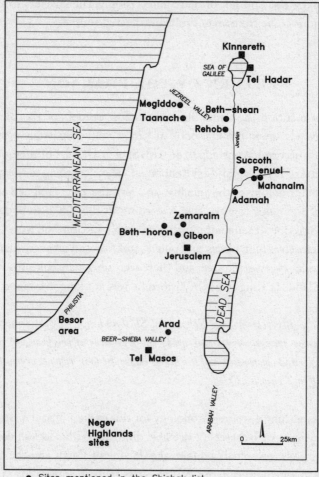

● Sites mentioned in the Shishak list
■ Other sites

The Shishak (Sheshonq I) campaign

role as a great world power, Sheshonq I embarked on a military campaign to the north—into the land of Canaan—that is recorded on the outer wall of the Hypostyle Hall in the great temple of Amun at Karnak. This is significant, for the consensus among Egyptologists and biblical scholars has long been that the Egyptian Sheshonq I and the biblical Shishak are the same historical personality.

In the Karnak relief, a gigantic image is shown of Sheshonq smiting his enemies and leading off a large group of prisoners of war. Each figure is identified with the name of a place that the pharaoh claimed to have conquered. This list of place-names provides apparent evidence for the likely route of Sheshonq's invasion, though it has no clear geographical order. The places mentioned are organized in three groups in widely separated regions. The first group includes villages or towns in the coastal plain, in an area of the central hill country north of Jerusalem, in a sector in Transjordan along the Jabbok River, and in the Jezreel Valley. The second group includes places in the south, including the Beer-sheba Valley and, possibly, the Negev highlands. And the third, on a part of the relief that is damaged, seems to have included places along the southern coast. As we will see, it is highly significant that Jerusalem and the highlands of Judah—in fact the entire land of Judah—which are the pharaoh's main target in the biblical story, are conspicuously absent from the Karnak list.

The biblical text puts Shishak's campaign in the fifth year of Rehoboam, 926 BCE according to the widely accepted chronology of the Judahite monarchs. Yet this date is far from reliable, because of another case of circular reasoning. Due to the very fragmentary nature of Egyptian records in this period, it is difficult to provide the pharaohs of the Twenty-first and Twenty-second Dynasties with exact dates. The reign of Sheshonq I has always been dated by his identification as Shishak, according to the traditional biblical chronology of the Judahite kings' reigns. And to make things even more questionable, scholars seeking to confirm the historical accuracy of the Bible have done so by evincing the evidence of the

Sheshonq relief. Neither one proves the other. Neither provides any independent dating evidence. So even though it is safe to say that Sheshonq and Shishak are, in fact, the same person, and that he ruled in the tenth century BCE, we are left with a considerable measure of uncertainty about when his famous northern campaign took place.

Moreover, it is unclear whether he carried out his campaign in his early years on the throne or in his later days. There is even a serious debate among Egyptologists whether Sheshonq I carried out one or more northern campaigns. If we take into consideration all these factors, the Sheshonq campaign could have taken place almost any time in the mid to late tenth century BCE, not necessarily during Rehoboam's reign.*

What was the purpose of this campaign? Many biblical scholars have traditionally described the Egyptian invasion as a *razia*—little more than a destructive raid, designed to cause maximum damage but leave no permanent presence, but a reexamination of the evidence suggests that it should be seen as the revival of a centuries-long ambition by the pharaohs of Egypt to reconquer and control its former Canaanite possessions.

SHISHAK'S HIDDEN STRATEGY

For centuries the great pharaohs of Egypt's New Kingdom (the Late Bronze Age in the fifteenth to twelfth centuries BCE) had placed

---

* The reason why the Shishak invasion was linked in the Deuteronomistic History to the reign of Rehoboam may be more theological than historical. It is a vivid example of the Deuteronomistic principle of sin and divine retribution, since Rehoboam permitted idolatry and was punished by a foreign assault on his land. The biblical author living in the late seventh century BCE could have known about this distant event from several possible sources, such as an inscribed hieroglyphic stele still standing somewhere north of Jerusalem (like the one found at Megiddo); from local oral traditions; or from migrant Judahites who lived in the late seventh century in the Delta, near Tanis, capital of Sheshonq I, where his monuments and historical achievements were still remembered.

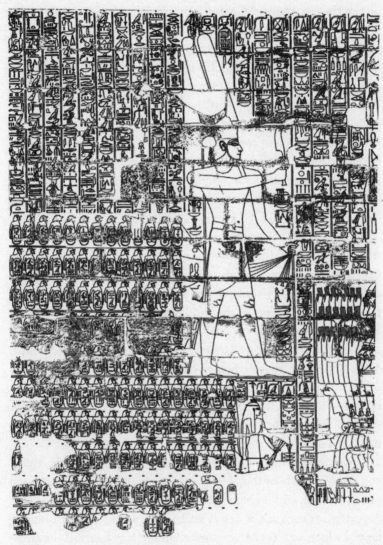

The Sheshonq I relief from the temple of Amun at Karnak, Upper Egypt

great importance on their empire in Canaan for its strategic military and trade routes and its agricultural wealth. In times of Egyptian power, the city-states of Canaan were administered by the pharaohs, either directly, through the establishment of Egyptian garrisons and government centers, or indirectly, by vassal princes. Yet Egyptian domination of Canaan crumbled in a time of great upheaval at the end of the Late Bronze Age, around the mid–twelfth century BCE. The destruction of the old palace-based culture of the Canaanite cities and the arrival and settlement of the Sea Peoples—with the Philistines prominent among them—created an entirely new political landscape. In the period that followed, when the northern highlands experienced dramatic demographic expansion, some of the old Canaanite cities in the fertile and strategically important valleys seem to have experienced a revival of urban life.

In the Jezreel Valley, the once great city of Megiddo slowly rose from the ruins of Late Bronze Age destruction. Signs of a neo-Canaanite renaissance are also visible at the nearby city of Taanach, at Rehov in the Beth-shean Valley, and at Kinnereth and Tel Hadar by the Sea of Galilee. On the basis of the pottery vessels produced at these centers, as well as metal and stone objects, cult remains, and architecture, it is clear that the old Canaanite traditions continued. More important, new carbon 14 dating results from Megiddo and other sites place this period of presumably independent Canaanite revival squarely in the tenth century BCE. And this neo-Canaanite system in the northern valleys came to a violent end, with devastation by fire recorded at every excavated site.

Far to the south, in the desert regions of the Beer-sheba Valley and the highlands of the Negev, an entirely different phenomenon was occurring, and it challenged Egyptian control in another way. An extensive network of desert settlements arose, the most important of which was Tel Masos, located in the very heart of the Beer-sheba Valley on the ancient east-west caravan route, near a group of freshwater wells. Excavations there revealed evidence for cultural contacts with the Philistine and Phoenician coast in the west and northwest, and with the copper production centers of the Arabah and southern Transjordan on the southeast. A small settlement was also established for the first time at Arad, a place specifically mentioned in the Sheshonq I topographical list.

Archaeologically, Tel Masos and the other sites in this area seem to represent the emergence of a desert chiefdom, created when favorable economic conditions associated with trade-related prosperity brought about the sedentarization of pastoral nomads in this area. Located along the trade routes connecting the Arabah and the Dead Sea with the Mediterranean, Tel Masos apparently served as a way station for the overland transport of copper from the Arabah Valley and possibly also goods from Arabia to the trading centers on the Mediterranean coast.

It is therefore fairly easy to see the possible motivations for two major objectives of Sheshonq I's campaign. Though many biblical scholars have traditionally described it as a one-time raid (particularly because the traditional chronology placed it after the creation of the biblically described vast and powerful kingdom by David and Solomon), reanalysis of the archaeological evidence suggests that it should be seen as an attempt by Egypt to revive its empire in Canaan.

In the northern valleys, an obvious goal would have been to assume control over the main cities. In the south, Sheshonq's goal would have been to take over the emerging desert polity of Tel Masos and to establish control over the southern trade. The fact that these Egyptian goals were at least partially achieved is shown by the discovery of a fragment of a large victory stele set up by Sheshonq at Megiddo, a place mentioned in the Karnak relief. The wave of abandonment evident at Tel Masos in the Beer-sheba Valley and at a group of sites to its south in the Negev highlands suggests that the independence of the rising desert trading chiefdom was also shattered at this time.

But what of a list of place-names in the central and northern highlands and on the Transjordanian plateau that also appear on the Karnak relief? From the time of the New Kingdom in the Late Bronze Age, Egyptian pharaohs had generally refrained from sending troops into the sparsely settled, wooded, rugged hill country, where chariots would be more of a military burden than an advantage, and hostility from the isolated, mobile population could be anticipated. Yet the Karnak relief mentions such place-names as Adamah, Succoth, Penuel, and Mahanaim, all located along the Jabbok River, an area in Transjordan that had never been of great interest to the Egyptian pharaohs. It also mentions places in a very restricted area of the highlands immediately to the north of Jerusalem, including Gibeon, Beth-horon, and Zemariam (near modern Ramallah).

Could it be just a coincidence that both these areas of especially intense Early Iron Age settlement—which had never before been of particular interest to the Egyptians—were closely connected with Saul's activities in the biblical tradition? Could it be a coincidence that the Sheshonq list mentions Gibeon, which many scholars see as the hub of the Saulide family and territory? Could it be a coincidence that the area to the north of Jerusalem is exactly the one where we find (in sharp contrast to the situation elsewhere in the highlands) a cluster of sites that were abandoned in the tenth century?

Something attracted the attention of the Egyptian pharaoh to these remote areas of relatively little geopolitical importance. A reasonable possibility is that the area around Gibeon and the settlements along the Jabbok River in Transjordan were the main centers of an emerging territorial-political entity strong enough to endanger the renewed Egyptian interests in a direct way.

WHY IS JERUSALEM NOT MENTIONED?

The Bible, for its part, knows only one target for Shishak's campaign. In the terse report of 1 Kings 14:25–26, the pharaoh's only mentioned objective is to attack Jerusalem, the capital of the Davidic dynasty. At this point in the Deuteronomistic History,

Jerusalem had been a powerful and prosperous capital for about eighty years. David had reigned there as king of all Israel and had established a great empire. His son Solomon succeeded him and greatly embellished the capital city, constructing an elaborate palace and Temple complex. Since Solomon's wealth was legendary it is little wonder that the Bible reported Shishak's great haul of Temple booty from his attack on Jerusalem, including "the shields of gold which Solomon had made."

Biblical scholars have long considered the Shishak invasion mentioned in 1 Kings to be the earliest event described in the Bible that is supported by an extrabiblical text. Yet Jerusalem—target of the pharaoh's march into the highlands—does not appear on Sheshonq's Karnak list.

For some scholars, the reason is simple. The name Jerusalem has simply not been preserved on the weathered Karnak relief. This is possible, but highly unlikely, since the rows of bound figures that designate captured places in the highlands just to the north of Jerusalem are in a relatively good state of preservation, and since no other Judahite town—in the highlands or in the Shephelah—appears in the list. It is thus not just a case of a single name that is missing; the entire land of Judah does not seem to be mentioned at all. And yet the urge to harmonize the Bible with the Karnak inscription has been persistent and has led some scholars to suggest that because Jerusalem was saved from destruction by a heavy ransom and left standing (according to the Bible), it was not included in the official list of conquered towns.

Yet if the biblical account is reliable about the greatness of tenth-century BCE Jerusalem and about the sheer scale of booty Sheshonq plundered from the Temple, would he and the carvers of his triumphal inscription have been so modest as not to mention this humiliation of the rulers of such a prominent city and formidable state? Such modesty would be out of character with centuries of Egyptian tradition in presenting the conquests of their pharaohs in outlandishly bombastic and self-laudatory ways.

Indeed, the problem goes far beyond selective preservation of data or rhetorical styles. As we have seen, new analyses of the archaeological data from Jerusalem have shown that the settlement of the tenth century BCE was no more than a small, poor highland village, with no evidence for monumental construction of any kind. And as we noted in examining the rise of David, archaeological surveys have revealed that at that time the hill country of Judah to the south of Jerusalem was sparsely inhabited by a few relatively small settlements, with no larger, fortified towns.

At the time of the Sheshonq campaign, Judah was still a marginal and isolated chiefdom in the southern highlands. Its poor material culture leaves no room to imagine great wealth in the Temple—certainly not wealth large enough to appease an Egyptian pharaoh's appetite. From the archaeological information, we must come to a conclusion that undermines the historical credibility of this specific biblical narrative. The reason that Jerusalem (or any other Judahite town or even village) does not appear on the Karnak inscription is surely that the southern highlands were irrelevant to Shishak's goals.

The central highlands sites that *do* appear in the list are clustered closely together in the area just to the north of Jerusalem, precisely where Early Iron Age settlements were densest—and precisely where the Bible places the home region of Saul. Here we can see evidence for a north Israelite entity that was completely different in nature from the dimorphic bandit chiefdom to the south. The hub of this northern entity—described in the Bible as Saul's "kingdom"—was located around Gibeon, which was probably the center of a highland chiefdom of considerable power. From the example of Labayu in the Amarna letters (and also, in fact, from what we know about highlands-lowlands relationships in later times) we can read the archaeological and historical evidence as indicative of a highlands polity with an expansionist intent.

The biblical narrative describes Saul's military protection of the settlements in Gilead, his campaigns against the Philistines, his stunning raid against the desert-dwelling Amalekites, and his last fateful

battle in the Jezreel Valley. If we recall the description of the territories bequeathed to Saul's heir, Ish-bosheth, we see that it closely
matches the Sheshonq list in linking a cluster of places in the hill
country north of Jerusalem with the Jabbok River area in Transjordan—a phenomenon *not known in other periods*. This can hardly be a
coincidence. What we have here is a unique glimpse at a dramatic—
and heretofore unrecognized—conflict between a resurgent Egypt
and an aggressive highland entity that biblical traditions associate
with Saul.

This northern highland polity—it was still too decentralized and
informal to call it a kingdom—may also have endangered the security of the trade routes in the coastal plain and across the Jezreel
Valley. Egypt apparently recognized the threat. With its hundreds
of villages and relatively large population, this was an area that had
to be brought under control, despite the long reluctance of Egyptian forces to venture into the rugged, forested highlands.

The archaeological evidence suggests that this actually happened: the places just to the north of Jerusalem that appear on the
Karnak list (and that the biblical tradition describes as the core of
Saul's activity) were the scene of a significant wave of abandonment
in the tenth century BCE.

The conclusion seems clear: Sheshonq and his forces marched
into the hill country and attacked the early north Israelite entity. He
also conquered the most important lowland cities like Megiddo and
regained control of the southern trade routes. But his triumphal
inscription did not and would not have mentioned Jerusalem or
Judah, an isolated chiefdom that posed no immediate threat—or was
already resigned to the reality of Egyptian rule.

THE FORGOTTEN BETRAYAL

We can only hypothesize what kind of a relationship might have
existed between the northern and southern highland chiefdoms in

the tenth century BCE, and we need to remember that most probably there was no sense of shared Israelite identity yet. There were important differences between the two regions. Certainly the population and potential power of the northern highlands far outweighed the resources of the scattered pastoralists and few villages of the south. Northern domination—or perhaps occasional northern attempts at domination of the southern highlands—seems plausible. Yet in the Bible, David and Saul are not depicted as regional rivals, but as characters in a single drama, in which their individual stories are closely intertwined. David was Saul's young minstrel, his all-too-popular warrior, his son-in-law, and ultimately his successor to the throne of all Israel. David's activities in Judah and his employment as a Philistine vassal occurred only when he was forced to flee for his life from the growing madness of Saul.

In the case of David, we have already suggested that the early folktales incorporated into the biblical narrative preserve memories of the rise of a bandit chief to the rulership of Judah, which itself matches a pattern of political leadership in the highlands that had gone on for centuries. Likewise, the emergence of a northern highlands alliance—associated with Saul in the biblical tradition—is also consistent with the archaeological and Egyptian textual evidence. But one last element must be accounted for before we can attempt a historical reconstruction of the interactions of the northern and southern leaders, Saul and David. Nowhere in the biblical story of the early Israelite kingdom is there a hint of any serious threat from Egypt.* The Philistines are the most prominent enemy. Their raids against the towns of Judah prompt David's saving actions; their attempts at domination in the northern highlands provide the context for some of Saul's most memorable military feats. It was the Philistines who won the final, great victory over Saul at Mount Gilboa, and it was they who hung the headless bodies of Saul and

---

* There is one possible, vague memory in the heroic tales of 2 Samuel 23, a mention in passing that Benaiah the son of Jehoiada "slew an Egyptian" (verse 21.)

his sons from the wall of the great fortress city of Beth-shean nearby (1 Samuel 31:10).

What were the Philistines doing so far away from their coastal enclave? What were they doing in the heart of the highlands? There is no extrabiblical clue—archaeological or historical—that the Philistines ever formed a united army that could intervene so far away from their home territory. What were they doing in the northern stronghold of Beth-shean? This towering site, located at a strategic crossroads of overland trade routes south of the Sea of Galilee, has been repeatedly excavated and has been recognized as one of the most important Egyptian fortresses and administrative centers in Canaan in the Late Bronze Age, with its complement of Egyptian-style residency and shrines. In the tenth century, Beth-shean had far declined from its former splendor, but apparently remained a potential strongpoint for renewed Egyptian rule. The reason for the biblical reference to Philistine presence at Beth-shean and the highlands in this period may lie in the Philistines' relationship to Egypt—and that might shed new light on the historical realities of the careers of David and Saul.

It is important to note first of all that no Philistine cities are mentioned in the triumphal list of Sheshonq. This omission may be due to the damaged state of the Karnak inscription, but it may have a strategic explanation as well. Though their coastal enclave could potentially have tried to block the passage of Egyptian troops northward, apparently no fighting took place there. The takeover of the southern desert trade routes could only have been in the interest of the coastal Philistine cities, with their access to Mediterranean maritime commerce. The weakening of the aggressive northern chiefdom would have allowed them wider territorial security. The coastal Sea Peoples, including Philistines, had long served as Egyptian mercenary forces, and their role as Egyptian allies in this campaign and its aftermath seems quite plausible.

But why were the Egyptians forgotten in this part of the biblical tradition? Over the centuries, as the heroic stories of this period were told and retold among the people of Judah, Egypt again slipped into a period of historical eclipse, whereas the Philistines remained present and grew stronger. By the time of the compilation of the stories, when the scattered local traditions were collected and woven into a single narrative, hostility to the Philistines was as strong as ever. So they were portrayed as the main villains of the piece. It is possible that the Bible's reference to the Philistines attacking the hill country and establishing garrisons at Geba (1 Samuel 13:3) and Bethlehem (2 Samuel 23:14), and to the great Philistine-Israelite battle at Beth-shean, may, in fact, preserve a memory of the Egypto-Philistine alliance.

The biblical tradition contains another secret that it only clumsily tries to hide. David fought back Philistine attacks on the western borders of Judah, but he also served as a vassal to Achish, the king of the Philistine city of Gath. He mustered with his men at the great gathering of Philistine troops at Aphek as they prepared to set off and deal a death blow to the forces of Saul. As a former Philistine vassal and chief of a region that was not attacked in the campaign of Sheshonq, David had a great deal to gain from a decline in the power of the northern highlands. A blow to the cluster of settlements in the Benjaminite plateau would have afforded the southern chiefdom a convenient opportunity to expand its territorial control northward in coordination with the Egyptians, or once the Egyptians had withdrawn.

In short, the southern chiefdom could have been a passive partner in the Egypto-Philistine alliance. This could be the reason that—like the Philistine cities—it is not mentioned in the Sheshonq I list at Karnak. It could also have been the origin of a northern accusation that David cooperated with the Philistines and was, at least indirectly, responsible for Saul's demise. David and Judah may have benefited from the fall of the northern polity and expanded to control some of the highland territories that Saul once led. A memory that in the early days of the Davidic dynasty Jerusalem ruled over areas in the northern highlands beyond the traditional borders of Judah could well have been the historical kernel behind the idea of the "united monarchy" that David ruled from Jerusalem.

We do not know how long the Egyptians remained in the region or whether they managed to reestablish—even briefly—direct rule over Canaan/Israel. But sooner or later the Egypto-Philistine presence faded, and David and his heirs could have continued to dominate at least a part of the northern highlands. Thus in the immediate aftermath of Sheshonq's attack on the northern chiefdom, David's greatest danger might well have come not from outside enemies but from the hostility and accusations among the people of the northern highlands that he had betrayed or at least taken advantage of the defeat of their own leader, Saul.

SAINT, OR TRAITOR?

Saul, the first king of Israel, is depicted in the Bible as a painfully, even tragically conflicted figure. On one hand he is portrayed as a shy, modest, "handsome young man" (1 Samuel 9:2), a hero who saves the people of Israel from all their enemies:

> *When Saul had taken the kingship over Israel, he fought against all his enemies on every side, against Moab, against the Ammonites, against Edom, against the kings of Zobah, and against the Philistines; wherever he turned he put them to the worse. And he did valiantly, and smote the Amalekites, and delivered Israel out of the hands of those who plundered them. (1 Samuel 14:47–48)*

On the other hand Saul is described as hotheaded, prone to fits of violent anger, and tormented by evil spirits. He twice tried to murder his faithful servant David and pursued him relentlessly. In his transgression of cultic law, he disqualified himself as a righteous ruler. The first book of Samuel puts it this way: "And the Lord repented that he had made Saul king over Israel" (1 Samuel 15:35).

How to explain these contradictions? Many biblical scholars have seen them as evidence for the existence of two different sources in the text. The stories that look at Saul favorably have generally been considered to have arisen in the northern kingdom of Israel and preserved genuine, though vague, memories of the time of the first king of the north. Like the stories of David the bandit in the southern highlands, they contain quite specific geographical details that include what may be memories of events in the tenth century BCE. Saul's bravery, courage, and tragic demise at the hands of his enemies would have long been repeated and elaborated as a commemoration of the emergence of the first powerful highlands chiefdom and a mournful reflection on the dream of a united Israel ruled from the north that came to a sudden and unexpectedly violent end.

The anti-Saul, pro-David elements in the narrative reflect an entirely different perspective. They continually remind us why Saul was doomed to failure and why David became Israel's rightfully anointed king. The two voices represent two sides in a now-silenced argument that has been woven into the overall biblical narrative. Indeed, some scholars have suggested that the entire story of David's rise—detailing his replacement of Saul as God's anointed—is written in the form of an apology, a literary genre well known in the ancient Near East, used by usurpers who had to legitimize their accession to the throne. Yet this theory makes sense only if the texts were written in the tenth century. This is highly unlikely: not only is there no evidence of an elaborate royal administration (of the type that might have been expected to possess literary scribes and court bards) in the isolated hilltop village of Jerusalem; there is no sign of extensive literacy or writing in Judah until the end of the eighth century BCE.

What we have in this early phase, instead, is a conflict of local, oral traditions that would only much later be integrated in a single written work. The assertions of one are contradicted by the other. The accusations of one side are countered by other side's new explanatory detail. The partisans of Saul—the voice of whom can be found only in the background of the stories—would have maintained that David was no more than a bandit, a nobody who was accepted to the circles of the king and then betrayed him, an illegitimate usurper who undermined the throne of Saul and his family. To them, David was a traitor, a Philistine agent, who participated—actively or passively—in the military expedition that resulted in the death of the first great king of the north.

The supporters of David had to answer these accusations. David would never have taken up a life of banditry had it not been for the jealous rage of Saul. Moreover, at every opportunity that David had to kill his pursuer, he refrained from taking that action, for the greater good of Israel. In one of the incidents, David is reported to have said:

> Do not destroy him; for who can put forth his hand against the Lord's anointed. . . . As the Lord lives, the Lord will smite him; or his day shall come to die; or he shall go down into battle and perish. The Lord forbid that I should put forth my hand against the Lord's anointed; but take now the spear that is at his head, and the jar of water, and let us go. (1 Samuel 26:9–11)

No less meaningful are the words (regarding David) put in the mouth of Saul himself:

> You are more righteous than I; for you have repaid me good, whereas I have repaid you evil. . . . And now, behold, I know that you shall surely be king, and that the kingdom of Israel shall be established in your hand. (1 Samuel 24:17, 20)

The biblical narrative explains why David's alliance with the Philistine king was only halfhearted, little more than a ruse to protect his Judahite countrymen. When he and his troops were mobilized by the Philistines to march against Saul's forces, he was conveniently excused from Philistine service on the grounds of possible double loyalty (1 Samuel 29:3–10). No less significant, when David hears the news of the death of Saul and his sons at Mount Gilboa, he laments them in the most beautiful, moving words:

> *Thy glory, O Israel, is slain upon thy high places! How are the mighty fallen! Tell it not in Gath, publish it not in the streets of Ashkelon; lest the daughters of the Philistines rejoice, lest the daughters of the uncircumcised exult. Ye mountains of Gilboa, let there be no dew or rain upon you, nor upsurging of the deep! For there the shield of the mighty was defiled, the shield of Saul, not anointed with oil. From the blood of the slain, from the fat of the mighty, the bow of Jonathan turned not back, and the sword of Saul returned not empty. Saul and Jonathan, beloved and lovely! In life and in death they were not divided; they were swifter than eagles, they were stronger than lions. Ye daughters of Israel, weep over Saul. . . . How are the mighty fallen in the midst of the battle. (2 Samuel 1:19–25)*

Most important of all, the biblical tradition asserts that the events were all divinely directed and thus perfectly lawful. God himself rejected Saul and elected David to replace him. It was he who transferred the throne to David from Saul. All these charges and counterarguments still bear the painful memories of the events of the tenth century BCE. Yet they are neither completely impartial history nor even the spontaneous back-and-forth argument between the grieving supporters of a fallen leader and the partisans of an up-and-coming highland chief. They are the result of an extraordinary period of creativity—at this stage still oral, not written—and thus represent another layer of folkloristic material that would contribute to the biblical tale.

By the end of the tenth century BCE, it was no longer enough just to cherish and celebrate the legends and achievements of local heroes. After the death of Saul and David's establishment of a dynasty in Jerusalem, a wider highland identity may have begun to emerge in which the legendary figures of *both* Saul and David loomed large. At least in the area of Judah and the highlands immediately to its north, a new cycle of stories began to spread among the villages in which early heroic tales were merged into a psychological drama about the right of a particular dynasty to rule. In these early days and as we will see even more so in later centuries when a considerable wave of northern refugees came to the south, it was impossible for the southerners to disregard the inspiring tales of Saul's election and the sheer scope and daring of his attempt to unite the northern highlands. Likewise, it was inconceivable that northerners would not be aware of the legends of David and his mighty men. What resulted was an embryonic national tradition that would be considerably expanded in every period when the rulers of Judah felt it necessary to counter northern accusations of betrayal and to contradict any challenge to the historical legitimacy of the Judahite claim to northern territories.

These historical developments have always been seen through the lens of the biblical tradition—and in the countless works of art portraying the tormented Israelite king and the innocent shepherd boy from Judah—as due to David's greatness and Saul's tragic flaws. Yet the archaeological and historical context shows that David's destiny was neither clear nor unambiguous in a chaotic period of regional conflict in the Early Iron Age. Violence, domination, and betrayal were the indelible memories of the struggle of Egyptians, Philistines, and rival highland chieftains to forge a new world in the tenth century BCE. And an understanding of that unfolding drama is not of mere antiquarian interest. In the struggle for survival by the people of the northern and southern highlands of Canaan, the concept of a shared identity—the People of Israel—was born.

PERIOD	STAGES IN DEVELOPMENT OF BIBLICAL MATERIAL
9th Century BCE	Stories about David's rule in Jerusalem, transformed into 9th century ballads recited in the court of David's successors; elaboration of oral legends of David's conquests to match the territorial extent of the North Israelite, Omride state.

HISTORICAL BACKGROUND	ARCHAEOLOGICAL FINDS
Judah slowly develops from highland chiefdom to kingdom, but lives in the shadow of the Omride state. The Davidic Dynasty survives the rise of Damascus and fall of the Omride Dynasty.	Jerusalem expands, but still limited to the City of David. First administrative centers in Lachish, Beth-shemesh, Beer-sheba, and Arad. Gath the dominant Philistine city until its destruction by Aram Damascus.

CHAPTER 3

Murder, Lust, and Betrayal

Legends of the Davidic Court in Jerusalem

— NINTH CENTURY BCE —

FROM BITTER WIVES TO A RAVISHED PRINCESS, TO cold-blooded killers and traitors; from secret lovers to betrayed confidants to out-and-out scoundrels—there is perhaps no more fascinating cast of characters in the Bible than the close circle that surrounded King David in his court in Jerusalem. The biblical narrative known to scholars as the "Succession History" or the "Court History" (2 Samuel 9–20 and 1 Kings 1–2) follows yet differs in tone from the narrative of "David's Rise to Power." It is a drama of strong desires and their painful suppression. It is the story of a royal court continually falling prey to the basest temptations of power, with a king who is noble enough to repent his own unrighteous acts, and thereby receive atonement for his sins.

This part of the biblical story begins in the aftermath of Saul's death at Mount Gilboa, when David is crowned king at Hebron

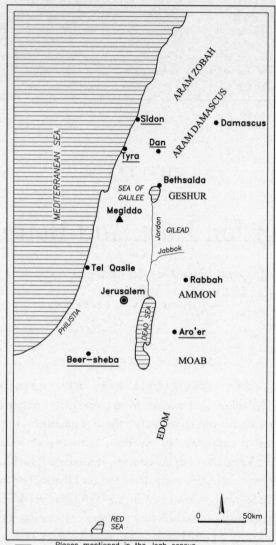

David's wars and his state's territorial extent
according to the Joab census

by the people of Judah; his followers launch a campaign of assassinations to liquidate the house of Saul. Ish-bosheth, Saul's surviving heir, and Abner, Saul's faithful military commander, are both murdered by David's lieutenants, allowing David himself to disavow any blame. Representatives of *all* the tribes of Israel come to see David in Hebron and anoint him king over the entire nation of Israel. With his daring band of warriors, David then proceeds to march on Jerusalem and seize it. Residing in the stronghold now called the City of David, the king strengthens Jerusalem's fortifications. Hiram of Tyre, the powerful Phoenician ruler, acknowledging David's greatness, sends precious cedar beams and skilled carpenters and masons to construct a proper royal palace for David in his new capital. Amidst his newfound opulence, David gathers a glittering entourage of scribes, military officers, mercenary bodyguards, priests, retainers, wives, and concubines as his inner circle. They become the cast of characters of the "Court History."

Until very recently, many biblical scholars accepted the "Court History" as a reliable and largely accurate historical record. It was assumed that the biblical narrative was written in the court of either David or Solomon—close in time to the events it described. One of the primary reasons was its extraordinary wealth of detail. For King David is not portrayed as a typical Egyptian or Assyrian king-god—perfect, aloof, and above the rest of humanity—as in most royal biographies in the ancient Near East. Instead, he is a man with strong urges and painful weaknesses, which the text does not try to hide. He benefits from the execution of his bitterest rivals; he steals another man's wife and has her husband killed; he weeps uncontrollably at news of the death of his rebel son, Absalom, who tried to kill him; and he fades into a cold, lonely senility as his various courtiers and heirs squabble over who will succeed him to the throne.

Such details—along with the quite specific geographical descriptions of David's sweeping conquests*—create an intensely realistic story. Thus, scholars have thought that at the time of writing, the memories of David's reign must still have been quite fresh. And there was an obvious political logic to its composition: the official "Court History" was an act of royal spin control, intended to explain (and put the best possible light on) David's actions and the selection of Solomon—who was not the first in line to the throne—as David's legitimate successor. Taking the biblical lists of David's court officials at face value, scholars have assumed that the mention of the offices of "recorder" (2 Samuel 8:16) and "secretary" ("scribe" in the Hebrew text of 2 Samuel 8:17) proved that written records were compiled and maintained in tenth-century BCE Jerusalem.

This is another case of circular argumentation, in which the biblical text serves as the primary evidence that its own historical reportage is true. We have repeatedly mentioned the lack of any archaeological evidence for extensive literacy in Judah until the late eighth century BCE. Now we must ask another question: on the basis of what we know about the general archaeological situation in Jerusalem, does the "Court History" speak with a tenth-century voice? Do the descriptions of David's wars and building projects mesh with the archaeological reality of that era? Are the dynastic intrigues that play such a major role in the "Court History" conceivable in David's time?

AN ABSENCE OF EVIDENCE

The answer is certainly negative. First, with regard to the physical background, there is little evidence in Jerusalem of any impressive tenth-century BCE royal constructions or, for that matter, much con-

---

* Although 2 Samuel 8, which describes some of David's wars, is not usually considered part of the "Court History," nonetheless, since military triumphs are an important element of David's biblical image, we include it in our discussion of royal traditions of the Davidic dynasty.

struction of any kind. Although it is possible that some structures of Davidic or Solomonic Jerusalem may have been destroyed or buried under the massive platform of Herod's Temple, the evidence of great royal expansion elsewhere in the area of the City of David is nonexistent. The three main monuments that have been associated with the events of David's reign—Warren's shaft (identified by some as the water shaft mentioned in connection with David's conquest of Jerusalem in 2 Samuel 5:8); the Stepped Stone Structure (proposed as the Millo mentioned in connection with David's rebuilding of Jerusalem in 2 Samuel 5:9); and the tombs of the kings of Judah (the rock cuttings identified by some as remains of the royal tombs of the Davidic dynasty)—have nothing to do with tenth-century BCE building efforts and hardly provide conclusive independent proof of the biblical narrative.*

The suggestion of some scholars that "absence of evidence is not evidence of absence" can be easily countered when we consider the general picture. Over a century of excavations in the City of David have produced surprisingly meager remains from the late sixteenth to mid–eighth centuries BCE. They amount to no more than a few walls and a modest quantity of pottery sherds, mostly found in erosion debris. The situation has been found to be the same at every excavated site in Jerusalem. The suggestion that substantial tenth-century BCE building remains *did* exist in Jerusalem but were obliterated by erosion or massive building activity in later generations is simply untenable, since impressive structures from both the earlier Middle Bronze Age (c. 2000–1550 BCE) and the later Iron Age II (c. 750–586 BCE) *have* survived.

The evidence clearly suggests that tenth-century Jerusalem was a small highland village that controlled a sparsely settled hinterland. If it had been the capital of a great kingdom with the wherewithal to muster tens of thousands of soldiers, collect tribute from vassals,

---

* For more detail on the archaeological search for the monuments of David's Jerusalem, see Appendix 2.

and maintain garrisons in Aram Damascus and Edom (as the biblical narrative informs us it did), one would expect the presence of administrative buildings and storehouses, even outside the royal compound at the summit of the ridge. One would also expect to see changes in the villages of Judah—from which a significant portion of David's armies were presumably mobilized and which would stand to benefit at least indirectly from the kingdom's great wealth. Yet there is not the slightest evidence of any change in the landscape of Judah until the following century. The population remained low and the villages modest and few in number throughout the tenth century BCE.

And what of David's sweeping conquests described in great detail in 2 Samuel 8, 10, and 12:26–29? If the descriptions of these wars and conquests are reliable, there should be evidence of violent military destructions in the area of his enlarged realm. Indeed in the early days of biblical archaeology, that is precisely what many scholars believed they had found. At sites throughout the areas of David's supposed military expansion—first and foremost along the coast and in the northern valleys—virtually every destruction level that could be vaguely dated to David's time was ascribed to his conquests, especially since these destruction layers usually marked the transition from a Philistine or a Canaanite city to a new material culture identified as "Israelite."

Thus at the lowland site of Tell Qasile, a Philistine settlement located within the boundaries of modern Tel Aviv, the excavator Amihai Mazar declared, "The violent destruction of the flourishing Stratum X . . . at the beginning of the 10th century B.C., was part of a series of destructions in various parts of the country," most probably caused by "an Israelite invasion under King David." Likewise, the Canaanite city-state of Megiddo, in the Jezreel Valley in the north, was thought to provide another example for the sweeping Davidic conquests. The Iron I city, still featuring Canaanite material culture, was conventionally dated to the eleventh century BCE. It came to an end in a conflagration so intense that it baked the mudbricks of its various buildings and covered the floors with a deep layer of collapsed upper-story beams, smashed artifacts, and ash. The Israeli archaeologist Yigael Yadin, who excavated at Megiddo in the 1960s, interpreted this as evidence of a Canaanite city "completely destroyed, probably by David," and then replaced by an Israelite city of the time of Solomon.

But all these images were the result of that familiar kind of circular reasoning—using the biblical narrative as the basis for archaeological interpretation and then using the interpreted remains as proof of the Bible's historical accuracy. The evidence of destruction at Tell Qasile, Megiddo, and other sites seemed, at that time, to fit the biblical story, but it is clear today that the archaeological proof of the conquests of David was illusory. We now know from new excavations and reanalysis of pottery assemblages, architectural observations, and radiocarbon dating that Philistine life in the southern coastal plain and Canaanite life in the northern valleys continued uninterrupted well into the tenth century BCE. The wave of destruction that had previously been dated to around 1000 BCE and attributed to the expansion of the united monarchy in the days of King David actually came later, by almost a century.

So if we take all the evidence together and again ask if the biblical "Court History" of David is historically appropriate for the tenth century BCE, the answer would have to be no. There is no clear archaeological evidence for Jerusalem's emergence at that time as the capital of a powerful empire with elaborate administrative institutions and a scribal tradition capable of composing such an elaborate chronicle of events.

Nor are the destructions long ascribed to David's wars of conquest a secure basis for historical reconstruction. The few thousand farmers and herders of Judah—a number including women, children, and old people—could probably provide no more than a few hundred able-bodied fighting men, which is hardly enough for any military adventure beyond a local raid. A major social and political transformation—the emergence of a state with its various offices and institutions—would have to occur before the events of the "Court History" could possibly ring true. Such a transformation can indeed be traced in the archaeological record, but as we will suggest, it occurred first in the northern highlands rather than Judah—and only with the passage of several generations *after* the presumed reigns of both David and Solomon.

THE FIRST ISRAELITE ROYAL COURT

Even as village life in the highlands of Judah continued without significant alteration through the tenth and early ninth centuries BCE, major transformations were under way in the highlands to the north. Despite the abandonment of the cluster of settlements in the highlands of Benjamin (significantly, sites connected with the area of the biblical stories of Saul), archaeology hints at a steady growth in the population and agricultural capacity of the hundreds of villages scattered through the northern highlands that would profoundly influence the course of political developments.

In contrast to the situation in the Judahite highlands, the north witnessed the steady expansion of the area of settlement—both in the small, fertile valleys in the heart of the highlands and in the marginal areas to the east and west. New settlements on the eastern desert fringe hint at the growth of village-based herding; the establishment of villages on the rocky western slopes facing the Mediterranean suggests the renewal of terrace agriculture for vineyards and olive groves after a hiatus of hundreds of years. Larger villages emerged as regional centers and trade with the Phoenician coast was revived.

Then, suddenly, much more elaborate administrative centers appeared at important sites throughout the region, the largest being the vast compound built at Samaria in the northwestern hills. A huge podium, requiring massive leveling and filling operations, was constructed over the site of a former village. The podium was surrounded by an impressive casemate wall, with rooms that were probably used for storage. Other elaborate, specialized structures were constructed within the large area enclosed by the walls. The most noteworthy was a palace beautifully built of ashlar blocks, the largest structure ever found in Iron Age Israel. This imposing compound—and the others like it that were constructed at selected sites throughout the northern valleys—served both as administrative centers and impressive monuments to the power of their occupants. In anthropological terms, it is clear what was happening: the society of the northern highlands was undergoing a transformation from a dispersed village culture to the centralized regimentation of a full-blown state.

When we say "full-blown state," we must be clear. Earlier we characterized tenth-century BCE Judah as a "chiefdom," namely a loose network of more or less equal communities (both settled and pastoral) bound in largely ceremonial alliance with a strongman or chief and his family. The power of the chief was limited to dealing with neighboring peoples, mustering local forces to counter local threats and incursions, and cultivating and preserving the kin alliances of the chiefdom itself. The economic and military capacity of a chiefdom was severely limited; the key to its very survival was stability. That seems to have been the initial situation with the establishment of the earliest Iron Age villages in the north as well. But when the population grew and expanded into new areas—specializing in certain crops and animal products—exchanges grew increasingly complex.

To trade grain for olives, and wool for grain and wine, required permanent structures for administration and storage; thus regional centers emerged. The final stage in this transformation was the creation of a state—or a "kingdom"—to impose a centralized system of control. It is only at this level of organization that large professional armies, foreign conquests, and extensive building projects are possible, due to the existence of a specialized core of state officials and laborers, who are themselves supported by the surplus of the region's agricultural and commercial wealth. It is a system with great power and many obligations for its inhabitants.

These are precisely the developments that we can see in the archaeological evidence of the emergence of a center at Samaria in the early ninth century BCE. And for the first time, we can associate archaeological evidence with identifiable biblical characters: the Omride dynasty of the kingdom of Israel, which ruled, according to the biblical and ancient Near Eastern chronology, between 884 and 842 BCE, several generations *after* the reported time of David and Solomon.

According to 1 Kings 16:15–24, Omri, the dynasty's founder, came to power in a military coup d'etat and established his capital on the hill of Samaria, from which he and his son Ahab ruled a vast kingdom. We have supporting testimony from independent, outside sources that confirms the main outlines of this biblical account. This report is substantiated by a number of contemporary inscriptions—the earliest extrabiblical records ever discovered to directly document the existence of biblical characters.

The Assyrians indeed refer to the northern kingdom as "the House of Omri," confirming the biblical testimony that he was the founder of the dynasty and the capital. And in the monolith inscription of the Assyrian king Shalmaneser III, we read of a great coalition of kingdoms that confronted the Assyrian armies at the battle of Qarqar on the Orontes River in Syria in 853 BCE. One of the most powerful participants in this coalition was a ruler referred to as "Ahab the Israelite," who contributed two thousand chariots and ten thousand foot soldiers to the anti-Assyrian force. Even if this royal text is typically exaggerated, it still suggests an entirely new scale of military power possessed by the kingdom of Israel. And at the height of their power, the Omrides apparently extended their rule eastward into Transjordan and north into Syria as well.

The famous Mesha inscription, inscribed on a black stone monument, was discovered in the nineteenth century in Dibon, the ancient capital of Moab (in southern Transjordan). The text records that "Omri, king of Israel, humbled Moab many days." It goes on to note that the Israelite occupation of the area continued under

Omri's son and included the construction of two new strongholds in the Moabite territory. Furthermore, the expansion of the Omrides into Syria is referred to in the Tel Dan inscription, in which Hazael, king of Aram Damascus, reports that Israel had formerly occupied parts of his land.* From both archaeological and historical perspectives, we can therefore recognize the emergence of the first true kingdom of Israel in the early ninth century BCE. Could it be just a coincidence that the Omride struggle for centralized power, its lavish building projects, its royal court, its advanced professional army, and its sweeping foreign conquests in Transjordan and Syria call to mind the unforgettable stage scenery of David's "Court History"?

THE RISE OF JUDAH

In the first half of the ninth century BCE, Israel was one of the most powerful states in the region. The question that immediately comes to mind is, if the Omrides used their military might to expand in the northeast and east, why didn't they expand toward the south, in the direction of Judah? The biblical narrative, with its descriptions of the might and prestige of David and Solomon's great kingdom, portrays the later struggle between north and south as one of equals. But as we have seen, the evidence for any great empire under David is utterly lacking. All we can say is that material life went on much as before and the dynastic line in Jerusalem continued without interruption after the death of David. Solomon, Rehoboam, Abijam, and Asa are listed in the book of Kings as David's successors and we have no independent evidence either to confirm or to challenge this sequence. But something else was happening, implied by the Bible and clearly suggested by the archaeological evidence. By the time of David's great-great-great grandson Jehoshaphat (who reigned according to

---

* The importance of the Tel Dan inscription and its mention of the "House of David" is discussed in Appendix 1.

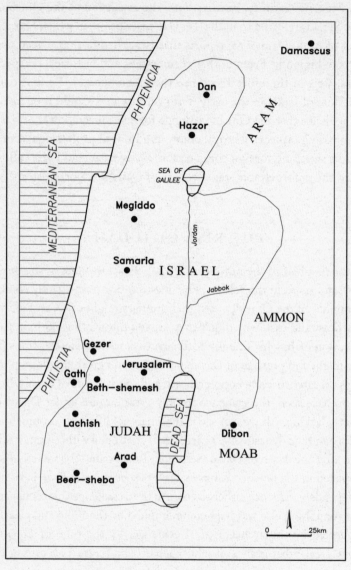

Israel and Judah in the ninth century BCE

the biblical chronology from 870 to 846 BCE), Judah seems to have become a virtual vassal to the kingdom of Israel.

The Bible reports that Jehoshaphat, a contemporary of Ahab, offered manpower and horses for the northern kingdom's wars against the Arameans. He strengthened his relationship with the northern kingdom by arranging a diplomatic marriage: the Israelite princess Athaliah, sister or daughter of King Ahab, married Jehoram, the son of Jehoshaphat (2 Kings 8:18). The house of David in Jerusalem was now directly linked to (and apparently dominated by) the Israelite royalty of Samaria. In fact, we might suggest that this represented the north's takeover by marriage of Judah. Thus in the ninth century BCE—nearly a century after the presumed time of David—we can finally point to the historical existence of a great united monarchy of Israel, stretching from Dan in the north to Beer-sheba in the south, with significant conquered territories in Syria and Transjordan. But *this* united monarchy—a real united monarchy—was ruled by the Omrides, not the Davidides, and its capital was Samaria, not Jerusalem.

It is precisely at this time that the first archaeological signs of state formation are evident in Judah. Archaeological surveys have revealed that the number of scattered agricultural villages (though still modest) was steadily growing. In the Judahite lowlands, permanent centers of administration, controlling specific regions or specialized aspects of the economy, were first constructed in the ninth century BCE. In the rich grain-growing lands of the Shephelah in the west—the traditional breadbasket of Judah—two impressive citadels were constructed, requiring the organization of considerable labor, and were far more imposing in appearance than any previous settlements in that region in the Early Iron Age. At Lachish, excavations by British archaeologists in the 1930s and a subsequent Israeli expedition directed by David Ussishkin revealed a massive podium that supported a fortified complex containing storerooms and a palace; at Beth-shemesh, slightly farther to the north, evidence of another massive construction effort has recently been uncovered by a Tel

Aviv University team headed by Shlomo Bunimovitz and Zvi Lederman. It includes a system of massive fortifications and an elaborate
subterranean water system that would enable the residents of this
important site in the rich Sorek Valley to withstand a protracted
siege.

Even more telling is the sudden appearance of evidence for centralized administration in the Beer-sheba Valley, which had for centuries been the active route of overland trade between Transjordan
and the Mediterranean coast. At both Arad, on the eastern end of
the valley, and Tel Beer-sheba in the west, permanent fortresses
were constructed in the ninth century BCE. They seem to represent
an effort to take control over the trade routes that passed through
the Beer-sheba Valley and to protect the southern borderlands of
the kingdom. Was this achieved by the kings of Judah under the
auspices of the Omrides? The story (in 1 Kings 22:48–49) of
Jehoshaphat's attempt to engage in southern trade with the help of
the northern kingdom, even if grossly exaggerated and confused
with later Red Sea trading efforts, may represent a vague echo of
this period.

And what of Jerusalem? Here too, the first signs of elaborate construction seem to appear in the ninth century BCE. Though the date
of the famous Stepped Stone Structure has long been a matter of
contention, it was clearly the support for a structure that must have
been much more elaborate and impressive than the earlier buildings
on the city's southern edge. A close examination by the Dutch
archaeologist Margreet Steiner of the datable potsherds retrieved
from the mantle of the Stepped Stone Structure included red
slipped and burnished types of the ninth century BCE.

An important clue to the nature of the building that originally
stood on top of the Stepped Stone Structure—and was obliterated
by later occupations—may have been found immediately to the
north. In the 1950s the British archaeologist Kathleen Kenyon
uncovered a pile of ashlar blocks there, including a beautiful proto-
Aeolic capital, characteristic of the distinctive architectural decora-

tion at the royal compound of Samaria, the capital of the northern kingdom. These blocks were found at the foot of the Stepped Stone Structure and may have collapsed from a building that stood on the platform farther up the slope. Indeed, David Ussishkin proposed that a Samaria-like government compound, which included a palace and a temple, was built on the Temple Mount in Jerusalem in the ninth century BCE. Similar to Samaria's, it must have featured massive operations of leveling and especially filling in order to create a flat platform for a royal quarter, surrounded by a casemate wall.*

Unfortunately, that hypothesis cannot be confirmed archaeologically, as the huge Herodian podium for the Second Temple built in the Roman period has completely eradicated or buried any sign of earlier structures on the Temple Mount. Yet it remains an intriguing possibility that the domination of the royal house of Judah by the northern kingdom was expressed in Jerusalem by architectural imitation—with the construction of an elaborate royal compound on the Temple Mount, on the model of the Samaria acropolis.

Thus from archaeological and historical evidence it is likely that the first structures and institutions of statehood appeared in Judah in the ninth century, most likely under the influence of the more developed royal institutions of the north. According to the Bible, the marriage of the Davidic king Jehoram to the Omride princess Athaliah produced a royal heir named Ahaziah, who was a product of *both* royal lines. With Ahaziah's succession to the throne—and even more so after his death, when Athaliah eliminated the surviving Davidic heirs and ruled in Jerusalem alone as a queen mother (2 Kings 11)—the Israelite nobility was more close-knit than ever, representing what must have been functionally a single polity, dominated by Samaria.

Despite the contention of some biblical scholars that David's "Court History" was composed in tenth-century Jerusalem by David

---

* This does not suggest, however, that a more modest temple and palace built by the earlier highland chiefs of Judah did not stand there before.

or Solomon's personal spin doctors, we will soon see that the world described in the biblical stories of David's conquests and court politics far more accurately evokes the social and political landscape of Omride and post-Omride times in the ninth century BCE. Those stories, in their vividness and wealth of detail, profoundly altered the image of David. Why was this done?

RESHAPING THE PAST

In a detailed study of the biblical stories of David's wives Bathsheba and Michal, and the later Queen Athaliah, the German biblical scholar Axel Knauf underlined the importance of the art of storytelling in the inner life of the Judahite court. He pointed out that official feasts and gatherings were important occasions for social and political interaction between the ruling family and the lineages associated with it. They provided an opportunity for boasting, critique, and competition, expressed in stories, legends, and folktales.

We have already suggested that the earliest stories of David as an outlaw were the product of his followers' eagerness to celebrate the courage and cunning of their chief. We have also suggested that the interlocked cycle of David and Saul stories was the expression of an imaginative counterattack by the supporters of David against the damning accusations of betrayal by the supporters of the fallen Saul. But in the "Court History" and other chapters in the second book of Samuel there is another, entirely different kind of tale. Its stories are about court politics, royal rivalries, internal uprisings, and foreign conquests, played out on the stage of royal bedrooms and throne rooms,* and in pitched battles between royal armies equipped with specialized units of infantry, cavalry, and chariotry.

---

* Knauf particularly stressed the central role played in ancient Near Eastern courts by stories expressing the viewpoint of the queen mother, whose main political challenge was to maintain the primacy of her line in the struggle for succession to the throne.

A biblical passage relates that after clearing the Philistines from the Jerusalem area and securing his rule in his capital city, David ordered that the holy Ark of the Covenant be brought to Jerusalem in a joyous procession to mark the establishment of the nation's eternal core.* David's wild, ecstatic behavior at the head of the marchers—"leaping and dancing before the Lord" (2 Samuel 6:16)—revealed his unkingly demeanor and enraged his royal wife Michal, daughter of King Saul. As Knauf pointed out, the story of Michal's harsh rebuke to the dancing David ended with the cryptic statement "And Michal the daughter of Saul had no child to the day of her death" (2 Samuel 6:23)—a classic dynastic jibe, explaining why the Saulide line died out in Jerusalem.

Yet the sarcastic words of the aristocratic Michal to David— "How the king of Israel honored himself today, uncovering himself today before the eyes of his servants' maids, as one of the vulgar fellows shamelessly uncovers himself!" (2 Samuel 6:20)—are hardly conceivable in the context of a rustic highland chiefdom where social bonds, rather than social differences, needed to be stressed. Whether there was a real woman named Michal, daughter of Saul, who was married to the historical David, we may never know. But we can be safe in assuming that the story did not take its present form—and certainly its meaning—before the rise of a class-conscious aristocracy in Jerusalem.

Likewise, the complex love story of David and Bathsheba hardly makes any sense outside a distinctly courtly atmosphere. In the midst of the fierce fighting against the neighboring kingdom of Ammon, the biblical narrative described how King David, remaining in his palace in Jerusalem, is ensnared by his own lust.

It happened, late one afternoon, when David arose from his couch and was walking upon the roof of the king's house, that he saw from

---

* It is contained in the final chapter of what scholars describe as the "Ark Narrative," the story of the wandering of the Ark from Shiloh to captivity in Philistine cities, and back to Kiriath-jearim and finally Jerusalem—1 Samuel 6–7:1; 2 Samuel 6.

*the roof a woman bathing; and the woman was very beautiful. And
David sent and inquired about the woman. And one said, "Is not this
Bathsheba, the daughter of Eliam, the wife of Uriah the Hittite?" So
David sent messengers, and took her; and she came to him, and he
lay with her. (Now she was purifying herself from her uncleanness.)
Then she returned to her house. And the woman conceived; and she
sent and told David, "I am with child." (2 Samuel 11:2–5)*

The woman's husband, Uriah, was engaged in the fierce battle for
Rabbah, the capital of Ammon. Immediately David recalls him to
Jerusalem, but all of his attempts to persuade the good soldier Uriah
to sleep with his wife, Bathsheba (and thereby provide a cover for
her adulterous pregnancy), fail. In an act of cold calculation that
would forever cast a shadow on David's reputation, he sends Uriah
back to the front with a letter to his commander, ordering Joab to
"Set Uriah in the forefront of the hardest fighting, and then draw
back from him, that he may be struck down, and die" (2 Samuel
11:15). In the bitter fighting beneath the walls of Rabbah, Uriah
perishes and after a brief period of mourning the beautiful Bathsheba becomes David's wife. But David soon faces the consequences
of his actions. Reproached by the prophet Nathan, he bitterly
repents his actions and watches helplessly as the child born of
Bathsheba dies. This reversal of fortune proves to be a passing
episode, for then "David comforted his wife, Bathsheba, and went
in to her, and lay with her; and she bore a son, and he called his
name Solomon" (2 Samuel 12:24).

Every detail of the story—from the king spying the bathing
beauty from the roof of his palace to the notes dispatched by mes-
senger from the royal palace, to the death of the cuckolded husband
in the fierce siege of the heavily fortified city of Rabbah, capital of
Ammon—is drawn from the scenes and events of royal life of a type
that emerged only in the ninth century BCE. We cannot know if
David actually had an affair with a woman named Bathsheba, but
the story of how David repented for his sin and how Bathsheba's

son, Solomon, succeeded to his father's throne was, as many scholars have noted, a powerful political statement legitimizing Solomon's line.* That legitimation is argued in a detailed and realistic setting that only those who were familiar with the life of a royal court and the field procedures of a standing, professional army could possibly recognize.

So too, the tragic story of Absalom's rebellion is deeply dependent on the morals and etiquette of a royal court. The Bible relates that despite great wealth, stunning military victories, and vast armies of conscripted royal laborers, all is not well in the closed circles of David's court. Rivalries begin among the princes. The rape of Tamar, David's daughter, by his hotheaded eldest son, Amnon, initiates a chain of events that reveals David's growing weakness, if not as a king then as a man. Enraged by the crime, Tamar's brother Absalom murders Amnon and flees northward to spend years in exile with the Arameans. Upon returning to Jerusalem he hatches a conspiracy to overthrow his father's increasingly rigid rule. David, growing emotionally weak, is forced to flee Jerusalem for his life. The revolt is finally suppressed, David returns to his capital, and Absalom is hunted down and killed by David's forces. Yet this victory is at the same time David's greatest personal disaster.

Learning of Absalom's death, "the king was deeply moved, and went up to the chamber over the gate, and wept; and as he went, he said, 'O my son Absalom, my son, my son Absalom! Would I had died instead of you, O Absalom, my son, my son'" (2 Samuel 18:33).

The deadly rivalry of princes and the conflict and defection of trusted royal advisers all bespeak a far more complex social background than was apparent in tenth-century BCE Jerusalem. There are many more examples—King Hiram of Tyre's provision of building supplies for David's palace (2 Samuel 5:11); David's diplomatic

---

* Baruch Halpern explained this story as a sophisticated work of propaganda by the supporters of Solomon, aimed to counter rumors that he was not the son of David, and thus not of royal Davidic blood. We would argue that even if the story were old, it assumed its present form only much later in Judah's history.

marriage to the daughter of the king of Geshur (2 Samuel 3:3); David's bestowal of an agricultural fiefdom to Saul's surviving grandson, the crippled Mephibosheth (2 Samuel 9); David's stationing of garrisons in the territory of Aram of Damascus and in Edom in southern Transjordan (2 Samuel 8:6, 14); and Joab's detailed royal census of David's far-flung domains (2 Samuel 24:1–9). All these vivid details seem out of place for the context that the historical David, ruler of a modest chiefdom in the southern highlands, would have known.

MORE GEOGRAPHICAL CLUES

But why date these stately descriptions specifically to the ninth century and not later? In this case the answer again lies in geography. Take the kingdom of Geshur as an example. It is mentioned as an ally of David (2 Samuel 3:3) and as the place where Absalom (the son of the Geshurite wife of David) found refuge after the killing of Amnon. Geshur appears in these biblical texts but is not mentioned in the eighth-century BCE Assyrian records. The large, fortified site of Bethsaida on the northeastern shore of the Sea of Galilee may have been its capital. It was established in the ninth century and initially shows clear Aramean material culture, while in the eighth century BCE, when perhaps it was conquered by the northern kingdom, its Aramean character ends. The only logical chronological setting for a story in the land of Geshur is therefore in the ninth century BCE.

The description of the extent of the census carried out by Joab toward the end of David's reign offers additional ninth-century geographical evidence:

> So Joab and the commanders of the army went out from the presence of the king to number the people of Israel. They crossed the Jordan, and began from Aroer, and from the city that is in the middle of the valley, toward Gad and on to Jazer. Then they came to Gilead, and

to Kadesh in the land of the Hittites; and they came to Dan, and from Dan they went around to Sidon, and came to the fortress of Tyre and to all the cities of the Hivites and Canaanites; and they went out to the Negeb of Judah at Beer-sheba. (2 Samuel 24:4–7)

According to this description, David's kingdom encompassed all of the central highlands as well as the Transjordanian plateau from Aro'er in the south to the Golan in the north. Aro'er is located on the northern cliff of the deep valley of the Arnon River in Moab, and the only possible historical reality for the mention of this place is the conquests of the Omrides in Moab. Jazer and Gilead apparently refer to the northern areas of Transjordan. To the west of the Jordan, the northern boundary extends from Dan to the border of the Phoenician cities of Tyre and Sidon. And in the south, it extends to the Beersheba Valley, where the first evidence of royal control appears only in the ninth century. Some minimalist scholars have argued that this description of the borders of the Davidic state is a late and completely imaginary creation, yet it uncannily retraces the combined territories of the emergent kingdoms of Israel and Judah *together*, at the time when their royal lines were at least temporarily merged.

Such is also the case with the biblical accounts of David's great military victories against the neighboring powers, detailed in 2 Samuel 8, 10, and 12. Moab is the first foreign conquest, a foreshadowing of the conquests of the Omrides in the same area:

And he defeated Moab, and measured them with a line, making them lie down on the ground; two lines he measured to be put to death, and one full line to be spared. And the Moabites became servants to David and brought tribute. (2 Samuel 8:2)

Next comes the war with the Arameans of Syria in the north:

David also defeated Hadadezer the son of Rehob, king of Zobah, as he went to restore his power at the river Euphrates. And David took from him a thousand and seven hundred horsemen, and twenty thousand foot soldiers; and David hamstrung all the chariot horses, but left enough for a hundred chariots. And when the Syrians of Damascus came to help Hadadezer king of Zobah, David slew twenty-two thousand men of the Syrians. Then David put garrisons in Aram of Damascus; and the Syrians became servants to David and brought tribute. (2 Samuel 8:3–6)

In addition to the mention of massive forces of chariotry and infantry that recall Ahab's contingents at the battle of Qarqar in 853 BCE, the general perspective is of the ninth century, as noted by the Israeli biblical historian Nadav Naaman. First of all, the stories describe Aramean states, whose independent existence was short-lived, ending with their annexation to the Assyrian empire in the eighth century BCE. The Aramean states that are mentioned in the story, except for Damascus, are missing from the eighth- and seventh-century BCE records. More important, these were areas that were fought over and at least partially controlled by the Omrides at the height of their power in the mid–ninth century BCE. Lastly, the main figure in the story, Hadadezer, corresponds to the Aramaic name Adad-idri, who was the king of Damascus in the mid–ninth century BCE. Adad-idri appears in the monolith inscription of Shalmaneser III as one of the prominent figures in the coalition of Levantine states that faced the Assyrians at Qarqar. Another powerful king in that coalition, as we mentioned earlier, was Ahab the Israelite.

The "Court History" of David thus offers a whole series of historical retrojections in which the founder of the dynasty of Judah in the tenth century is credited with the victories and the acquisitions of territory that were in fact accomplished by the ninth-century Omrides. But why would a *Judahite* author model the achievements of his kingdom's founding father on the wars of the later Omride kingdom of *Israel*?

THE DEATH AND REBIRTH OF
THE DAVIDIC DYNASTY

As things turned out, the dynastic marriage of the house of Omri and the house of David had a violent and unhappy ending that, at least briefly, threatened the survival of the Davidic dynasty. By the mid–ninth century BCE, the heyday of the Omride kingdom was already passing. One by one, its imperial possessions were falling away. By this time, there are enough external historical sources that, with due caution, we can confirm at least the main historical outlines of the biblical accounts. The Mesha inscription (and 2 Kings 3:5) records an armed uprising in Moab that swept away its control by the kingdom of Israel after Ahab's death. The major blow is recorded in the Tel Dan inscription (described in Appendix 1)—the earliest nonbiblical evidence for the name David—which confirms the defeat of the Omrides by Hazael, king of Damascus. With differences in circumstances and detail from the biblical account in 2 Kings 9, it reports the killing of the Judahite king Ahaziah and his more powerful contemporary, the Israelite king Joram. Destruction layers in many sites in the north may provide gloomy evidence for the subsequent Aramean assault. Within the northern kingdom itself, a new pretender, the army commander Jehu (whose name also appears in contemporary Assyrian records), arose to oust and exterminate the surviving members of the Omride line.

What happened in Judah, after Israel was attacked? According to 2 Kings 11, in Jerusalem things took their own violent turn. The queen mother, Athaliah, the Omride princess sent south in a diplomatic marriage, seized power. To ensure her position against her most dangerous local rivals, she ordered the massacre of all surviving Davidic heirs. We have no independent evidence of the historical reliability of this report. But we do know from subsequent historical developments that the Davidic line survived. The biblical account credits the dedication and quick thinking of a Davidic princess in the midst of Athaliah's bloodbath:

But Jehosheba, the daughter of King Joram,* sister of Ahaziah, took Joash the son of Ahaziah, and stole him away from among the king's sons who were about to be slain, and she put him and his nurse in a bedchamber. Thus she hid him from Athaliah, so that he was not slain; and he remained with her six years, hid in the house of the LORD, while Athaliah reigned over the land. (2 Kings 11:2–3)

The loyalists of the house of David eventually gain their revenge. Jehoiada the priest secretly reveals the existence of a surviving Davidic heir to the still-loyal palace guards in Jerusalem, and conducts a well-planned coup d'etat:

Then he brought out the king's son, and put the crown upon him, and gave him the testimony; and they proclaimed him king, and anointed him; and they clapped their hands, and said, "Long live the king!" When Athaliah heard the noise of the guard and of the people, she went into the house of the LORD to the people; and when she looked, there was the king standing by the pillar, according to the custom, and the captains and the trumpeters beside the king, and all the people of the land rejoicing and blowing trumpets. And Athaliah rent her clothes, and cried, "Treason! Treason!" Then Jehoiada the priest commanded the captains who were set over the army, "Bring her out between the ranks; and slay with the sword any one who follows her." For the priest said, "Let her not be slain in the house of the LORD." So they laid hands on her; and she went through the horses' entrance to the king's house, and there she was slain. (2 Kings 11:12–16)

Thus, according to the Bible, ended the life of the last of the Omrides.

For Jehu, the new ruler of the reconstituted kingdom of Israel,

---

* Though the name is spelled this way in the Revised Standard Version of the Hebrew Bible, his name is properly Jehoram; he reigned as king of Judah, according to the traditional biblical chronology, 851–843 BCE. Likewise Joash's name is properly spelled "Jehoash." (See chart on p. 18.)

things were also not going well. Where once King Ahab faced the Assyrian king Shalmaneser with two thousand chariots and ten thousand foot soldiers, his dynasty's successor, King Jehu, is pictured as a pitiful supplicant at Shalmaneser's feet on the famous Black Obelisk, discovered in the nineteenth century at Nimrud in Iraq. Its cuneiform inscription records that Shalmaneser received from his new vassal, among other things, "silver, gold, a golden *saplu*-bowl, a golden vase with a pointed bottom, golden tumblers, golden buckets, tin, a staff for a king. . . ."

By contrast, other important events soon happened in the Shephelah that offered an opportunity for Judahite expansion there. The account in 2 Kings 12:17 reports that Hazael, king of Damascus, "went up and fought against Gath, and took it." Recent archaeological excavations at the site of this powerful Philistine center, Tell es-Safi in the western Shephelah, by Aren Maeir of Bar Ilan University, have revealed dramatic confirmation for the destruction of the city that had threatened Judah's western villages since David's tenth-century bandit days. Ninth-century Gath was a huge city that stretched over an area of about a hundred acres. It was surrounded by a sophisticated siege system, put to the torch, and completely destroyed. Though eventually partially resettled, the city never fully recovered, living on in the biblical tradition as the home of Goliath, the Philistine giant, and David's erstwhile lord, King Achish—from an increasingly distant, legendary age.

For a short while in the second half of the ninth century, Judah found itself with suddenly expanded political possibilities. In the north, Israel was severely weakened by the Arameans; its northern territories were taken, and Jehu and his son Jehoahaz were pressed by Damascus. Their rule was restricted to the highlands around Samaria. In the west, Gath, the most powerful Philistine city, was destroyed by Hazael. Judah took advantage of this situation by expanding the administrative centers of Beth-shemesh and Lachish.

There may be more to it than that. The second book of Kings (12:18) tells us that in the same campaign, Hazael extracted tribute from Jehoash king of Judah. It seems that the king of Damascus played a major role in the history of Judah: his assault on Israel and destruction of Gath relieved the pressure on Judah from both north and west. Is it possible that all this was a coincidence; or did Judah strike a deal with Damascus to become its vassal in exchange for its help in its attempt at liberation from the dominance of the Omrides?

The liberation from Omride rule, the return of the Davidides to power, and the ensuing prosperity created a new situation—one that was reflected in the continuing elaboration of royal tales. The structures and customs of monarchy were now firmly in place in Jerusalem, and the court bards of Judah gave expression to their new independence. They explained that the great united monarchy of Israel and Judah—known at their own time to have ruled from Samaria—actually had its roots in the distant, legendary time of their own King David. They claimed that their great founding father had anticipated the Omrides' later victories and had never suffered their crushing defeats. David, they said, conquered and completely subdued all the bitter enemies of Israel, enemies that defeated and humiliated the northern kingdom in the mid–ninth century. He crushed Damascus, slew many Moabites, and conquered the capital of Ammon. In the tales told in court circles—and later put into writing—the founder of the Jerusalem dynasty was pictured as strong as, in fact much stronger than, the greatest of the northern kings. The power and logic of these stories indicated that David's descendants were the only worthy contenders for rule over the once-great kingdom of Israel.

There may well have been historical characters named Michal, Bathsheba, Joab, and Absalom, whose personal lives and political survival were entwined with the historical David. We simply have no way of reconstructing what events and conflicts may have occurred within the close circle of David's family and companions in his highland chiefdom in the tenth century BCE. However, the biblical "Court History" offers a richly costumed period-piece epic, a series of courtly stories that evoke the atmosphere of a newly established kingdom on the rise. Even as the villagers of Judah still regaled in the retelling of the rough-and-ready tales of the outlaw David and his band of cutthroats, even as the arguments continued among the villagers of Bethel and Gibeon about the tragic death of Saul and the succession of David, a new context of power and glory was added to the chorus of memories.

In the royal court of the house of David, in the feasts and dynastic gatherings of princes, princesses, courtiers, and queen mothers, new legends were—still orally—woven to inspire them for future triumphs while recalling a largely legendary past. The great wars of conquest, the details of battles, besieged cities, and vast chariot forces were not history but contemporary reality. Even the most intimate details of David's personal stories evoke the dangerous liaisons of the new court life that was unknown in Jerusalem in the tenth century BCE. Updating the legends was necessary and accomplished with consummate skill. For in their legendary transformation of the rugged founder of the dynasty into a thoroughly great monarch—portraying his life as a series of royal victories, courtly conflicts, and aristocratic dilemmas—the bards of ninth-century BCE Jerusalem provided later western kings and princes with a vivid, poetic justification for both their own human weaknesses and their unshakable right to rule.

PART II

THE EVOLUTION OF A LEGEND

PERIOD	STAGES IN DEVELOPMENT OF BIBLICAL MATERIAL
Late 8th Century BCE	First written version of the tales and ballads about Saul, David, and Solomon's succession, combining earlier southern and northern oral traditions; serves as a unifying national epic for Hezekiah's kingdom.

HISTORICAL BACKGROUND	ARCHAEOLOGICAL FINDS
Judah becomes an Assyrian vassal. Israel falls. Torrent of refugees from the north. Judah emerges as a full-blown, bureaucratic state, with a mixed population of Judahites and Israelites.	Dramatic growth of Jerusalem: fortifications, elaborate tombs, the Siloam Tunnel. Impressive demographic growth in the entire territory of Judah. Olive-oil industry. Spread of scribal activity and signs of developed administration.

CHAPTER 4

Temple and Dynasty

The Birth of the First Written Epic

— LATE EIGHTH CENTURY BCE —

THE BIBLICAL ACCOUNT OF DAVID'S RISE, HIS REIGN, and Solomon's succession is far more than a haphazard collection of ancient folklore. Though its main narrative building blocks were drawn from oral traditions of various historical periods, its biblical form is a sweeping literary saga that weaves together all its memorable incidents and unforgettable characters into a coherent and masterful narrative. Extending from the first book of Samuel to the first book of Kings—with a complex plot line punctuated by betrayals, assassinations, and divine guidance—it explains how David was selected by God to become Israel's king and savior, how Jerusalem became Israel's sacred capital, and how Solomon succeeded him to the throne.

As we have suggested in earlier chapters, "The History of David's Rise" contains a number of early elements—particularly David's career as a bandit and his rivalry with Saul—that preserved authentic memories of tenth-century BCE events in oral form. Likewise, we have suggested that the stage setting of the "Court History" reflects the aristocratic culture of Jerusalem palace circles during the ninth century BCE, almost a hundred years after David and Solomon's time. It was presumably conveyed orally, in the form of courtly ballads, under the influence of the Omride dynasty of northern Israel.

These oral sources contain a significant amount of unflattering material about David. "The History of David's Rise" tells of his cooperation with Israel's enemies the Philistines, his bitter rivalry with Saul, and his conspicuous absence from the fateful battle at Mount Gilboa in which Saul was killed. It concludes with the grisly annihilation of the house of Saul.* The "Court" or "Succession History" is a bloody tale of betrayals and assassinations, which eliminated all of Solomon's major rivals to succeed David to the throne.

As we have said, this is quite unusual among the official chronicles of ancient Near Eastern kings, where the object was generally idealization, rather than journalistic accuracy. Many scholars argue—though we disagree—that "David's Rise" and the "Court History" were put into writing in the tenth century BCE within or very close to the lifetime of David, when the memories of his alleged crimes and misdemeanors were still vivid. They see the basic biblical narrative as a work of apologetic history that was meant to answer the charges and accusations of David and Solomon's contemporary opponents and to provide a persuasive explanation of the legitimacy of the Davidic dynasty.

The full David and Solomon story is indeed a sophisticated work of dynastic propaganda, but we can point to another, later period in the history of Judah when such an ambitious text was

---

* The list of targeted liquidations of northern figures is painfully long: David is indirectly linked to the death of Abner, the loyal general of Saul (2 Samuel 3:27); to the killing and then beheading of Ish-bosheth, the son of Saul (2 Samuel 4:7); to the hanging of seven other members of the house of Saul (2 Samuel 21:7–9); and the beheading of the northern rebel Sheba the son of Bichri (2 Samuel 20:22).

needed and *could have been written* at least in an initial form. Archaeology has revealed a far-reaching series of changes that took place throughout the kingdom of Judah in the late eighth century BCE— a full two centuries after David and Solomon's time. Jerusalem suddenly grew into a huge metropolis. In the countryside of Judah, many new villages appeared, and existing villages and towns experienced a period of widespread expansion. Fortresses, storehouses, and administrative centers were built throughout the kingdom. The appearance of inscriptions and official seals testifies to the importance and widespread use of the written word. Public literacy was obviously the essential precondition for the compilation of the biblical David and Solomon story as a written text intended to influence public opinion in favor of the Davidic dynasty.

A closer look at the wider political and economic developments throughout the ancient Near East in the late eighth century BCE brings us a step closer to understanding why the kingdom of Judah suddenly changed its character—and why the written narrative of David's life and the early days of Solomon's reign was initially composed.

THE NEW ASSYRIAN ORDER

Developments far from Judah were the main impetus for its dramatic transformation. By the middle of the eighth century BCE, the vast Assyrian empire, expanding from the Tigris and Euphrates Valley to the Mediterranean coastlands, had begun to construct what we would today call a "globalized" political system and economy, perhaps the first known to history. This great Mesopotamian empire, centered in the massive palace cities of Calah, Dur Sharrukin, and Nineveh, gradually projected its power, by a combination of military moves, political pressure, and economic incentives, into every facet of the region's political and economic life. By devastat-

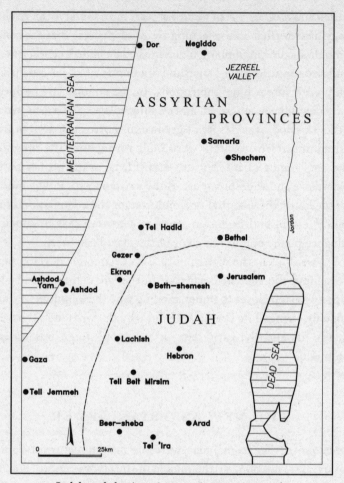

Judah and the Assyrian provinces to its north
in the late eighth century BCE

ing cities and destroying independent kingdoms that refused to
become compliant vassals, the Assyrians gradually created a com-
plexly interconnected trading network in which all the lands, animals, resources, and peoples of the areas they had conquered could
be moved or exploited to serve the best interests of the Assyrian

state. The peoples and kingdoms that came under the threat of Assyrian domination were faced with a difficult decision: either willingly to become a part of the Assyrian world system or to risk destruction and exile.

This Iron Age superpower would have a decisive effect on the history of both Judah and the northern kingdom of Israel, though not all at once. At first Assyria's impact on the southern highlands of Judah was negligible. As far as we know from the silence of historical sources and archaeological evidence, Judah—with only limited resources and set off from the major trade routes—remained a remote and primitive highland kingdom throughout the ninth and early eighth centuries BCE. It evaded even indirect Assyrian control, probably due to the simple fact that the southern highlands, with their limited resources and largely pastoral population, possessed nothing worthy of control.

Yet the situation was entirely different in the northern kingdom, which from the late ninth century BCE onward was viewed by the Assyrians as a tempting prize. After the fall of the Omrides, Israel became a loyal vassal to the fearsome Assyrian superpower—as graphically depicted on the Black Obelisk of Shalmaneser III, with the Israelite king Jehu groveling before the Assyrian throne. That fealty eventually brought participation in the Assyrian economy. By the early eighth century BCE, the northern kingdom, though dominated by Assyria, reached its peak economic prosperity, territorial expansion, and diplomatic influence. Archaeologically, this is seen in the inscribed Hebrew ostraca found in the palace of Samaria, whose lists of agricultural commodities and royal officials attest to a highly organized, bureaucratic economy. Likewise the elaborately carved Samaria ivories are evidence of a flowering of Phoenician-influenced artistic styles. The magnificent Shema seal from the time of the northern king Jeroboam II (784–748 BCE), bearing the image of a roaring lion with the inscription "Belonging to Shema, servant of Jeroboam," also represents a developed regional bureaucracy. At Megiddo, the stables that likely served as a horse-breeding complex show the extent of lucrative specialized trading activity.* And the impressive underground water systems, city gates, and fortifications at both Hazor and Megiddo are evidence of extensive public works.

To the people of the kingdom of Judah, the cosmopolitan society of the north must have seemed like an alien world. At that time Jerusalem was still restricted to the narrow ridge of the City of David, which remained unfortified. Despite its emerging royal culture, there was not a single real urban center in the entire southern highlands, which was still relatively sparsely settled. A few fortresses had been established in the Beer-sheba Valley and the Shephelah, yet the number of such sites was extremely limited. Evidence of meaningful scribal activity in Judah in the early eighth century is lacking. Very few inscriptions and personal seals can be assigned to this period. There is no evidence for a specialized production of agricultural commodities or mass production of pottery, which was characteristic of the north. In short, Judah in the early eighth century BCE was still in a relatively low state of economic and social development.

That situation would change suddenly and explosively. In 744 BCE, the great Assyrian king Tiglath-pileser III dramatically shifted Assyrian imperial policy from remote domination to direct military assault and control. The kingdom of Israel and the kingdom of Damascus became newfound allies in a desperate attempt to resist this new imperial policy. The Bible describes their march southward to Jerusalem to pressure Judah to join them in an open revolt against the Assyrians (2 Kings 16:5). The beleaguered Judahite king Ahaz, fearing Assyrian wrath, on the one hand, and conquest and deposition by the northern rebel alliance, on the other, took an un-

---

* For more on the evidence for horse breeding and trading at Israelite Megiddo, see chapter 5.

precedented step. He abandoned Judah's long isolation and actively sought the protection of the Assyrians by pledging his loyalty to Tiglath-pileser (2 Kings 16:5–9; Isaiah 7). In so doing, he affirmed Judah's status as an Assyrian vassal state. This biblical report has been confirmed by archaeological finds. Ahaz's name is specifically mentioned in an Assyrian building inscription that boasts of abundant income from the empire's faithful vassals, who sent to Assyria "all kinds of costly objects, be they products of the sea or of the continent, the choice products of their regions, the treasures of their kings."

Judah was now protected, and Assyria's wrath against the region's rebels was not long in coming. In a series of campaigns westward, Tiglath-pileser brought the coastal cities of Philistia under Assyrian control, and turned his sights on the rich territory and resources of the kingdom of Israel. In 732 BCE, after conquering Damascus, deposing its king, and making it an Assyrian province, Tiglath-pileser marched into Israel, conquered some of its most fertile agricultural areas, and formally annexed them as an Assyrian province. Megiddo and Hazor were both conquered and transformed into centers of direct Assyrian rule. And for the kingdom of Israel, the loss of the Galilee and Assyrian control of the Mediterranean coast were economic and political catastrophes that could never be overcome.

The northern kingdom of Israel—isolated, partially dismembered, and fighting for its very existence—raised the banner of rebellion again. This time it was suicidal. In 722 BCE, Shalmaneser V, king of Assyria, laid siege to Samaria, and after Shalmaneser's death, his brutal successor Sargon II completed the work. The rump kingdom of Israel, now largely restricted to the vicinity of Samaria, was annexed as an Assyrian province—called Samerina—and Assyrian provincial officers were dispatched to regulate its economy and political life. At least a portion of the Israelite population was deported and new peoples were brought from Mesopotamia and settled in their stead.* Sargon refers to the reorganization of the new province of Samerina, noting that he "settled therein people from countries which I myself had conquered . . . and imposed upon them tribute as is customary for Assyrian citizens."

The second book of Kings (17:24) confirms the arrival of new settlers, describing how "the king of Assyria brought people from Babylon, Cuthah, Avva, Hamath, and Sepharvaim, and placed them in the cities of Samaria instead of the people of Israel." Scattered archaeological evidence seemingly confirms this. A papyrus written in Aramaic mentions deportees settled at the ancient Israelite cult center of Bethel. Seventh-century cuneiform texts found in the Israelite border town of Gezer and at a site nearby bear Babylonian names.

The political landscape had suddenly shifted. In the wake of the conquest of the northern kingdom of Israel, Judah became the only autonomous state in the highlands. Its long life in the shadow of the larger, wealthier kingdom of Israel was over. Judah emerged from this great historical watershed transformed almost beyond recognition. By the end of the eighth century BCE, it had all the hallmarks of a proper kingdom: massive building activity, mass production of commodities, centralized administration, literacy, and, most important, a new understanding of its own historical destiny.

---

* Despite the legendary stories of the exile of the "Ten Lost Tribes" of Israel in this period, we cannot be sure that Sargon's claim of deporting almost 30,000 Israelites after the fall of Samaria is accurate. In the eighth century BCE the population of the northern kingdom living west of the Jordan can be estimated at about 225,000. Even if we were to take Sargon's figure of 27,290 Israelite exiles at face value and add to it the 13,500 Israelites claimed by Tiglath-pileser III to have been deported from the Galilee, the overwhelming majority of the rural Israelite population was not deported. Many undoubtedly remained in their ancient villages in the immediate wake of the conquest and continued to cultivate their land.

AN ECONOMIC AND
SOCIAL REVOLUTION

The composition of the David and Solomon story as a written narrative—and indeed the composition of biblical texts as we now have
them—would not have been possible were it not for this dramatic
change in Judah's character as a society. The changes can be seen
first and foremost in Jerusalem itself. The city underwent a period
of explosive expansion.* The ancient core of settlement, perched for
millennia on its narrow ridge near the Gihon spring, was heavily
fortified. New suburbs sprang up outside the walls of the original
City of David, on the broad, formerly unoccupied hill to the west.
The built-up area eventually spread to cover much of the western
hill. This new suburb was surrounded with a fortification wall even
more formidable than the newly built defenses of the City of David,
with a thickness of more than twenty feet.

The process of expansion seems to have been fairly rapid. From
the pottery types recovered on the western hill it is clear that it took
place during the few decades that preceded and immediately followed the Assyrian conquest of the kingdom of Israel. In the span of
just a few years, Jerusalem grew from a modest hill country town of
about ten to fifteen acres to a large, fortified city of almost 150 acres.
The population spiked accordingly. A rough estimate of the demographic growth that took place in this period, based on a ratio of
people to the size of the built-up area, would suggest that Jerusalem's
population skyrocketed from around one thousand inhabitants to
approximately twelve thousand. That made it a significant urban
population by the standards of the ancient Near East—and far and
away the largest city that ever existed in the southern highlands. At
the same time, many farmsteads were built in the vicinity of the city,

---

* The discovery of this major episode in Jerusalem's history is due to the excavations
of Nahman Avigad in the Jewish Quarter in the 1970s and more recent excavations
by Ronnie Reich and Eli Shukron in the City of David.

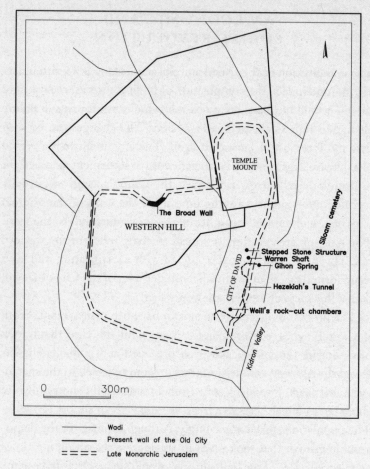

TEMPLE
MOUNT

The Broad Wall

WESTERN HILL

Siloam cemetery

CITY OF DAVID

Stepped Stone Structure
Warren Shaft
Gihon Spring

Hezekiah's Tunnel

Weill's rock—cut chambers

Kidron Valley

0   300m

—————— Wadi
—————— Present wall of the Old City
= = = = Late Monarchic Jerusalem

The expansion of Jerusalem in the late eighth century BCE

presumably to provide Jerusalem's swollen population with agricultural produce. Many more farms and villages appeared all over the
southern highlands of Judah as well.

The construction of massive fortifications in the City of David
and around Jerusalem's western hill would have required massive,
conscripted labor—as would the impressive seventeen-hundred-
foot-long subterranean tunnel used to bring water into the City of

David, known as the Siloam tunnel. Outside Jerusalem, there is also evidence of extensive public construction. At the regional center of Lachish in the Shephelah, the city gate system, the podium of the palace, and a complex of stables were enlarged and expanded. At Tell Beit Mirsim and Beth-shemesh in the Shephelah, excavations have uncovered unusual complexes of stone olive oil presses. Far to the south in the Beer-sheba Valley, where overland trade routes led from Transjordan to the port cities on the Mediterranean, fortresses and well-planned storehouses were built at the strategic way stations of Arad, Tel Ira, and Beer-sheba itself.

What was the impetus for this extensive building program? From where did the resources come? The decision of the Judahite king Ahaz (c. 743–727 BCE) to become an Assyrian vassal represented something more than political submission; it marked Judah's formal entrance into a wider economy as an active participant in long-distance commerce. The archaeological finds of the late eighth century BCE show clear evidence of this economic activity. The construction of fortresses and storehouses in the Beersheba Valley is undoubtedly connected with the Arabian spice trade, now conducted under Assyrian auspices. The appearance of olive oil processing complexes at Tell Beit Mirsim and Beth-shemesh also seem connected with regional commerce, for neither site is located in the traditional highland areas where olives were grown. Either groves were intentionally planted around the new olive oil production centers or, more likely, harvested olives were transported from throughout the Judahite highlands to be transformed into a valuable and potentially tradable commodity—lacking in Assyria—and then shipped to the Assyrian-controlled commercial centers on the coast.

The archaeological dating of these developments is not precise enough to pinpoint exactly when in the late eighth century BCE they started, but it is likely that they began in the time of Ahaz, picked up speed during the much longer reign of his son and successor Hezekiah (c. 727–698 BCE), and were substantially intensified after the fall of the kingdom of Israel. As the last autonomous kingdom west of the Jordan, Judah took advantage of the great economic opportunities presented by its status as a vassal kingdom. And in the midst of this apparent economic activity there appeared the first signs of extensive state-level activity and an important new form of public communication: *the written word.*

The sudden appearance at many sites of inscribed signet seals bearing personal names shows a new concern with ownership and economic status. Standardized, inscribed weight stones are clear evidence of the regulation of commercial exchange. A well-known class of storage jars from this period, produced in large quantities, bears distinctive seal impressions on the handles. They contain an emblem in the shape of a winged sun disc or scarab beetle (which may have been a royal Judahite insignia), a short Hebrew inscription reading *lmlk* ("belonging to the king"), and the name of one of four cities: Hebron, Socoh, Ziph, and a still unidentified place designated by the letters *mmst*. Scholars have suggested several alternative explanations: that they contained the products of royal estates; that they were used as official containers for tax collection and distribution of commodities; or that the seal impressions were merely the identifying marks of pottery workshops where official royal storage jars were manufactured. In any case they represent a kingdom-wide network of regulation and communication. And as is also seen in the appearance of a growing number of inscribed potsherds in the fortresses of Arad and Beer-sheba, it was a network of connections and exchanges made possible only by the spread of literacy out into the countryside, presumably from royal secretaries and scribes in Jerusalem.

In Jerusalem, seals, weight stones, and standardized store jars have been found in significant numbers. There are additional indications of the expanding functions of literacy in the kingdom's capital: the elaborate family tombs hewn into the steep cliffs to the east and south of the city and in large rock-cut burial chambers a few hundred yards to the north of the city. Some are freestanding monolithic monuments, while others are carefully carved subterranean chambers with finely finished walls and gabled ceilings. There is little doubt that these tombs were used for burial of nobility, for one of them bears an inscription with the name of the deceased and his royal office: ". . . *yahu*, who is in charge of the house . . ." Biblical scholars have identified him with Shebna (the full biblical Hebrew form would be *Shebnayahu*) the royal steward, whom the prophet Isaiah (22:15–16) condemned for arrogance in hewing an elaborate tomb in the rock.

Perhaps most significant is the first use of writing in Iron Age Jerusalem for a public pronouncement. The hewing of the Siloam water tunnel was commemorated by a unique ancient Hebrew inscription chiseled into its bedrock wall, celebrating in a dramatic literary narrative the skill of the engineers and the courage of the two teams of diggers, who worked from opposite ends of the tunnel's course:

> . . . *when the tunnel was driven through. And this was the way in which it was cut through: While [. . .] were still [. . .] axe(s), each man toward his fellow, and while there were still three cubits to be cut through, [there was heard] the voice of a man calling to his fellow, for there was an overlap in the rock on the right [and on the left]. And when the tunnel was driven through, the quarrymen hewed [the rock], each man toward his fellow, axe against axe; and the water flowed from the spring toward the reservoir for 1,200 cubits, and the height of the rock above the head[s] of the quarrymen was 100 cubits.*

This inscription caused a great sensation at the time of its accidental discovery in 1880. It was immediately seen as archaeological verification of the biblical reference to how King Hezekiah "made the pool and the conduit and brought water into the city" (2 Kings 20:20). Yet it is important for far more than biblical confirmation: it is the earliest archaeological evidence for extensive literary activity in Jerusalem.* The archaeological picture of Judah in the closing decades of the eighth century is of a populous, prosperous, and *literate* kingdom. Jerusalem had become a heavily fortified city with a large population and a special class of royal officials, scribes, and administrators, who could conscript workmen for public projects and private memorials. In fact, this picture uncannily resembles the biblical descriptions of Jerusalem under David and Solomon in its general context and in many specific details.

Writing for the first time in the Iron Age thus became an important tool in creating and establishing the state's coherence. That was the essential precondition for the compilation of the biblical David and Solomon story as a written text. Only then were court secretaries and scribes in a position to compile an ambitious literary epic about the dynasty's founding fathers. This is a crucial fact for any discussion of the evolution of the biblical tradition: the first signs of widespread literacy in Judah mark the earliest possible time when ancient oral traditions could be collected, reworked, and edited together in the form of written texts.

A FLOOD OF REFUGEES

As a skillful example of royal self-promotion and historical legitimation, the biblical account of David's rise and Solomon's succession could not have been written earlier than the late eighth century BCE. But why did it take the particular form that it did? It is significant that many of the accusations against David concern the killings of figures from the northern highlands, in particular, related to the house of Saul. The accusations undoubtedly came from northern

---

* Two personal seals of officials of the Judahite king Uzziah (785–733 BCE) were discovered in the nineteenth century, but they are isolated examples of official writing in Judah, probably heavily influenced by the extensive literacy in the court of Uzziah's contemporary King Jereboam II of the northern kingdom (784–748 BCE).

traditions, but why were they kept in the text? Why were they of special significance in this period?

Our main clue is demographic, for the explosive growth of the city of Jerusalem and indeed all of Judah at the end of the eighth century cannot be explained on the basis of sheer prosperity or natural growth alone. The more than tenfold increase in Jerusalem's population seems to have been closely tied to the contemporary chain of events, specifically the conquest of the northern kingdom of Israel. The Israeli archaeologist Magen Broshi long ago suggested that the sudden population explosion in Jerusalem at the end of the eighth century BCE—far greater than could be explained by natural population increase—was the result of a wave of refugees from the former kingdom of Israel fleeing southward to avoid conscription in the new Assyrian order. There is clear evidence that the population of the Judahite countryside also grew dramatically. Archaeological surveys have noted that the number of settlements in the hill country to the south of Jerusalem swelled from around thirty in the ninth and early eighth centuries BCE to more than 120 in the late eighth century. In the Shephelah, the number increased from twenty-one to 276. Beyond the increase in the number of sites, the existing sites seem to have grown bigger and become more densely inhabited. All in all, it would not be an exaggeration to estimate that Judah's population more than doubled in the late eighth century BCE.

Where precisely did these refugees come from? We can now suggest a particular region on the basis of archaeological surveys in the northern highlands. A word of caution is in order: pottery collected in surveys is limited in quantity and variety. Hence in most cases it can be dated to a general period rather than to a very specific, short span of time. In examining the demographic patterns of the northern highlands—in particular the territory of the northern kingdom—it is relatively easy to distinguish between pottery types from Late Iron II (the eighth to seventh centuries BCE) and the much later Persian period (the fifth to fourth centuries BCE), but very difficult—

if not impossible—to distinguish chronological phases in Late Iron II survey collections. The data are nevertheless of great significance: clear patterns of population growth and decline emerge.

In the area of northern Samaria, between Shechem and the Jezreel Valley (the northern sector of the kingdom of Israel in its last stage of existence), the number of sites did not change dramatically between the Late Iron II and the Persian period. There were 238 settlements in the eighth century and 247 in the Persian period.* Yet the situation is utterly different in southern Samaria—the area between Shechem and Bethel, just to the north of Jerusalem. The number of sites there decreased from 238 in the eighth century to 127 in the Persian period and the total built-up area shrank even more spectacularly, from approximately 420 to 111 acres (170 to 45 hectares). Translating these figures into estimated population suggests a striking, 75 percent drop, from a population of about thirty-four thousand to nine thousand. Even if there were several oscillations between the two eras of comparison, it is clear that southern Samaria suffered a major demographic decline after the conquest of the northern kingdom of Israel by Assyria.

Another source of evidence points to the same conclusion. In the eighth century BCE southern Samaria was an important olive oil producing region that required a substantial population to maintain this industry. It is significant that this was a place where the Assyrians settled Mesopotamian deportees after their conquest of the kingdom of Israel. As we have mentioned, the Assyrians left most of

---

* Israeli archaeologist Adam Zertal has attempted to reconstruct the settlement pattern of the seventh century BCE (to differentiate from the eighth) in northern Samaria according to a few pottery types and has argued for a significant decline in the number of sites after the fall of the north. Yet most of these types can also be found in the eighth century BCE. His main—probably only—criterion was a type of decorated bowl that he linked to the Cuthean deportees who were settled by the Assyrians in the region. Without dealing with the question if this identification is valid, the presence or absence of a single pottery type in survey sites (some of which produce a limited number of sherds) can be random and misleading. We believe that Zertal's interpretation of the situation in the seventh century is therefore based on very shaky grounds.

the Israelite rural population in place, exiling only a small proportion, presumably the elite. Yet in this region there seems to have
been a calculated effort to replace a vanished population. Cuneiform
tablets from Gezer and nearby Tel Hadid attest to the presence of
Babylonian deportees in the area in the early seventh century BCE.
The name Avvim, which appears in a biblical list of Judahite towns
(Joshua 18:23), seems connected with the name Avva—one of the
places of origin of the Mesopotamian deportees (2 Kings 17:24);
Avvim is located in the highlands of Benjamin, around Bethel. A
papyrus written in Aramaic mentions deportees who were probably
settled in Bethel itself. This planned settlement may have had two
motivations: to restore the economic output of a depopulated area
and to establish a docile population (entirely dependent on the
Assyrians) near the border of the vassal kingdom of Judah, as a measure of caution against future unrest.

In any case, the evidence seems to converge on the southern part
of the northern kingdom and the vicinity of Bethel as the source of
many of the refugees who swelled the population of Judah and
Jerusalem at the end of the eighth century BCE. This is precisely the
area where there is evidence for a tenth century BCE highland polity
related to the biblical traditions of Saul. Those traditions, like the
tales about David, would have been orally transmitted for centuries,
and as local memories and expressions of regional identity, would
hardly have vanished from the consciousness of the people of the
region, even if they were to leave their ancestral lands and become
refugees in Judah.

Thus two traditions—of Saul and Israel, of David and Judah—
would have been thrust together in the midst of the far-reaching
social and economic changes that transformed the kingdom of
Judah after the fall of Israel. Not only did Judah develop from an
isolated highland society into a fully developed state integrated into
the Assyrian economy; its population dramatically changed from
purely Judahite into a mix of Judahite and ex-Israelite. Perhaps as
much as half of the Judahite population in the late eighth to early

seventh century BCE was of north Israelite origin. And as we will see, the composition of an official dynastic history, in which the concept of a *united* monarchy was central, was only one of the ways that the rulers of Judah attempted to bind together the new society that had been created within the span of just a few decades.

ONE PEOPLE, ONE TEMPLE

The biblical story of David and Solomon places great emphasis on their role in centralizing the Israelite cult in their capital city and on the special sanctity of that place. David orders the holy Ark of the Covenant to be brought to Jerusalem in a joyful procession (2 Samuel 6) and Solomon is credited with constructing the great Temple as the center point of united Israel's worship. The insistence on the centrality of Jerusalem was a theological process that would continue to develop for several centuries, but there is some suggestive archaeological evidence for the beginnings of cultic centralization at the end of the eighth century BCE. It is noteworthy in that respect that King Hezekiah, son of Ahaz, is remembered in the Bible as one of the most righteous kings of Judah, who "did what was right in the eyes of the Lord, according to all that David his father had done" (2 Kings 18:3). From the Bible's perspective, his achievement was primarily religious:

> *He removed the high places, and broke the pillars, and cut down the Asherah. And he broke in pieces the bronze serpent that Moses had made, for until those days the people of Israel had burned incense to it; it was called Nehushtan. He trusted in the LORD the God of Israel; so that there was none like him among all the kings of Judah after him, nor among those who were before him.* (2 Kings 18:4–5)

Scholars have debated the historicity of this description, some accepting it as reliable, others raising doubts or rejecting it altogether on purely textual grounds. We have no archaeological information about the possible changes made to the Jerusalem Temple in this period, as it lies inaccessible to excavation beneath the Muslim shrines on the Temple Mount. Yet there is suggestive evidence in some of the outlying fortresses and administrative centers of the kingdom that dramatic changes in the nature of public worship in Judah were under way at the end of the eighth century BCE.

At the eastern end of the Beer-sheba Valley, the fortress of Arad was maintained, as we have suggested, in an effort by the rulers of Judah to extend their control over the passing caravan trade. It contained an elaborate sanctuary, with an altar for sacrifices in the outer courtyard and internal chambers for rituals. In the course of subsequent research, a member of the Arad excavation team, Zeev Herzog, suggested that the sanctuary had functioned during the eighth century BCE. Its end came not in violent destruction, but in intentional replanning: the shrine and its altar were dismantled and the area they formerly occupied was covered with a layer of soil, over which new structures were built. The ritual significance of the objects from the dismantled shrine was nevertheless respected; small altars used for burning incense within the sanctuary were laid on their sides and carefully buried in the place where the sanctuary once stood. These alterations were undertaken just before the end of the eighth century BCE.*

Farther to the west at Tel Beer-sheba, a similar alteration in ritual practice seems to have taken place. Although no sanctuary was identified in the excavations, the building blocks of a large horned altar were found, suggesting that a sanctuary or a freestanding place for sacrifices had once stood in this royal citadel. Some dismantled pieces of this altar were found discarded in the earthen ramparts of the city's fortifications and some were reused as building material in storehouses. Significantly, both the ramparts and the storehouses

---

* For more detail about the stratigraphy and archaeological arguments concerning the dismantling of shrines in Judah in this period, see Appendix 5.

were constructed at the end of the eighth century BCE—suggesting that the shrine had been dismantled by that time.

Finally, at Lachish, the most important regional center of the Shephelah, a parallel development took place. A pit containing cult objects was uncovered in the excavations immediately beneath the level of the palace courtyard, which was expanded and paved in the late eighth century BCE. The cult objects are difficult to date and it is impossible to know precisely *when* in the late eighth century the courtyard was resurfaced, but it fits the general context of activities we have been describing. The finds at Arad, Beer-sheba, and Lachish seem to point to a similar picture: all three present evidence for the existence of sanctuaries in the eighth century BCE, but in all three, the sanctuaries fell into disuse before the end of the eighth century. It is noteworthy that none of the many seventh- and early-sixth-century BCE sites excavated in Judah produced evidence for the existence of a sanctuary.

Archaeology cannot provide an exact date within this general time frame for the removal of the countryside shrines, but a look at the broader events—and the tradition preserved in 1 Kings 18:4–5—points to the days of Hezekiah as a likely context. It seems plausible that during this time, Judah experienced a sweeping reform of cultic practices, in the course of which countryside sanctuaries were abolished, destroyed, and buried, probably as part of an effort to centralize the state cult in Jerusalem. Yet this process should be seen from socioeconomic and political—rather than strictly religious—perspectives. It probably aimed at strengthening the unifying elements of the state—the central authority of the king and the elite in the capital—and at weakening the old, regional, clan-based leadership in the countryside.

Simultaneous with the sudden appearance of standardized weights and measures, royal seals and uniform storage jars, the institutions of state-directed administration grew more complex and more centralized. All this served the new need to unify Judah's diverse population. The kingdom contained not only distinctive regional cultures (from desert, highlands, and foothills) but also

large numbers of immigrants from the territory of the former kingdom of Israel. These people must have brought to Judah their
northern cult traditions and attachments to ancient northern
shrines, the most important of which was the Bethel temple, situ-
ated in the midst of their ancestral villages. Located just a few miles
north of Jerusalem, it was now in Assyrian territory, but still probably reachable for ceremonies and festivals.

This must have posed a serious religious challenge to Judahite
authority. It seems that the solution was a ban on all sanctuaries—
countryside shrines in Judah and the Bethel temple alike—except
for the royal Temple in Jerusalem. In short, the cult "reform" in the
days of Hezekiah, rather then representing puritan religious fervor,
was actually a domestic political endeavor. It was an important step
in the remaking of Judah in a time of a demographic upheaval and
economic reorganization. In the new conditions of the late eighth
century BCE, Judah gained a growing sense of authority and responsibility over all the people of the central highlands—as the last kingdom left with even nominal autonomy. Jerusalem was its capital city
and the Davidic dynasty was its ruling family. Jerusalem may have
always been a small town in comparison to the great cities of the
northern kingdom, but its newfound destiny was to become the
center of all the people of Israel.

This sudden realization of Jerusalem's historical centrality now
seemed to demonstrate God's favor. It was an essential precondition
to compiling an authoritative history of the Davidic dynasty—in
which divine will, rather than happenstance or realpolitik—played
the central role in the elevation of Jerusalem and its Davidic kings
to leadership over all Israel.

THE FIRST AUTHORIZED VERSION

Uniformity of ritual at a central Temple was one way to encourage
the integration of the population, and it is possible that an early ver-

sion of the construction of the Temple by Solomon may have been written as early as the days of Hezekiah. Yet the writing of a national history was another important tool. Assyrian kings had popularized and dignified the compiling of official chronicles—developing from terse building inscriptions into elaborate texts of thanksgiving for military victories or civil achievements, to bombastic and totally self-serving dynastic histories. It is likely that the spread of Assyrian military and political power encouraged the adoption of Assyrian cultural characteristics throughout the region, including chronicle writing as the high-status accessory of every respectable Assyrian vassal king. But Judah's dynastic history was to be something different—and it would survive and be remembered long after even the greatest kings of Assyria had faded into obscurity.

The biblical story of David and Solomon is not just a standard work of self-serving royal propaganda. It was—and is—a passionate and sophisticated defense of Davidic legitimacy, powerful enough to be argued in the public squares or meeting places to still the voices of criticism with the skill of its argument and its considerable narrative art.

What was the reason to put the oral traditions about David into writing? Why was it necessary for the southerners to deal with accusations from the north regarding the founder of their ruling dynasty? Why was it necessary to state that David was not a traitor and a collaborator with the Philistines; that he was not a simple thug; that he bore no responsibility for the death of the first northern king in the battle of Gilboa; that he did not participate in the killing of Ish-bosheth the son of Saul; that he was not responsible for the death of Abner; that he did not unjustly order the liquidation of all of Saul's immediate descendants? Why the need to explain that Solomon, who was not first in line to the throne of his father, came to be his successor? More important, *when* was it necessary to insist that David and his descendants were the only legitimate rulers over all the people of Israel?

At the time of Hezekiah, when half if not more of the Judahite population was in fact Israelite, Judah could not ignore, or eradicate, the historical traditions of the north. In order to unify the kingdom, it had to take all of them into consideration, to incorporate them in a single official story that would defuse the impact of the traditions that were hostile to the expansion of royal Judahite rule.

That was done first and foremost with popular culture: with the legends and memories that were cherished in the villages of Judah, in the traditions of the northerners, and in the Jerusalem court. As the single, national account of the beginnings of monarchy in Israel, a new narrative wrapped a northern-centered anointment of Saul around the tales of the bandit and showed how David innocently acted only in the best interests of his people. It explained how David was a great patriot and father of his country who time and again saved Israelites from the hands of the Philistines; that he was forced to run for his life because of Saul's faults, faults that the northern king himself admitted (1 Samuel 26:21); that he was always loyal to Saul. It showed that he was in no way responsible for the death of Saul, for he was not even present at the battle of Gilboa; that it was God's power and will that unseated Saul and anointed David; that it was Joab, not David, who carried out the bloody purge of the Saulides and their loyalists; and that regarding territory and military exploits, David was greater than any of the northern kings, including the mighty Omrides, in the extent of his legendary conquests. Most important of all was the idea of a divine promise—that the Davidic dynasty was under the protection of the God of Israel.

This unbreakable connection between the God of Israel and the house of David is expressed most succinctly in God's words to David:

When your days are fulfilled and you lie down with your fathers, I will raise up your offspring after you, who shall come forth from your body, and I will establish his kingdom. He shall build a house for my name, and I will establish the throne of his kingdom for ever. I will be his father, and he shall be my son. When he commits iniquity, I will chasten him with the rod of men, with the stripes of the sons of men; but I will not take my steadfast love from him, as I took it from Saul, whom I put away from before you. And your house and your kingdom shall be made sure for ever before me; your throne shall be established for ever. (2 Samuel 7:12–16)

This promise and the dynastic chronicle that leads up to it are not history, but the expression of a new economic, social, and demographic reality in Judah that gave birth to the idea of the united monarchy, now projected back into Israel's distant past.

We know very little about the process of scribal activity in this period or about the kinds of groups who might have been responsible for collecting the traditions and composing a unified text. What we have in the Bible is the result of continued elaboration and editing; what we suggest for the time of Hezekiah is an initial version of the text that continued to be elaborated in subsequent decades. Was it kept only in a temple or palace library? Was it made in many copies distributed throughout the kingdom, or was the story retold to the public on the basis of just a few original texts? Whatever the answers, the earliest version of the biblical story of Saul, David, and the accession of Solomon—and possibly also his construction of the Temple—was created not solely or even primarily for religious purposes, but for a now-forgotten political necessity—of establishing Temple and Dynasty as the twin foundation stones for the new idea of a united Israel.

HEZEKIAH'S REVOLT

The death of Sargon II on the field of battle in 705 BCE may have raised hopes that the plan for a united Israel could be realized. Judah adopted a new strategy toward Assyria that replaced its more deliberate policy of vassal status with a daring, if dangerous, course.

Times of royal succession in Assyria were always filled with tension and uncertainty throughout the empire since the authority of the new king was not yet established. This was clearly the case with the succession of Sennacherib, Sargon's son. Almost immediately upon his taking the throne, a serious revolt broke out against Assyrian rule in Babylonia, the spiritual heartland of Mesopotamia and a vital component of the Assyrian state. Taking advantage of the uprising in Babylon, the rising Twenty-fifth Dynasty of Egypt sought to extend its influence along the Philistine coast. King Luli of the Phoenician city-state of Sidon also considered challenging Assyria. The combination of apparent Assyrian weakness and the possibility of an uprising emboldened the Judahite king Hezekiah to participate in planning for a regionwide rebellion. It proved to be a risky and ultimately disastrous course for Judah to take.

Facing the Assyrian armies in direct confrontation required courage and intensive, large-scale preparation. In Jerusalem, the impressive fortification walls protecting the eastern slope of the City of David and the "broad wall" on the newly settled western hill were almost certainly constructed during the years that followed Sargon's death. Any such massive defensive preparations would have been seen as an obvious threat to Sargon, who campaigned in Samaria in 720 and in Philistia between 720 and 711. Likewise these massive preparation works would have been unthinkable after the Assyrians arrived on the scene to confront Hezekiah in 701 BCE. The fact that this huge construction project was a matter of urgency is evident in the signs of the hurried building: the broad wall on the western hill passed right through an existing suburb in which standing houses had to be razed. That was not the only or even the most impressive preparation for war. The Siloam tunnel, the 1,750-foot-long, winding subterranean channel that brought freshwater into the fortified city, was of vital strategic significance. Its inscription recording the frantic work of the diggers in completing the tunnel both celebrates their successful achievement and reveals the urgency of the work.

In light of Assyria's complete military dominance of the region, Hezekiah and his allies were taking an enormous risk. And once the rebellion in Babylon had been suppressed, they faced the consequences of their decision. In the spring of 701 BCE, Sennacherib finally turned his full attention westward and marched in their direction with Assyria's devastating military might.

SENNACHERIB'S REVENGE

As Sennacherib's army proceeded down the Mediterranean coast to restore Assyrian control of the vital trading ports in Phoenicia and Philistia, all of Hezekiah's allies were crushed, one by one. After conquering Sidon and recapturing the coastal cities, Sennacherib moved inland to the Philistine city of Ekron, conquering it and deposing its king. In panic, the rebel allies called for assistance from Egypt, but an arriving Egyptian relief force was quickly smashed. Now it was time for Assyria's final attack on Judah, aimed first at the strong and prosperous cities in the Shephelah that had grown dramatically in the previous decades. As related on the Prism of Sennacherib:

> *As to Hezekiah, the Judahite, he did not submit to my yoke: forty-six of his strong, walled cities, as well as the small towns in their area, which were without number, by leveling with battering rams and by bringing up siege engines, and by attacking and storming on foot, by mines, tunnels, and breeches, I besieged and took them; 200,150 people, great and small, male and female, horses, mules, asses, camels, cattle, and sheep without number, I brought away from them and counted as spoil.*

The archaeological evidence of destruction in the late eighth century BCE is eloquent testimony to the thoroughness of the devastation that the Assyrians wrought. Intense destruction layers have been noted at most of the major sites in the Shephelah, whose economic importance to Hezekiah's kingdom was great. In 2 Kings 18:14, 17 there are references to the presence of Sennacherib with "a great army" at Lachish. The battle there was later commemorated in an elaborate wall relief in Sennacherib's palace in Nineveh, now displayed in the British Museum. It includes such vivid details as the desperate defenders shooting arrows and hurling torches from the city's battlements down upon the attacking soldiers; the Assyrian siege ramp and armored battering ram breaching Lachish's defenses; the rebels captured and impaled on tall pikes placed around the city; and the pitiful exodus of Judahite women and children taken from their conquered city off into exile. Excavations at Lachish by David Usisshkin uncovered evidence of the city's complete destruction, as well as the Assyrian siege ramp and other remains of the siege.

Sennacherib took glee in the humiliation he imposed on the rebel Judahite king in his own capital, unable to come to the aid of his besieged cities and towns: "[Hezekiah] himself I made a prisoner in Jerusalem, his royal residence, like a bird in a cage. I surrounded him with earthwork in order to molest those who were leaving his city's gate."

The second book of Kings offers a different version of the story, in which the Assyrian siege of Jerusalem was miraculously lifted when an angel sent by God killed 185,000 of the besieging soldiers in their sleep, an account that biblical scholars have explained as describing a plague. One fact seems clear in both versions: instead of devastating Jerusalem, the Assyrian army besieged it, but withdrew without destroying it or even deposing Hezekiah from the throne.

The cost of his survival was enormous. According to the Bible, a crippling payment of tribute was paid to the Assyrian king.

And the king of Assyria required of Hezekiah king of Judah three hundred talents of silver and thirty talents of gold. And Hezekiah gave him all the silver that was found in the house of the LORD, *and in the treasuries of the king's house. At that time Hezekiah stripped the gold from the doors of the temple of the LORD, and from the door-posts which Hezekiah king of Judah had overlaid and gave it to the king of Assyria. (2 Kings 18:14–16).*

According to the Prism of Sennacherib, the price paid by Hezekiah was not only treasure but the loss of some of the most fertile lands in his kingdom, the territory in the Shephelah on which the kingdom's newfound prosperity was based:

His cities, which I had despoiled, I cut off from his land, and to Mit-inti, king of Ashdod, Padi, king of Ekron, and Silli-bêl, king of Gaza, I gave [them]. And thus I diminished his land. I added to the former tribute, and I laid upon him the surrender of their land and imposts—gifts for my majesty. As for Hezekiah, the terrifying splen-dor of my majesty overcame him, and the Arabs and his mercenary troops which he had brought in to strengthen Jerusalem, his royal city, deserted him. In addition to the thirty talents of gold and eight hundred talents of silver, gems, antimony, jewels, large carnelians, ivory-inlaid couches, ivory-inlaid chairs, elephant hides, elephant tusks, ebony, boxwood, all kinds of valuable treasures, as well as his daughters, his harem, his male and female musicians, which he had brought after me to Nineveh. . . .

Thus Sennacherib's campaign and its aftermath effectively destroyed the economic system that Ahaz and Hezekiah constructed over the previous years. Judah was now territorially shrunken, demographically swollen, completely subjected to Assyria, and bur-dened by a crippling debt. Yet the Davidic kingship survived and Jerusalem remained standing. The twin pillars of Judahite society—Temple and Dynasty—endured.

The faith that despite temporary reverses, their dynastic founder, David, was chosen by God and that the city of Jerusalem was divinely protected—even after being besieged by the greatest of empires—was unique testimony to the resilience of Judah's new sense of identity and destiny. But with the devastation of the Sheph-elah and the enormous burden of tribute that had to be paid, the rulers of Judah now had to develop different strategies for survival. And as these new strategies were formulated and put into action in the following decades, several more layers of the David and Solomon story would be added—to produce an even more elaborate narrative of the united monarchy of Israel, substantially in the form that we have in the Bible today.

PERIOD	STAGES IN DEVELOPMENT OF BIBLICAL MATERIAL
Early 7th Century BCE	Written chronicle of the reign of Solomon as a wise, rich monarch in the high Assyrian imperial style; stress on his wise rule, building activities (including the construction of the Temple), and trade expeditions to foreign lands.

HISTORICAL BACKGROUND	ARCHAEOLOGICAL FINDS
Assyrian domination continues, after Sennacherib's devastating campaign in Judah in 701 BCE. In an attempt to recover, Manasseh fully incorporates Judah into the Assyrian world economy.	Assyrian activity in the southern coastal plain and Edom. In Judah, revival of cities destroyed by Sennacherib. Early return to the Shephelah. Strong activity in the Beer-sheba Valley and the Judean Desert. Signs of developed administration intensify: seals, seal impressions, weights, ostraca, etc. Rise of Ekron the main Philistine center in the Shephelah with evidence for olive-oil industry.

CHAPTER 5

Solomon's Wisdom?

Client Kingship and International Trade

—EARLY SEVENTH CENTURY BCE—

THE BIBLICAL DESCRIPTION OF KING SOLOMON'S FORTY-year reign of royal prosperity and grandeur (1 Kings 3–10) has provided western civilization with some of its most glittering images of enlightened kingship, guided by wisdom and blessed with unparalleled wealth. With a regal bearing unmarred by David's violent background and warrior image, Solomon serenely establishes an efficient bureaucracy to administer his vast kingdom and presides over a court and palace that is renowned for its opulence and refinement. He judges the most difficult cases—even of disputed babies—with consummate wisdom. He marries a pharaoh's daughter and constructs the great Jerusalem Temple. His possessions are boundless: thousands of horses and chariots (1 Kings 4:26) and a harem of seven hundred wives (1 Kings 11:3). He conscripts work gangs to refortify Jerusalem and other regional centers, and commissions far-flung trading expeditions for "gold, silver, ivory, apes, and peacocks" (1 Kings 10:22). His reputation as a wise and powerful ruler is unparalleled; when the queen of Sheba travels to Jerusalem from her far-off land to test King Solomon's wisdom, she finds that Solomon's wealth and splendor far

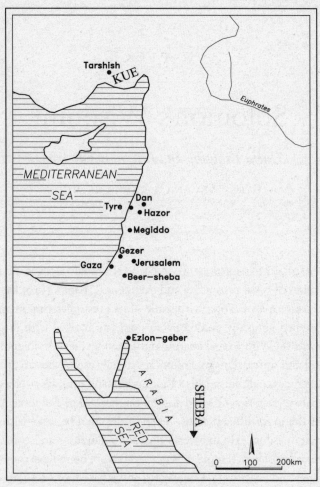

The biblical world of King Solomon

surpass even her grandest expectations, so that "there was no more spirit in her" (1 Kings 10:5).

As a story of royal manners and aristocratic deportment, the biblical narrative of Solomon has for centuries provided artists, poets, and theologians with timeless images of royal leadership. But as an accurate chronicle of tenth-century affairs—describing the actual life and works of Solomon—it has no historical value at all. The grandiose descriptions of Solomonic wealth and unchallenged royal power are absurdly discordant with the historical reality of the small, out-of-the-way hill country kingdom that possessed no literacy, no massive construction works, no extensive administration, and not the slightest sign of commercial prosperity. Of course one might argue that admiration for the kinds of achievements attributed to Solomon might have been conceivable in even the poorest or most backward of kingdoms. But the biblical narrative is filled with so many specific details about trade transactions, monetary values, and complex royal administration that its authors seem to be describing a reality they knew from personal experience—not merely dreaming of an invented or imagined utopia.

It is a world of effortless international connections and the celebration of commercial prosperity, in which the labor of skilled craftsmen and common workers (for building the Temple), no less than cedar logs or spices, is seen as a commodity whose price is open to negotiation. The profit to be made on the resale of imported chariots and horses (1 Kings 10:28–29) and the precise accounting of the kingdom's annual income "from the traders and from the traffic of the merchants, and from all the kings of Arabia and from the governors of the land" (1 Kings 10:15), assume an understanding of and appreciation for great administrative and commercial detail. Indeed, the stories of Solomon's negotiations with King Hiram of Tyre to help build the Temple, his international trade in thoroughbred horses, his lucrative maritime expeditions, and the gifts of precious goods from the queen of Sheba enthusiastically celebrate the values and vision of what we would call today a globalized economy.

As we will see in this chapter, the most famous episodes of the Solomon story reflect an accurate historical memory not of Solomon, but of the dramatic era when the kingdom of Judah recovered from Sennacherib's destructive campaign by plunging headlong into the world of imperial commerce. Judah's economic development in the era of Ahaz and Hezekiah was just the beginning. The Solomon story refers to the next act. It does not merely dress an old tale of a founding father in late-eighth- and seventh-century costume. As we will see, Assyrian-era details and values are central to understanding the motivations for composing the tale of Israel's most prosperous king.

RISING FROM THE ASHES

The biblical Solomon sits majestically enthroned at the summit of a lofty pyramid of royal power. His kingdom—stretching from Dan to Beer-sheba (1 Kings 4:25), or, according to another verse, from the Euphrates to the border of Egypt (1 Kings 4:21)—boasted a sophisticated administration directed from Jerusalem by the king and a coterie of priests, secretaries, scribes, palace administrators, army officers, and overseers of conscripted labor gangs. Twelve district officers, identified by name and connected with clearly delineated territories, were stationed throughout the kingdom with the task of providing "food for the king and his household; each man had to make provision for one month in the year" (1 Kings 4:7). Grain, cattle, sheep, and wild game flowed into Jerusalem to provide the king's daily provision. Thousands of laborers were conscripted to carry out the king's ambitious building projects, including the fortification of Jerusalem, the construction of Megiddo, Hazor, and Gezer, the establishment of new settlements in the wilderness, and the construction of "all the store-cities that Solomon had, and the cities for his chariots, and the cities for his horsemen, and whatever Solomon desired to build in Jerusalem, in Lebanon, and in all the land of his dominion" (1 Kings 9:19). The kingdom was secure and united. As the Bible puts it, "Judah and Israel dwelt in safety, from Dan even to Beer-sheba, every man under his vine and under his fig tree, all the days of Solomon" (1 Kings 4:25).

This idealized vision clearly has nothing to do with the poor villages and the rugged conditions in tenth-century BCE Jerusalem, nor is it an accurate description of the rapidly growing kingdom of Ahaz and Hezekiah. Its picture of well-established and far-reaching royal organization more closely resembles, at least in its broad outlines, if not in all its hyperbole, the increasingly organized and centralized kingdom of Judah in the early seventh century BCE. The instruments of royal power—trade, building projects, and administration—that begin to emerge during the reign of Hezekiah were exercised more extensively during the reign of his son and successor Manasseh (698–642 BCE). If any historical character resembles the biblical Solomon, it is he.

Sennacherib's invasion resulted in far-reaching destruction, devastating Judah's main regional centers and richest agricultural areas. By the time of Manasseh's accession, the economy of Judah was in ruins. The city of Jerusalem was isolated in the midst of a depopulated countryside; it had become the lonely "lodge in a cucumber field" described by the prophet Isaiah (1:8)—a huge, crowded city in the midst of an overwhelmed agricultural hinterland. Archaeological excavations throughout the Shephelah and the Beer-sheba Valley have exposed the extent of the destruction in ash layers, smashed pottery, and the tumbled stones of collapse uncovered at virtually every settlement that flourished during the reign of Hezekiah at the end of the eighth century BCE.

This, then, was King Manasseh's great double challenge: a huge yearly tribute was demanded by the Assyrians, and the agricultural potential of Judah was severely impaired. Hezekiah's son and successor had to formulate a new economic strategy for survival. With its vital grain-growing region of the Shephelah lost, Judah had to find alternative means of agricultural production. Since the towns and villages in the central mountain ridge—which specialized in horti-culture—could not be relied on to make up the difference, other places in the kingdom would have to be found to supply the kingdom with vital grain and field crops. Still other sources of income would be needed to meet the obligations of Assyrian tribute. There are archaeological indications that Manasseh met the challenge. The sweeping changes and economic revival that took place in early-seventh-century BCE Judah—evident in the archaeological record—uncannily mirror the descriptions of planned royal colonization and administration that the story of Solomon so enthusiastically cele-brates.

First came the development of environmentally marginal areas. Even in the time of Manasseh's immediate predecessors, the wilder-ness of Judah had been a desolate area of deep ravines, caves, and iso-lated landmarks in the Dead Sea region, a wild and dangerous backdrop to the stories of David's flight with his band of outlaws from the vengeance of King Saul. Yet in the seventh century BCE, farms and small settlements were established in this arid, virtually rainless region, where herding had long been the main way of life. On the basis of archaeological finds here, there is good reason to suggest that during the long reign of Manasseh, settlements were established at En Gedi and at small sites along the western coast of the Dead Sea. At the same time, agriculture began in the arid Buqei'a Valley south of Jericho, and on the arid slopes east of Jerusalem.

Far to the south, in the Beer-sheba Valley—another dry and sparsely populated area of the kingdom dotted only with a few fortresses to guard the caravan routes—settlement dramatically increased in the seventh century BCE. New sites were established at Tel Masos, Horvat Uza, and Horvat Radom, and the settlements of Tel Ira and Aro'er expanded. Surface surveys have revealed the pres-ence of many more. As in the wilderness of Judah, the goal was clearly agricultural. In good years, the Beer-sheba Valley alone could produce over five thousand tons of grain per annum through traditional dry farming methods, while the basic needs of its population required no more than 5 percent of that amount. Thus, if the agriculture in both the Beer-sheba Valley and the wilderness of Judah was well organized—with maximum cultivation in years of adequate rainfall, irrigation, and efficient storage in times of drought—these two regions could replace at least a portion of the grain yield of the now-lost Sephelah and supply a significant proportion of Judah's agricultural needs.

The expansion into the arid regions was a matter of survival. It seems to have been part of a carefully planned and directed royal policy. In the wilderness of Judah especially, there is evidence of ambitious agricultural constructions, including the hewing of cisterns and the construction of dams to retain the precious winter floodwaters. And in the newly settled Negev communities, evidence for the reconstruction of the royal fortress at Arad and the construction of another fort at Horvat Uza testifies to a high level of administration and royal control. Moreover, the steady increase in the number of seals and seal impressions on storage vessels and bullae in Judah during this same period shows that commercial transactions and careful accounting of agricultural shipments had become a high priority.

As Manasseh reorganized his kingdom, the main elements of a well-planned royal administration materialized on the landscape and in the lives of the officials, workers, and settlers who were marshaled and organized to carry out his commands. It was only at this time that a detailed description of royal officers, regional fortresses, and district capitals would have begun to acquire a recognizable significance in celebrating the achievements of Solomon.*

Of course there were obvious differences between seventh-

---

* The distinctly Assyrian-era description of Solomon's time could equally fit the conditions in Judah during the reign of Josiah (639–609 BCE), during which (as we will see in the next chapter) the Deuteronomistic History was compiled. Yet the decidedly negative image of Solomon in 1 Kings 11, reflecting the distinctive ideology of Deuteronomy, seems to be a critique of an *already-existing* description of Solomon's cosmopolitan reign.

century Judah and Solomon's vast biblically described domain. In Manasseh's time, Judah was restricted to the southern hill country and the desert fringes, with the territory of the former kingdom of Israel under direct Assyrian rule. The biblical descriptions, by contrast, depict a Solomonic administration that stretches across the

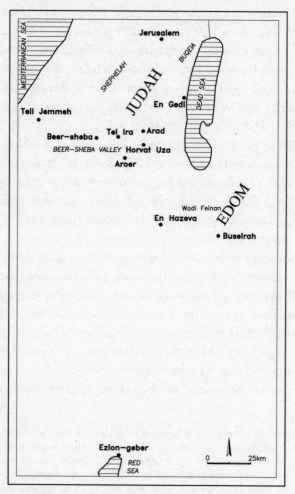

The main sites of King Manasseh's realm

entire land of Israel, encompassing all of Israel's northern lands and tribes. This obviously calls for an explanation. If the intention was to celebrate persuasively a new and more efficient kind of royal administration in Judah, why was the geographical extent of Solomon's kingdom described as so vast?

HAZOR, MEGIDDO, AND GEZER

In contrast to the great administrative achievements of the fallen kingdom of Israel, Manasseh's efforts at reorganization would have seemed puny. But in the crafting of the pan-Israel ideology in Hezekiah's time, the David tradition—and by extension the birthright of Solomon—had been expanded to cover the territory of *both* Judah and Israel. Thus the geographical expansion of Solomon's extensive administration to encompass the north would have been a logical and necessary step in legitimizing the new Judahite royal order—and its Davidic pedigree—as a venerable tradition that stretched back to the origins of the dynasty.

Until recently, a single biblical verse plucked from the Solomonic narrative, which deals with three celebrated northern sites, convinced many archaeologists that Solomon's great empire was a historical fact:

> *And this is the account of the forced labor which King Solomon levied to build the house of the LORD and his own house and the Millo and the wall of Jerusalem and Hazor and Megiddo and Gezer. (1 Kings 9:15)*

The excavation of similar six-chambered gates at Hazor, Megiddo, and Gezer—linked with this single biblical verse and thus dated to the tenth century BCE—established the foundation for the traditional archaeology of Solomon and his united monarchy. Yet this interpretation has been conclusively disproved both on stratigraphic

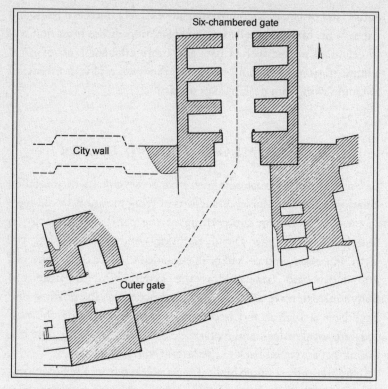

The six-chambered gate of Megiddo (courtesy of Zeev Herzog)

and chronological grounds.* The supposedly Solomonic gates date to different periods of time, in the ninth and eighth centuries BCE, and strikingly similar city gates have been found *outside* the borders of the kingdom of Solomon, even according to a territorially maximalist view. But the specific mention in the Bible of Solomon's building of Hazor, Megiddo, and Gezer is significant in an entirely different respect. All three cities were located in the territory of the northern kingdom and were probably its most important administrative centers after its capital in Samaria. Hence, the historical real-

---

* For more details on the debate over the historical reliability of the great Solomonic building activities, see Appendix 3.

ity behind 1 Kings 9:15 should probably be sought in how the Solomonic tradition assimilated cherished memories from the history of the north.

Megiddo first prospered as a northern Israelite city under the Omrides in the ninth century BCE, when two beautiful ashlar palaces were constructed there. In the eighth century, presumably in the time of Jeroboam II, the city was equipped with an elaborate six-chambered gate and housed an extensive complex of stables, surrounded by a massive city wall. It had a sophisticated water system—a deep shaft and a tunnel that led to a spring at the foot of the mound. Hazor, likewise, had been a prominent city in the time of the Omrides, was briefly occupied and embellished by the kingdom of Damascus, and was returned to Israelite rule and rebuilt on a grand scale in the time of the northern king Jeroboam II, in the eighth century BCE. At Hazor, too, an elaborate rock-cut water system was constructed in the early eighth century BCE. Gezer was also within the boundaries of the northern kingdom and reached its greatest extent in the eighth century BCE, when the town was surrounded by a massive stone wall, similar to the walls unearthed at Megiddo and Hazor. An existing six-chambered gate was then incorporated—as an inner gate—into an elaborate entrance system. Thus Megiddo, Hazor, and Gezer were all Israelite cities that flourished in the first half of the eighth century, the days of the great Jeroboam II, as the main administrative centers of the northern kingdom. There can be little doubt that their mention in the Solomonic narrative represented an attempt both to enhance Solomon's stature and to further integrate the prestige of the northern and southern kingdoms by anachronistically attributing their architectural grandeur to him.

The list of Solomonic district officers (1 Kings 4:7–19) likewise bears a close correspondence to the organization of the northern kingdom. It includes royal districts—all of which are located in the north—that roughly cover the geographical extent of the northern kingdom at its peak. West of the Jordan, these districts stretch from

Asher and Naphtali in Galilee to the area around the Valley of Aijalon and the highlands of Benjamin in the south. To the east of the Jordan, they extend from Gilead to northern Moab. Many of the main cities of the northern kingdom are explicitly mentioned, but Judah—with its highlands, the Negev, and the Shephelah—is excluded, which suggests that the list is most probably based on a northern administrative text. But this source was adjusted by adding Judah in a summary verse; it could then be put to service in celebrating the Jerusalem-based King Solomon as the father of organized statehood in all of Israel.

We seem to be faced here with a case of creative writing, in the inclusion of later northern administrative history into the biblical tradition of Solomon. For just as Hezekiah was faced with the influx of a significant refugee population from the conquered northern kingdom and sought to integrate them into a new Judah and Israel united into a single nation under the twin banners of Dynasty and Temple, his son Manasseh faced the problem of justifying the dramatic increase in royal power to the same mixed population, now resettled and regimented according to royal will.

If it could be shown that such kingly prerogatives were the natural fulfillment of the promise to the house of David, as well as the fulfillment of the venerable royal tradition of the north in the glory days of the Omrides and Jeroboam II, the Solomonic narrative would gain the authority of traditions from *both* Judah and Israel. The vision of the united monarchy under Solomon is thus an expression of seventh-century political, economic, and social objectives, reinforced by memories of the great administrative and political sophistication of the north. It was the ultimate expression of seventh-century BCE Judahite statism.

A closer look at another element of the Solomon tradition—his association with horses—suggests that the same process of legendary elaboration and assimilation of northern traditions was at work in regard to legitimizing Judah's increasingly vital participation in the international trade.

ALL THE KING'S HORSES

King Solomon is remembered in the biblical tradition as one of history's greatest horse traders:

> *Solomon also had forty thousand stalls of horses for his chariots, and twelve thousand horsemen. And those officers supplied provisions for King Solomon, and for all who came to King Solomon's table, each one in his month; they let nothing be lacking. Barley also and straw for the horses and swift steeds they brought to the place where it was required, each according to his charge. (1 Kings 4:26–28)*

> *And Solomon gathered together chariots and horsemen; he had fourteen hundred chariots and twelve thousand horsemen, whom he stationed in the chariot cities and with the king in Jerusalem. (1 Kings 10:26; see also 1 Kings 9:19, 22)*

In the 1920s, archaeologists mistakenly believed that the actual remains of Solomon's stables had been found at the great northern city of Megiddo. An expedition of the University of Chicago uncovered a series of elaborate pillared buildings, fitted with stalls and feeding troughs, that were identified as the stables of Solomon. Later research at Megiddo has disproved the Solomonic date of the buildings. It is now clear that they were constructed in the time of great prosperity in the northern kingdom in the first half of the eighth century BCE, under Jeroboam II. Though some specialists continue to question whether these structures really were stables, the American scholar Deborah Cantrell has convincingly proved that they were indeed used for horses. In other parts of the ancient Near East, similar structures have been uncovered. At Bastam in northern Iran, in the territory of ancient Urartu, then famous for its cavalry force, chemical investigation of the soil in a similar building revealed evidence for animal urine, further confirming the use of this type of structure as a stable. And near Nineveh, the capital of

Assyria, stone troughs similar to those at Megiddo were found bearing inscriptions explicitly identifying them as horse troughs.

Indeed the kingdom of Israel was well known for its equestrian skills. Assyrian texts testify to the special role of Israelite charioteers in the Assyrian royal army after the conquest of the north. The "horse lists" from Fort Shalmaneser dating to the days of Sargon II mention seven units, one of which—the second largest in size—consisted of chariot officers from Samaria. This Israelite force is the only one outside Assyria proper that is mentioned as a national unit, under its own city name. These Israelite charioteers were treated with special favor, with only a moderate tax imposed on them—similar to that levied on native Assyrians. The royal inscriptions of Sargon II mention a group of deportees with the same professional talent: "I formed a unit of 50 [200 in a parallel text] chariots from them, and I allowed the rest to pursue their own skills." The association of the kingdom of Israel with horses may even have been more extensive than its own chariotry and cavalry forces. Megiddo's complexes of pillared buildings equipped with stalls for hundreds of horses may actually represent an ambitious and successful Israelite involvement in the international horse trade.

What types of horses were traded in this period? Among all the warhorses so highly prized by the Assyrians, none was more sought after than the famous thoroughbreds from the region of Kush, south of Egypt, along the upper Nile. These Kushite horses were considered the best for chariots and are mentioned in Assyrian texts—as gifts or purchases—from the days of Tiglath-pileser III to Ashurbanipal. Starting in the late eighth century BCE, when Assyrian commercial centers had been established in Philistia, along the southern coastal plain, the Assyrians obtained their Kushite horses by direct trade with Egypt. A few decades later Egypt was at least nominally conquered by Assyria, and the great Assyrian kings of the seventh century BCE—Esarheddon and Ashurbanipal—obtained their Egyptian horses not through trade but through the imposition of an annual horse tribute. However, in the era before official Assyrian presence in the cities of Philistia and later in Egypt, the long-distance horse trade between Egypt and Assyria—so vital for military purposes—would have been indirect.

Here we may have the link between the Megiddo stables, the Assyrian records, and the Solomonic tradition. Throughout most of the eighth century BCE, it seems probable that the northern kingdom of Israel gained great prosperity by being the main importer and intermediary between the famed Egyptian—and especially Kushite or Nubian—horses and Assyria. The horses were bred and trained at the stable complex at Megiddo, the largest known anywhere in the ancient Near East, and were then sold to Assyria and

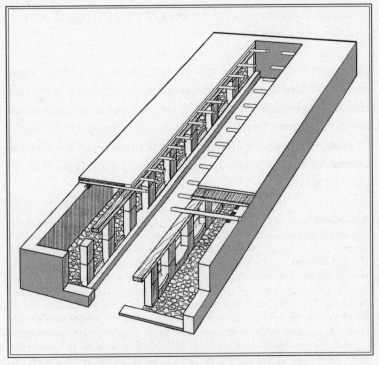

A Megiddo stable (reconstruction according to
Deborah Cantrell and Lawrence Belkin)

possibly to other clients during the reign of Jeroboam II. By the time of Manasseh there is no evidence of horse trading in Judah. Yet a memory of the profitable equine trade of the northern kingdom would have had positive value. It played a conspicuous role in enhancing the glamour and wealth of King Solomon. The anachronistic description of Solomon's dealings with horses suggests that it was based on vaguely remembered details of the eighth-century Israelite—and possibly more modest Judahite—trade:

> *And Solomon's import of horses was from Egypt and Kue, and the king's traders received them from Kue at a price. A chariot could be imported from Egypt for six hundred shekels of silver, and a horse for a hundred and fifty; and so through the king's traders they were exported to all the kings of the Hittites and the kings of Syria. (1 Kings 10:28–29)*

The mention of the marketing connections—acquired from Egypt and sold to northern kingdoms—may reflect a memory of the situation at Megiddo in the eighth century BCE, when horses were an enormous source of wealth and prestige.* Yet the specific details of the price, denominated in silver, as was the practice in the seventh-century Assyrian globalized economy, must be a reflection of the time of Manasseh.

---

* The role of Israel in the eighth-century horse business is elsewhere recorded in the biblical tradition, though with a decidedly negative twist. The eighth-century prophet Amos refers to the horses of Israel (4:10), and Isaiah—who prophesied in the days of Jeroboam II—condemns "those who go down to Egypt for help and rely on horses, who trust in chariots because they are many and in horsemen because they are very strong" (31:1). The northern prophet Hosea, who also lived in the eighth century BCE, seems to hint at the special horse relationship between Israel and Assyria in declaring that "Assyria shall not save us, we will not ride upon horses" (14:3). And the horse business with Egypt is condemned by Deuteronomy 17:16: "Only he must not multiply horses for himself, or cause the people to return to Egypt in order to multiply horses." We will see at the end of this chapter that the Solomonic tradition would also eventually be subject to this criticism.

At least in some circles in Jerusalem, the incorporation of that memory into the Solomonic tradition was another way to persuade the people of the kingdom of Judah that trade with Assyria was both economically beneficial and deeply seated in the traditions of the kingdoms of *both* Judah and Israel. The inflated numbers of horses, stalls, and chariots mentioned in the biblical verses can now be seen as legendary elements of a literary creation aimed to impress the reader or listener, rather than provide an accurate historical account.

CARAVANS, CAMELS, AND THE QUEEN OF SHEBA

According to the Bible, Solomon was the greatest of traders in other commodities as well. The description of his reign is filled with references to precious trade items from exotic lands. Solomon and King Hiram of Tyre built ships at "Ezion-geber, which is near Eloth on the shore of the Red Sea, in the land of Edom," and sailed from there to a place named Ophir in order to bring gold (1 Kings 9:26–28; also 10:11). Ezion-geber is located at the site of Tell el-Kheleifeh, on the northern tip of the Gulf of Aqaba. The identification of Ophir is less certain. Some scholars have suggested that it is no more than a legend—a Near Eastern equivalent of the mythical Eldorado. But in the table of Nations in Genesis 10:28–29 it appears together with Sheba, which should no doubt be located in southern Arabia. And none of Solomon's trading adventures is more famous than the queen of Sheba's state visit to Jerusalem with camels carrying spices, gold, and precious stones.

A cornucopia of precious spices, ivory, and incense, flowing northward from the Arabian Peninsula and the Horn of Africa, was eagerly sought by the kings, temples, and royal houses of the Mediterranean world. The outlets of the Arabian trade routes were controlled by the cities of Philistia, but the caravans shifted from one desert road to another according to changing political, economic, and security conditions. In the early eighth century BCE, the preferred route seems to have been from Arabia to the head of the Gulf of Aqaba, and from there to Gaza through northeastern Sinai. Assyrian records frequently refer to the various Arab peoples who inhabited the southern deserts and actively participated in the trade. It seems that the kingdom of Israel was also involved in the desert commerce. At the site of Kuntillet Ajrud on the caravan route between Aqaba and Gaza, a shrine was unearthed with a rich range of artifacts, drawings, and inscriptions, indicating the active cultural interchange in this remote and isolated place where wayfarers and commercial agents from Phoenicia, Israel, and Arabia stopped briefly in the course of their journeys, invoking their various gods to watch over them as they passed through the dangerous and unprotected desert routes.

As far as we can tell, however, the tiny, landlocked kingdom of Judah played no significant role in this early phase of the Arabian trade.

Things seem to have changed dramatically in the late eighth century BCE when the Assyrians moved decisively to exert their control. With their growing interest in the Arabian trade, the Assyrians diverted the main trade route to Edom and southern Judah, where its security could be more carefully monitored. The Assyrian method of controlling trade in the remote parts of the deserts was to forge agreements with the leaders of the Arab groups through whose territory the caravans passed. But in areas closer to the settled lands and the seaports, security of the routes could not be left to casual diplomacy. There the Assyrians established a system of strong forts and administrative centers, such as En Hazeva, southwest of the Dead Sea; Buseira, the capital of Edom, near Petra in Jordan; and Tell el-Kheleifeh, at the northern end of the Gulf of Aqaba. Judahite and Edomite personnel may have been deployed in those forts under Assyrian command. Finally, along the Mediterranean coast the Assyrians established several harbor emporia, from which the Arabian goods were shipped with the help of Phoenician intermediaries. Tiglath-pileser III counted Gaza "as a customhouse of Assyria" and Sargon II declares that he opened the border of Egypt to trade, mingled Assyrians and Egyptians, and encouraged mutual trade—no doubt referring also to the Arabian commodities. The archaeological remains of such trading emporia have been uncovered on the Mediterranean coast near Ashdod and to the south of Gaza.

Thus the growing activity in the Beer-sheba Valley expanded dramatically during Manasseh's reign. Together with the intensified settlement and agricultural production in this marginal region, the kingdom more actively participated and benefited from the thriving trade in the south under Assyrian domination. The regions along the caravan route, from the highlands of Edom through the Beer-sheba Valley, to the Assyrian-controlled coastal trading centers, experienced an unprecedented economic and demographic expansion during the seventh century BCE. In the Edomite highlands, many new settlements were founded and the built-up area in the towns of the Beer-sheba Valley more than doubled within just a few decades. The influence of Assyrian supervision could be felt far down the trade route, with the presence of characteristic Assyrian palace vessels or their imitations at almost every site excavated along its course.

Rich archaeological finds have confirmed the source of this commerce: south Arabian inscriptions and Hijazi artifacts have been found at several sites in the region, including Jerusalem. The mode of transport has also become clear with an analysis of the animal bones at the excavation of one of the most elaborate of the Assyrian trade stations, Tell Jemmeh, inland of Gaza. The remains of domesticated camels—while rare in previous eras—dramatically increase in the seventh century BCE, and the bones are almost exclusively of mature animals, which suggests that they were from traveling beasts of burden, not locally raised herds (among which the bones of young animals would also be found).

Controlling the termini of the Arabian trade routes and dominating the vassal states of Transjordan and Judah, the Assyrians no doubt took the lion's share of the trade revenues. But the sheer value of the precious goods shipped northward ensured that even Assyria's junior partners would also prosper from their involvement in the trade. Edom, an arid and once remote land, was strategically important to the Assyrians as a buffer zone against hostile desert tribes. Assyrian control centers were established there to ensure the security of the commerce and strengthen this semi-independent frontier state.

Judah likewise benefited from the prosperity in the towns and way stations of the Beer-sheba Valley—and there is some evidence that at least some of the trade was diverted to Jerusalem itself. Three ostraca with south Arabian script uncovered in the excavations of the City of David in Jerusalem were carved on local Judahite pottery, which suggests that at least a small community of Arabians had taken up residence there. A chance find of a seventh-century Hebrew seal bearing what is presumably a south Arabian name—and the hypothesis that King Manasseh's wife Meshullemeth, the daughter of Haruz of Jotbah (2 Kings 21:19), was an Arabian woman—strengthens the assumption that Manasseh was eager to expand his commercial interests in the south.

This was an increasingly vital economic strategy for Judah; evidence of its importance can be detected in the biblical story of the queen of Sheba's state visit to Jerusalem accompanied by a large caravan bearing precious trade goods. By Manasseh's time, the remote kingdom of Sheba, in the area of modern Yemen, was famous for its aromatics, which were brought by camel caravans to the Levant. It is mentioned in Assyrian sources of the late eighth century BCE, in the days of Tiglath-pileser III, Sargon II, and Sennacherib. Though recent archaeological research has apparently revealed earlier Iron Age remains in Yemen, it is clear that the Sabaean kingdom began to flourish only from the eighth century BCE onward. Little wonder that visions of Arabia assumed such great importance in the traditions of Judah.*

The fact that the book of Kings speaks about the visit of a queen (rather than a king) lends an additional note of credibility, for Assyrian records of the late eighth and early seventh centuries BCE (until c. 690 BCE) attest to the phenomenon of Arabian queens.

The biblical thousand-and-one-nights story of Solomon and Sheba is thus an anachronistic seventh-century set piece meant to legitimize the participation of Judah in the lucrative Arabian trade.

WHO BUILT THE TEMPLE?

Solomon is of course remembered as the builder of the great Temple in Jerusalem, but as we have noted, archaeology is completely mute regarding its early history. There is no doubt that the First Temple was built on the highest, northern sector of the ridge of the City of David. But this area—the Haram el-Sharif in Arabic—now houses two of the most sacred monuments of Islam, the el-Aqsa mosque and the Dome of the Rock, and for religious reasons it has not been possible to conduct any extensive archaeological excavations there.

Even if it were possible to excavate beneath the Dome of the Rock, it is doubtful that any significant Iron Age remains would be found. In the first century BCE, the Temple Mount was the scene of one of the greatest building operations in the history of the Holy

---

* Beyond the Solomonic tradition, Sheba figures prominently in the oracles of the seventh- and sixth-century BCE Judahite prophets. Isaiah predicts that a "multitude of camels shall cover you, the young camels of Midian and Ephah; all those from Sheba shall come. They shall bring gold and frankincense" (60:6). Jeremiah angrily asks, "To what purpose does frankincense come to me from Sheba?" (6:20) and Ezekiel charges Tyre that the "traders of Sheba and Raamah traded with you; they exchanged for your wares the best of all kinds of spices, and all precious stones, and gold" (27:22).

Land, when King Herod the Great erected the huge platform that still exists today (on which the el-Aqsa mosque and the Dome of the Rock stand). It was built as a typical Roman podium: the entire original hill was enclosed within huge supporting walls—including the Western Wall, or the Wailing Wall in Jewish tradition—and the area inside was leveled, filled, or constructed with support arcades and vaults. There is little possibility that Iron Age remains would have survived these immense operations.

Thus with no archaeological remains, we are forced to go back to the text. There can hardly be a doubt that the detailed description of the Temple in 1 Kings 6–7 was written by an author who had an intimate knowledge of the First Temple before it was destroyed by the Babylonians in the early sixth century BCE. But did Solomon build the original Temple? As the son of a local chief of a small, isolated highland polity, he would not have had access to resources to do much more than erect or renovate a modest local dynastic shrine of a type well known in the ancient Near East.

A more monumental Temple—of the kind described in the Bible—could only have been built by one of the later Davidic monarchs, at a time when Judah grew into a more complex state, with more significant manpower, economic resources, and construction skills. We simply do not know who built the first elaborate Temple in Jerusalem, which by the time of Hezekiah had already accumulated considerable wealth and expensive furnishings (of which it was stripped to provide tribute to Assyria—2 Kings 18:15–16). It is possible that the description in 2 Kings 12 of the extensive renovation of the Temple in the days of King Jehoash (c. 836–798 BCE) is significant. This was, as we have seen, a time when Judah was coming of age, after a period of intense interaction with the Omride dynasty of the north. Could the "repairs" on the House of the Lord mentioned in this biblical passage represent, in fact, the construction of the more impressive Jerusalem Temple that was still standing in the time of the compilation of the Solomonic narrative?

With no material remains, and no contemporary sources, any discussion of the architectural history of the Temple must remain pure speculation. The best (and perhaps only) support for a Solomonic origin of the Temple is the centrality of the Temple in Solomon's later image. Just as David was remembered as the founder of the Judahite dynasty, Solomon was remembered as the patron of Jerusalem's local cult place, which could have been little more than a rustic shrine in the tenth century BCE. Over the centuries, with the growth of Jerusalem and the development of its institutions, it became more impressive. Had Judahite popular tradition identified another Davidic king as the original builder, the credit given to Solomon for this achievement would have lacked even the most basic credibility.

KING SOLOMON'S MINES?

The biblical description of Solomon's building of the Temple—like the rest of the elaborated tradition—is also filled with chronological clues. King Hiram of Tyre is a case in point. Though he is mentioned several times in the book of Kings as the supplier of cedars of Lebanon for its construction and a trade partner of Solomon in various overseas expeditions, the existence of a historical figure by that name in the tenth century BCE cannot be verified from any contemporary or even later text.

The only certain historical Iron Age Hiram of Tyre was a king named Hirummu, who appears twice in the annals of the great Assyrian monarch Tiglath-pileser III in the 730s BCE as paying tribute to Assyria. He is mentioned together with Menahem king of Israel and Rezin king of Damascus. Scholars have labeled him Hiram II, to differentiate from (the hypothesized) Hiram I of the days of Solomon, but it is probable that the eighth-century Hiram traded with the northern kingdom, and that his name and deeds were used in order to praise Solomon as a great monarch—in yet another legendary assimilation of the fabled prosperity of the north.* The mention of ships of Solomon and Hiram sailing together to Tarshish (1 Kings 10:22)—probably Tarsus in southeastern Turkey—may reflect the trade cooperation of the northern kingdom with Tyre and the Phoenicians in the eighth century.

The text describing the construction of the Temple and palace in Jerusalem is full of references to copper items, another seventh-century BCE connection. Solomon himself is said to have smelted great quantities of copper in the Jordan Valley, "between Succoth and Zarethan" (1 Kings 7:46), and in the early days of biblical archaeology, in the 1930s, references to copper became a major issue in the search for the historical Solomon. Yet the discovery of "Solomon's mines" at Timna in southern Israel and his "smelting plants" at nearby Tell el-Kheleifeh (identified with biblical Ezion-geber and declared by the American archaeologist Nelson Glueck to have been the "Pittsburgh of Palestine") proved to be archaeological illusions. The Timna mines are now dated at least two centuries *before* Solomon. And it seems clear that Tell el-Kheleifeh was first settled—as a fort, not an industrial center—two centuries *after* Solomon in connection with the Assyrian-dominated Arabian trade.†

Another important source of copper is the area of Wadi Feinan, on the eastern margin of the Arabah Valley, approximately thirty miles south of the Dead Sea. Recent studies by German, American, and Jordanian scholars revealed evidence there for continuous activity in the Iron Age, with one of the intense periods of mining and production dated to the late eighth and seventh centuries BCE.

* The only extrabiblical support for the existence of a historical Hiram in the time of Solomon comes from the Jewish historian Flavius Josephus, who quotes the (now lost) works of Dius and Menander of Ephesus, two Hellenistic historians of the second century BCE. The Israeli historian Doron Mendels has labeled the works of these second-century historians "creative historiographies," which were drawn from existing sources. In the second century BCE the Bible was already known to Hellenistic writers and could have been the source for much of their information, including the legendary association of the two kings.

† For more detail on the reasons for these redatings, see Appendix 4.

Like all other lucrative economic activities in the region, this industry was carried out under Assyrian auspices. The mined copper must have been transported mainly to the west, to the Assyrian centers and ports in Philistia. Since the roads from Feinan to the west passed through Judahite territory in the Beer-sheba Valley, Judah—as a vassal of Assyria—would have participated in the lucrative copper industry.

All things considered, we have a situation where the conditions described in the great kingdom of Solomon closely resemble those of King Manasseh's realm. Well-administered districts and large numbers of corvee laborers building new royal cities; the trading connection with foreign leaders; caravans plodding northward through Judahite territory; and ambassadors from Arabia present in Jerusalem—when combined with the hazier, borrowed memories of northern Israel's commercial heyday—all bolstered belief in the antiquity and wisdom of King Manasseh's new strategy of whole-hearted participation in imperial commerce and diplomacy.

CREATING THE SOLOMONIC MYTH

The stories of Solomon in the Bible are uniquely cosmopolitan. Foreign leaders are not enemies to be conquered or tyrants to be suffered; they are equals with whom to deal politely, if cleverly, to achieve commercial success. The biblical tales of Solomon's dealings with Hiram of Tyre and the queen of Sheba are literary acts of self-promotion—in trade negotiations, in diplomatic relations, in the status of the king. Solomon's legend, first put into writing in the seventh century BCE, asserts Judah's greatness—and the essential skill of its monarch—in the brave new world of trade and cross-cultural communication of the Assyrian empire.

In ruling, administering, trading, and wisely judging his people, Solomon is presented as an ideal leader on the model of the Assyrian king: "And men came from all peoples to hear the wisdom of

Solomon, and from all the kings of the earth, who had heard of his wisdom" (1 Kings 4:34). "Thus King Solomon excelled all the kings of the earth in riches and wisdom. And the whole earth sought the presence of Solomon to hear his wisdom" (1 Kings 10:23–24). Even the extent of territory ruled by Solomon—in one version, from the Euphrates to Gaza (1 Kings 4:24)—reflects a vision of Assyrian kingship as the ultimate ideal. Though the dating of this verse is uncertain, the territory described is roughly equivalent to the western territories ruled by the Assyrian kings in the late eighth and seventh centuries BCE.

Closer to home, the Solomonic legend expresses nostalgia for the achievements of the fallen kingdom of Israel. Another description of the extent of Solomon's kingdom—from Dan to Beer-sheba (1 Kings 4:25)—actually fits the borders of Judah and Israel combined. While the stories of David were used to refute the accusations of the northerners, the image of Solomon borrows heavily from northern royal traditions—not refuting them but rather adopting them and depicting him as equal or even superior to the most powerful north Israelite kings. Just as *they* sailed the high seas in search of treasure; just as *they* traded in thoroughbred horses; just as *they* attracted the interest of the far-off Arabian kingdoms, so *our* cherished founding father Solomon had done on an even more massive and lucrative scale. Thus in addition to merging the cherished memories of the Israelites within the southern kingdom with the prestige of the Davidic dynasty, the Solomonic narratives were used to legitimize for *all* of Judah's people the aristocratic culture and commercial concerns of the court of Manasseh that promoted Judah's participation in the Assyrian world economy.

The Bible's composite vision of Solomon's wisdom, commerce, and far-flung international connections has filled a thousand church windows and illustrated Bibles for centuries. While David was a man of war, Solomon was the prince of peace through diplomacy and trade. Solomon's image promises security, stability, and happiness in a world in which boundaries are fluid and national glory is achieved through wisdom and commercial acumen.

Yet the circumstances that gave birth to this vision were not to last forever. As we will see in the next chapter, by the end of the seventh century, internal tensions within Judah and a change in the imperial landscape would sour belief in Solomonic-style globalization and bequeath to it a decidedly negative aspect. Those who sought to retreat from the imperial world into a puritanical, closed vision of ancient Israel would transform the entire David and Solomon story to serve a completely different set of values, infusing it with the messianic themes and apocalyptic tension that it still possesses today.

PERIOD	STAGES IN DEVELOPMENT OF BIBLICAL MATERIAL
Late 7th Century BCE	Elaboration of earlier written sources (History of David's Rise, Succession History, Solomonic traditions) and their incorporation into the Deuteronomistic History of Israel; edited to offer a unified theological message to serve aims of Josiah's religious reform; details such as David and Goliath combat and other Greek realities and condemnation of Solomon added.

HISTORICAL BACKGROUND	ARCHAEOLOGICAL FINDS
Weakening Assyria withdraws from the Levant. Religious reform in Judah; attempts at Judahite territorial expansion. Josiah is killed at Megiddo by the rising Twenty-sixth Dynasty of Egypt.	Judahite expansion in the Shephelah intensifies. Activity continues in the Beer-sheba Valley and the Judean Desert. More ostraca and seal impressions; evidence for increasing literacy. Egyptian presence (with Greek mercenaries) along the coast. Ekron olive-oil industry continues.

CHAPTER 6

Challenging Goliath

The Davidic Legacy and the Doctrine of Deuteronomy

— LATE SEVENTH CENTURY BCE —

THE BIBLICAL SOLOMON IS HAUNTED BY A GREAT CON-
tradiction. In 1 Kings 3–10, he is the great successor of David, a
larger-than-life ruler who builds the Temple in Jerusalem and who
provides the standards of wisdom and opulence that countless later
kings would attempt to achieve. Yet in 1 Kings 11:1–13 he is little
more than a senile apostate, who is led astray by the charms of his
many foreign wives.

> *He had seven hundred wives, princesses, and three hundred concu-*
> *bines; and his wives turned away his heart. For when Solomon was*
> *old his wives turned away his heart after other gods; and his heart*
> *was not wholly true to the LORD his God, as was the heart of David*
> *his father. For Solomon went after Ashtoreth the goddess of the Sid-*
> *onians, and after Milcom the abomination of the Ammonites. So*

Solomon did what was evil in the sight of the LORD. . . . Then Solomon built a high place for Chemosh the abomination of Moab, and for Molech the abomination of the Ammonites, on the mountain east of Jerusalem. (1 Kings 11:3–7)

In fact, his sins are so grave that they lead to a bitter split between Judah and Israel and the breakdown of the great Davidic state.

How can we assess these frankly conflicting biblical evaluations? Many scholars have accepted the positive chapters as representing old archival material, dating to the supposed great era of enlightenment in the days of the united monarchy. We have argued that this positive vision of Solomon was a product of the Judahite court in the early seventh century BCE. The tales of splendid Solomonic court life in Jerusalem, the impressive Temple, chariot cities, maritime commercial ventures, and lucrative trade with Arabia should be seen as a literary construct, a description of an idyllic and idealized figure that would have redounded to the credit of the entrepreneurial King Manasseh and warmed the hearts of the Judahite aristocracy who directly benefited from the new prosperity that was brought about by the incorporation of Judah into the Assyrian world economy.

But what is the source of this negative view of Solomon? In whose interest was it to blacken the reputation of the great king? The prosperity of the Assyrian trading system that Solomon came to personify would have had a very different aspect to those who were its unwilling pawns rather than its beneficiaries. Manasseh's strategy of international trading may well have devalued the traditional agricultural economy long shared by both the Judahites and many of the refugees from direct Assyrian rule in the north. The king's far-reaching intercultural contact amounted to an abandonment of time-honored ways—and not only in religion, but in social relations and economy. Those who supported his father, Hezekiah's, cult centralization and his nationalistic revolt against Assyria must have been appalled by the reign of Manasseh. And they were soon back in power—with pens in their hands.

The second book of Kings devotes a relatively brief and wrathful description to Manasseh's fifty-five-year reign that is preoccupied mainly with recounting his religious offenses and placing the blame for the greatest catastrophe that Judah would later experience directly on him:

> *And he did what was evil in the sight of the LORD, according to the abominable practices of the nations whom the LORD drove out before the people of Israel. For he rebuilt the high places which Hezekiah his father had destroyed; and he erected altars for Baal, and made an Asherah, as Ahab king of Israel had done, and worshiped all the host of heaven, and served them. And he built altars in the house of the LORD, of which the LORD had said, "In Jerusalem will I put my name." And he built altars for all the host of heaven in the two courts of the house of the LORD. And he burned his son as an offering, and practiced soothsaying and augury, and dealt with mediums and with wizards. He did much evil in the sight of the LORD, provoking him to anger. (2 Kings 21:2–6)*

Biblical scholars have traditionally interpreted the reports of Manasseh's fondness for pagan religious customs as evidence of the wholesale assimilation of Judah's ruling class into the religious syncretism of the Assyrian age. But in the ancient world, neatly dividing economics and politics from religion was not quite so simple.

For at least some of Manasseh's subjects, settled in new development towns and subject to royal regulation and taxation, his long reign must have been a source of misfortune and far-reaching social dislocation. We have seen the abundant evidence in the archaeological record of the emergence of a wealthy, literate, and influential ruling class in Jerusalem, but no evidence of great prosperity beyond that. Manasseh's new strategy brought survival to the state and prosperity to those who hosted trade ambassadors in their elegant houses. But for those who did not profit from this prosperity, the promise of safety and security—the day when every man would sit in contentment "under his vine and under his fig tree"—must have seemed further away than ever before.

The tension was clearly building. According to the Bible, after the death of Manasseh, in 642 BCE, and the succession of his son Amon, a violent series of events seemingly shattered the decades-long rule of the Judahite internationalists:

> *Amon was twenty-two years old when he began to reign, and he reigned two years in Jerusalem. His mother's name was Meshullemeth the daughter of Haruz of Jotbah. And he did what was evil in the sight of the LORD, as Manasseh his father had done. He walked in all the way in which his father walked, and served the idols that his father served, and worshiped them; he forsook the LORD, the God of his fathers, and did not walk in the way of the LORD. And the servants of Amon conspired against him, and killed the king in his house. But the people of the land slew all those who had conspired against King Amon, and the people of the land made Josiah his son king in his stead. (2 Kings 21:19–24)*

We cannot identify the "servants of Amon" who killed him, though they seem to have been a faction in the royal court of Jerusalem. Likewise the identity of "the people of the land" who installed the eight-year-old boy King Josiah has long been a matter of dispute by scholars, some of whom have suggested that they represent the countryside aristocracy, who supported Manasseh's policies.

In fact, opposition to Manasseh's rule seems to have come from a coalition of dissatisfied groups within Judah, whose political influence would rise as the power of Assyria began to wane. They would have a powerful effect in reshaping the institutions of the kingdom of Judah, and they would use their talents in the rewriting of the history of David and Solomon. During the reign of Josiah, all the preexisting traditions, poems, chronicles, and ballads about the first two kings of Judah were combined, producing the passionate and uncompromising tale of sin and redemption that remains a central message of the biblical story today.

THE DEUTERONOMISTIC VERSION

The complex, sprawling literary epic of David and Solomon, when read from its beginning in the first book of Samuel to its tragic conclusion in the first book of Kings—from the shepherd boy David's anointment to the death of the aged King Solomon amidst rebellion and tumult—offers a single, sobering moral: calamity inevitably follows disobedience of God's will. Saul, the troubled savior of Israel, loses his anointment and eventually his life for his cultic violations; David suffers family misfortune for his foibles; and Solomon, the resplendent monarch, pays for his sinful involvement with foreign wives and pagan ways with the loss of his greatness and the division of his vast kingdom.

These grim lessons are starkly contrasted with the rewards of righteousness. The united monarchy of David and Solomon, before its fall, in its moments of splendor, showed what the people of Israel could achieve when they were led by a righteous ruler and were perfectly faithful to God's laws. Yet this overarching moral scheme is not part of the original story. The separate cycles of folktales, heroic stories, and royal propaganda were distinct developments of the evolving ideology of Judah's ruling dynasty. It was only when the David and Solomon story was linked with a powerful religious message that the biblical narrative we now know finally began to take shape.

The editing and writing that occurred in Josiah's time were not the final stages of the writing of David and Solomon's stories, but they had a crucial impact on the Bible as we know it. Many biblical scholars argue that the composite narrative from 1 Samuel 16 to 1 Kings 11—from the anointment of David to the death of Solomon—is part of a longer saga, which spans the book of Joshua through the second book of Kings, and is known as the Deuteronomistic History. This sweeping chronicle of the people of Israel, from wandering to conquest to golden age to exile, has a clear connection with (in fact it clearly illustrates) the ideology expressed in the book of Deuteronomy. And the biblical narrative of David and Solomon bears the indelible stamp of the aggressive and uncompromising ideology not evident in earlier traditions: the Deuteronomistic doctrine of the worship of one God, in the Jerusalem Temple, under the auspices of a Davidic king, advanced through the zealotry of holy war.

The core of Deuteronomy's law code (Deuteronomy 4:44–28:68) has been convincingly connected by scholars with the "Book of the Law" suddenly "discovered" by the high priest Hilkiah in the Jerusalem Temple in the eighteenth year of the reign of the Judahite king Josiah, the grandson of Manasseh and son of Amon, in 622 BCE.

According to the biblical account (2 Kings 22:8–23:3), the dis-

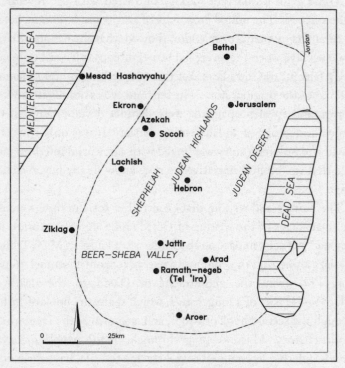

Judah in the days of Josiah

covery of the "Book of the Law" (or the "Book of the Covenant" as it is sometimes called) created an uproar and a spiritual crisis in Judah. When the book was read to King Josiah, he rent his clothes and declared, "Great is the wrath of the Lord that is kindled against us, because our fathers have not obeyed the words of this book, to do according to all that is written concerning us" (2 Kings 22:13).

Josiah's subsequent actions—at least as they are described in the Bible—bear a direct relation to Deuteronomy's explicit commandments. After "renewing" the exclusive covenant between God and the people of Israel, Josiah cleansed the Temple of all pagan cult objects; defiled the pagan high places and deposed idolatrous priests; commanded the people to keep "the Passover to the LORD your God, as it is written in this book of the covenant" (2 Kings 23:21); and banned the use of mediums and wizards. All of these actions—uncompromising law observance, aggressive prohibition of idolatry, and restriction of worship to a single place, namely, the Temple in Jerusalem—are expressed as strict commandments in Deuteronomy's law code.

For his pious actions in upholding this new scripture, Josiah, a seventeenth-generation descendant of David, is described in 2 Kings 23:25 as uniquely saintly: "Before him there was no king like him, who turned to the Lord with all his heart and with all his soul and with all his might, according to all the law of Moses; nor did any like him arise after him." He "did what was right in the eyes of the Lord, and walked in all the way of David his father" (2 Kings 22:2). In the biblical authors' opinion, David had embodied the idea of righteousness expressed in Deuteronomy; Josiah was his most righteous successor. The links between Josiah and David, between laws of Deuteronomy and the splendor of the united monarchy, are unmistakable. The anachronisms, narrative devices, and contemporary allusions woven through the final form of the David and Solomon story show how the narrative was shaped and whose interests it promoted as it reached its recognizable biblical form in the late seventh century BCE.

Understanding this crucial stage in the evolution of the Davidic tradition is central not only to an appreciation of the history of seventh-century Judah but also to an important innovation in the religious history of the western world. It was in the fateful reign of King Josiah that the mystique of the Davidic dynasty was suddenly, dramatically transformed from a collection of dynastic legends into a messianic faith that would long outlive the independence of the tiny Iron Age kingdom, to become the irreducible basis for Judeo-Christian religious belief.

EMPIRES IN TURMOIL

In order to understand the motivations for the ideological transformation of the David and Solomon tradition, we must briefly describe the dramatic events that swept over the region during King Josiah's reign. When Josiah came to the throne as an eight-year-old boy in 639 BCE, in the wake of his father's assassination, Assyria was still at the height of its power. The territory of the former northern kingdom of Israel was still under direct Assyrian administration and the coastal Philistine cities were administered by Assyrian client kings. Just a few years later, however, by around 630 BCE, the Assyrian empire was in a state of rapid disintegration. Pressures in the north and east severely strained the empire's resources. Its military might, though still formidable, had seriously declined.

Although the Assyrian chronicles from this period are fragmentary, the general picture is, nonetheless, unmistakable: after a century of unquestioned domination in the region, the power of Assyria became more distant as it withdrew to the east for its final—and ultimately unsuccessful—fight for survival. The once unchallenged and unchallengeable superpower that had dominated the economy and political life of the world gradually abandoned its claim to the provinces of the west.

The withdrawal of Assyrian garrisons and officials from the

Philistine cities and the districts of the former kingdom of Israel created a power vacuum. A new, rising dynasty in Egypt emerged as Assyria's successor, at least along the Mediterranean coast. During a reign of more than half a century, from 664 to 610 BCE, Psammetichus I, of the Twenty-sixth Egyptian Dynasty, gradually expanded his power base in the western Nile Delta to unite Upper and Lower Egypt, then marched north and annexed the prosperous trading cities of the Philistine plain.

This takeover seems to have been accomplished with tacit Assyrian agreement. In return for its control of the former Assyrian possessions, Egypt became Assyria's ally, agreeing to lend military support against anti-Assyrian uprisings and the growing influence of Babylonia in the north. However, though the Egyptians were now in control of the Philistine coast and the international highway that led inland past Megiddo to Syria and Mesopotamia, the peoples and cities of the highlands were of only marginal concern. As in the earlier era of Egyptian imperialism during the Late Bronze Age, over a half millennium earlier, the Egyptians seem to have left affairs in the highlands—in Judah and the former territory of Israel—to take their own course, as long as they did not threaten Egyptian control of the international highway along the coast and across the valleys of the north.

We know almost nothing of events in the territory of the former kingdom of Israel after the withdrawal of the Assyrians. The loosening of tight control over the region's people and agricultural production could have aroused hopes for political revival, but we have no indication of any attempt by the northerners to establish an independent kingdom again. In the south, on the other hand, we have the biblical reports of Josiah's zealous religious reform in the kingdom of Judah, culminating in his destruction of the northern cult place of Bethel.

These events are described in the Bible as purely religious actions, but in the changing political conditions of Assyrian withdrawal, they hint at something more than that. As long as Assyria remained dominant in the region, Judah's political independence and freedom of action was severely limited. With the Assyrians firmly in control of the northern highlands, there was no possibility of claiming rule over the remaining Israelite population, whose traditions had been at least partially incorporated in the pan-Israelite ideology of the south. Yet as the Assyrians withdrew, new possibilities beckoned. Archaeological evidence suggests that the kingdom of Judah took advantage of the new conditions by expanding both north and west.

The territorial expansion was apparently modest. Characteristic seventh-century BCE Judahite artifacts such as inscribed weights, pillar-shaped figurines, and distinctive types of ceramic vessels have been found only as far north as the area of Bethel, about ten miles north of Judah's traditional border. It is nonetheless noteworthy that evidence of Judahite presence extends to the site mentioned so prominently in the biblical story of Josiah's religious reform.

Archaeological finds also point to an expansion of Judahite influence in the west, in the area of the Shephelah—a movement that might even have started in the days of Manasseh. The major regional center of Lachish, which had lain in ruins for a while after its devastation by the armies of Sennacherib, was rebuilt and refortified in the seventh century, indicating the possible reassertion there of direct Judahite political control. Seventh-century BCE Judahite weights have been found throughout the surrounding region, suggesting the incorporation of this area into Judah's distinct system of trade. The rich farmlands of the Shephelah were not only economically and strategically vital; they were enshrined in Judahite tradition. It is highly significant that 2 Kings 22:1 reports that Josiah's mother came from Bozkath, a town in the Shephelah.

Can we say more about the goals of King Josiah and the opposition his attempts at territorial expansion would have faced? In the west, any hope of reasserting Judahite control of the lower Shephelah risked military confrontation with the emerging power of Egypt and the Philistine cities. To the north, successful Judahite expansion into the territories of the former kingdom of Israel, whose ruling dynasty had been deposed and exiled, lay in overcoming regional loyalties and asserting the claims of the Davidic dynasty over all the land of Israel. Indeed, when we examine the characteristic seventh-century BCE details that run through in the biblical stories of David and Solomon, a surprisingly clear picture of Judahite perceptions and intentions—and a new interpretation of the story of David and Solomon—can be seen.

DAVID AND THE PHILISTINES

The biblical David won his fame as a great warrior, toppling the mighty Goliath (1 Samuel 17), killing Philistine troops by the "ten thousands" (1 Samuel 18:7), and outwitting the Philistine king, Achish of Gath (1 Samuel 27–29). As we have seen, some of these stories undoubtedly have their origin in a very early period, for the prominent mention of Gath—as the hometown of Goliath, the capital of Achish, and the leading force among the Philistine cities—reflects the perceptions of a period before Gath was conquered and lost its political importance, at the end of the ninth century BCE. But the general picture provided by the biblical stories of David includes a number of important elements that reveal how deeply their final form reflected Josiah's time. Indeed, the Philistines whom David alternatively served under and fought against are described in terms dramatically different from what we know of the Philistines in the earlier phases of their history.

Our knowledge of the early Philistines, of the twelfth to tenth centuries BCE, comes from several sources, both historical and archaeological. An inscription and reliefs from the days of Pharaoh Ramesses III (1182–1151 BCE) commemorate his land and naval victories over a group named *Peleset* and other invading people, who "made a conspiracy in their islands" and simultaneously attacked Egypt by land and sea. A later Egyptian papyrus from the days of

Ramesses IV (1151–1145 BCE) reports that these defeated foes were settled in Egyptian strongholds. At that time Egypt still dominated the southern coastal plain of Canaan—exactly the place where the Bible locates the cities of the Philistines. Therefore, it has been widely accepted by scholars that the *Peleset* and Philistines were the same group of warlike migrants who were settled by the Egyptians in their garrison cities along the southern Canaanite coast. Indeed, archaeological excavations of levels from the era following Ramesses III have revealed the appearance of a new ceramic style, unmistakable for its elaborate painted decoration of geometrical shapes and stylized birds and fish, which is closely related to the pottery traditions of Cyprus and the Aegean—the area from which the *Peleset*-Philistines are believed to have come.

Yet despite the contention of many scholars that the Philistine stories in the Bible reflect a reliable memory from the days immediately after their invasion and settlement in Canaan, many important details about the early Philistines are inexplicably left out. There is no memory in the Bible of the upheaval that accompanied their arrival on the coast of Canaan; nor is their connection with the Late Bronze Egyptian administration in Canaan mentioned, except for a vague and contradictory assertion in the much later table of nations of the book of Genesis (10:13–14; also 1 Chronicles 1:11–12) connecting them genealogically with Egypt.* Nor is the Bible aware of other groups of Sea Peoples who arrived with the Philistines.† Special features in the material culture of the early Philistines—from pottery and cult to burial customs and culinary practices—also have no echo in the biblical text. The Bible could have been silent on many of these characteristics, but it is highly unlikely that it would have ignored *all* of them. While there is no question that the peo-

---

* An alternative biblical tradition (Amos 9:7 and Jeremiah 47:4) suggests that the Philistines came from Caphtor, a geographical name usually associated with Crete.

† Egyptian texts mention at least two more groups of Sea People—the Sikila and the Sherdani—who settled on the coast of Canaan.

ple of Judah were well acquainted with their Philistine neighbors, their *historical* knowledge about them seems to be based on oral traditions that were vague and imprecise.

Take the mention of King Achish, for example. Described as the ruler of the Philistine city of Gath, he plays a prominent role in the David stories, first barring the babbling David from admission to his city (1 Samuel 21:10–15) and then later welcoming him back as a trusted ally, even granting him his own territorial possession in the southern Shephelah at Ziklag (1 Samuel 27:2–6). And it was Achish who allowed David to depart in peace with his followers before the fateful battle between the Philistines and Saul (1 Samuel 29:6–11).

In the summer of 1996, a dramatic inscription was recovered by archaeologists Trude Dothan and Sy Gitin in their excavations at Tel Miqne in the western Shephelah, a site securely identified with the ancient Philistine city of Ekron. It was a late-seventh-century BCE dedication inscribed on a limestone block, bearing the name of Ikausu, ruler of the city at that time. This Ikausu is also mentioned in Assyrian records from the time of Kings Esarhaddon and Ashurbanipal as one of Levantine rulers who paid tribute to Assyria. The name Ikausu is linguistically similar to the name of the Philistine king Achish; many scholars have suggested it was a traditional Philistine royal name that had been used since the tenth century BCE.

Yet there is an obvious problem in establishing a direct connection between the Philistine king Ikausu (who ruled close to the time of King Josiah) and David's Philistine patron Achish. Ikausu was the king of Ekron, not Gath. Mighty Gath had been destroyed two centuries earlier; at the time of Ikausu, Gath was little more than a village; Ekron was by far the most powerful Philistine city-state. Perhaps the biblical authors simply used Achish as a convenient name for a powerful Philistine king. But in the seventh century BCE, the name Ikausu-Achish would have been too well known throughout Judah, with a clear contemporary significance. So the story of the alliance between David and an ancient Achish may have aimed at legitimizing the relationship between the "new David"—Josiah—and the city of the new Achish: Ekron.

There is clear archaeological evidence for this: the excavations at Tel Miqne have revealed an impressive period of urban development that transformed Ekron from a small town to one of the most important cities in the region by the time of Josiah. From the late eighth century BCE, and especially in the first half of the seventh century, under Assyrian domination, Ekron grew in size to become the most impressive olive oil processing facility known anywhere in the ancient Near East. Within its imposing city walls, over a hundred olive oil production units have been uncovered, including storerooms, presses, and vats. This ancient industrial zone stretched around the entire city, having an estimated production capacity of about a thousand tons a year. In the Assyrian economy, this was a significant asset.

Throughout the seventh century BCE Ekron experienced unprecedented prosperity as the center of oil production because of its convenient location on a main road network and its proximity to

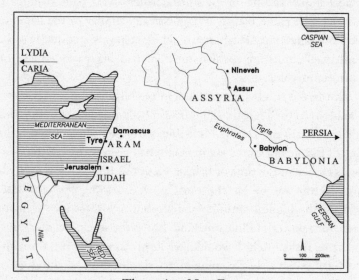

The ancient Near East

the olive groves in the Judahite hill country and the upper Shephelah. Indeed, the olive growers of Judah must have provided a significant part of Ekron's supply, first as part of its tribute to Assyria
after Sennacherib's invasion and later, under Manasseh, as he
sought to expand Judah's participation into the Assyrian imperial
economy.

Though there was a certain decline in the olive oil production at
Ekron after the Assyrians withdrew from the region around 630
BCE, the industry continued throughout the late seventh century
BCE under the hegemony of the Egyptian Twenty-sixth Dynasty.
For both economic and political reasons, Judah probably continued
to send its harvested olives to Ekron in the time of Josiah. There
was no better way to legitimate this continued economic connection with outsiders (clearly an abomination in the eyes of the puritan Deuteronomistic historians) than to "remind" the people of
Judah of the friendship and cooperation between the founder of
the Jerusalem dynasty—the pious David—with a Philistine king
named Achish.

NEW TERRITORIAL CLAIMS

The biblical stories of David and Achish contain another element of
direct concern in the days of King Josiah. Archaeological finds suggest gradual Judahite expansion westward to recover the lost lands
of the Shephelah, and it is significant that the authority of Achish is
marshaled in the biblical story to justify seventh-century Judahite
territorial claims. One of the most characteristic literary devices of
the Deuteronomistic History, betraying its seventh-century origins,
is the phrase "to this day." It is used on dozens of occasions, scattered through the books of Deuteronomy, Joshua, Judges, Samuel,
and Kings, to point out ancient landmarks or explain unusual situa-
tions that could still be observed in the time of the compilation of
the text. A typical use of this phrase is the description of David's

lawful acquisition of territory from the hands of the Philistine king Achish:

> *Then David said to Achish, "If I have found favor in your eyes, let a place be given me in one of the country towns, that I may dwell there; for why should your servant dwell in the royal city with you?" So that day Achish gave him Ziklag; therefore Ziklag has belonged to the kings of Judah to this day. (1 Samuel 27:5–6)*

Ziklag was located in the lower Shephelah, on the southwestern boundary of Judah, facing Philistia, in an area of major concern to the ruling circles of Judah in the late seventh century BCE. The biblical stories of David's time at Ziklag contain some other striking seventh-century anachronisms. After returning from the Philistines' war council, David finds that Ziklag has been plundered by the desert-dwelling Amalekites, whom he pursues, defeats, and from whom he claims abundant booty—which he subsequently distributes to his fellow Judahites (1 Samuel 30:26–31). Of the places that received the booty, a number were especially prominent in the time of Josiah, notably Bethel (which was apparently annexed by Judah after the withdrawal of Assyria), as well as Aro'er and Ramath-negeb in the Beer-sheba Valley on the southern border of Judah, facing Edom. Excavations have shown that both Aro'er and Ramath-negeb flourished only in late monarchic times. And significantly, another one of the places on the list, Jattir—identified with the site of Khirbet Yattir to the south of Hebron—was not even inhabited before the seventh century BCE.

All in all, the text reveals an elaboration and expansion of early traditions with a specific seventh-century purpose in mind: to validate Judah's territorial expansion toward the territory of the Philistine cities. It is the period of Josiah, indeed, that provides a surprising context for the single most famous story of David's early career.

WHO KILLED GOLIATH?

The mighty Philistine warrior Goliath of Gath is David's most famous foe. The mention of that long-destroyed city as Goliath's hometown reflects an early tradition, but at the same time, this timeless story also conceals a surprising chronological clue.

In the Bible, faith fuels the shepherd boy David's encounter with the Philistine giant, who is described in frightening detail:

> *And there came out from the camp of the Philistines a champion named Goliath, of Gath, whose height was six cubits and a span. He had a helmet of bronze on his head, and he was armed with a coat of mail, and the weight of the coat was five thousand shekels of bronze. And he had greaves of bronze upon his legs, and a javelin of bronze slung between his shoulders. And the shaft of his spear was like a weaver's beam, and his spear's head weighed six hundred shekels of iron; and his shield-bearer went before him. (1 Samuel 17:4–7)*

While Goliath rages and taunts his puny opponent,

> *David put his hand in his bag and took out a stone, and slung it, and struck the Philistine on his forehead; the stone sank into his forehead, and he fell on his face to the ground. (1 Samuel 17:49)*

This encounter bears all the marks of a distinctively Deuteronomistic story, including a faith-filled speech from the young David, declaring to the arrogant Goliath as he reaches the field of battle:

> *You come to me with a sword and with a spear and with a javelin; but I come to you in the name of the LORD of hosts, the God of the armies of Israel, whom you have defied. This day the LORD will deliver you into my hand, and I will strike you down, and cut off your head; and I will give the dead bodies of the host of the Philistines this day to the birds of the air and to the wild beasts of the earth; that all*

> *the earth may know that there is a God in Israel, and that all this*
> *assembly may know that the* LORD *saves not with sword and spear;*
> *for the battle is the* LORD's *and he will give you into our hand.*
> *(1 Samuel 17:45–47)*

The problem is that hidden in an earlier collection of heroic folk-tales about David's mighty men is another, quite different version of the death of Goliath, tucked away as an almost forgotten footnote:

> *And there was again war with the Philistines at Gob; and Elhanan*
> *the son of Jaareor-egim, the Bethlehemite, slew Goliath the Gittite,*
> *the shaft of whose spear was like a weaver's beam. (2 Samuel 21:19)*

Scholars have long speculated that either "David" was a throne name and he was originally called Elhanan, or another man named Elhanan was the real hero of the story, whose glory was stripped from him in the subsequent appropriation of the legend by the supporters of the Davidic dynasty.

Whether Elhanan or David did the killing in the original tale, the detailed description of Goliath's armor reveals the famous biblical story to be a late-seventh-century BCE composition that expresses both the ideology of holy war and the particular enemies faced by Judah in Josiah's time.

HOMERIC COMBAT AND GREEK MERCENARIES

Goliath's armor, as described in the Bible, bears little resemblance to the military equipment of the early Philistines as archaeology has revealed it. Instead of wearing bronze helmets the *Peleset* shown on the walls of the mortuary temple of Ramesses III in Upper Egypt wear distinctive feather-topped headdresses. Instead of being heavily armored and carrying a spear, javelin, and sword, they use a single spear and do not wear the metal leg armor known as greaves. Yet the biblical description of Goliath's armor is not simply a fanciful creation; every single item has clear parallels to archaeologically attested Aegean weapons and armor from the Mycenaean period to classical times. In all periods within this general time frame, one can find metal helmets, metal armor, and metal greaves. Yet until the seventh century BCE, these items were relatively rare in the Greek world. It is only with the appearance of the heavily armed Greek hoplites of the seventh through fifth centuries BCE that standard equipment comes to resemble Goliath's. In fact, the standard hoplite's accouterments were identical to Goliath's, consisting of a metal helmet, plate armor, metal greaves, two spears, a sword, and a large shield. And this suggests that the author of the biblical story of David and Goliath had an intimate knowledge of Greek hoplites of the late seventh century BCE.

What was the connection? Precisely at that time, Greek mercenaries from the coasts of Asia Minor came to play an increasingly important role in Near Eastern warfare. The Greek historian Herodotus reports that Carian and Ionian mercenaries served in the Egyptian army and were stationed in Egyptian border forts in the days of Psammetichus I, who took over the Philistine coast in the late seventh century BCE. This testimony is supported by Assyrian sources, which point to Lydia as the source of these troops, and by a wide range of archaeological evidence. Excavations in the Nile Delta revealed the unmistakable presence of seventh-century BCE Greek colonies through the evidence of imported Greek pottery and other artifacts. Greek and Carian inscriptions have been found at Abu Simbel; and a seventh-century BCE inscription found in the vicinity of Priene in western Asia Minor mentions Psammetichus I in a dedication left by a Greek soldier who served as a mercenary for him.* Although scattered units of Greek troops may have been used

* It is noteworthy that Herodotus (II:159) mentions that Pharaoh Necho II dedicated in the temple of Apollo in Didyma on the western coast of Asia Minor—not far from Priene—the armor in which he won battles in the Levant.

by the Babylonian kings in their massive armies of specialized fighting units, the Egyptian king Psammetichus I used them as a far more important striking and occupation force. With their heavy armor and aggressive tactics, the Greek hoplites embodied the image of a threatening, arrogant enemy that would have been all too well known to many Judahites of the late seventh century BCE.

There is another source of Greek influence in the story. The biblical account of Goliath and his armor has been compared to the Homeric description of Achilles (*Iliad* XVIII. 480, 608–12; XIX.153, 369–85). The *Iliad*, in its epic descriptions of warfare between Greeks and Trojans, provides several additional comparisons to the scenario of the David and Goliath story, especially in contests of champions from the opposing sides. The duel between Paris and Menelaus (*Iliad* III.21ff.) is told in the genre of a single combat that, like the biblical tale, decides the outcome of a war. The duel between Hector and Ajax (*Iliad* VII.206ff.) can be compared to the David and Goliath encounter in both general concept as well as the sequence of the events: a hero is challenged; his people react in horror; the hero accepts the challenge; the arms of the heroes are described; the combatants give speeches; and fight begins. Nestor of Pylos also fights a duel, and his opponent is described as a giant warrior.

Homeric influence on the biblical authors is highly unlikely before the very late eighth century, but it grows increasingly probable during the seventh century, when Greeks became part of the eastern Mediterranean scene. Interactions must have been fairly common. In places such as Ashkelon on the southern coast, and the small late seventh-century BCE fort of Mesad Hashavyahu north of Ashdod, Greek pottery testifies to the presence of traders, mercenaries, or immigrants. An ostracon written in Hebrew and found at the fort of Mesad Hashavyahu attests to the presence of Judahites at the site. In addition, a group called *kittim* is mentioned in ostraca, dated to c. 600 BCE, that were found at the Judahite fort of Arad in the Beer-sheba Valley. If the word *kittim* is understood—as some scholars suggest—to mean Greeks or Cypriots (from the place-name Kition in Cyprus), the ostraca may refer to Greek mercenaries in Egyptian service, guarding the vital trade routes that led to the coast. This would make Arad in particular and the Beer-sheba Valley in general other places of potential contact between Judahites and Greek hoplite mercenaries.*

There is no reason to deny the possibility that there was an ancient tale of a duel between a Judahite hero (David or Elhanan) and a Philistine warrior. But what message did the Deuteronomistic historian try to convey by dressing Goliath as a Greek hoplite and telling the story in a Homeric genre? In the late seventh century BCE two great revival dreams collided: Judah's fantasy to "reestablish" the united monarchy of David and Solomon and Egypt's vision of reviving its ancient empire in Asia. But Judah's dream of recapturing the rich lands of the western Shephelah was threatened by the power of Egypt that now dominated large parts of the Philistine plain. The duel between David and Goliath—dressed as one of the Greek hoplite mercenaries who protected Egypt's interests and might—symbolized the rising tensions between Josianic Judah and Egypt of the Twenty-sixth Dynasty.† To the Judahites of that era, with their awareness of the threatening Greek presence, the implications of the story were clear and simple: the new David, Josiah, would defeat the elite Greek troops of the Egyptian army in the same way that his famous ancestor overcame the mighty, seemingly invincible Goliath, by fighting "in the name of the Lord of hosts, the God of the armies of Israel" (1 Samuel 17:45).

---

* Jeremiah (44:1; 46:14) speaks about Judahites who lived in the Delta of the Nile. They too could have been in close contact with Greek mercenaries and merchants who established trading colonies there. For more evidence on Greek mercenaries and their possible connection to the David story, see Appendix 6 on the description of Cheretites and Pelethiles as David's royal bodyguard.

† It is noteworthy that the name Goliath has been compared etymologically to the Lydian (that is, west Asia Minor) name Alyattes. The historical Alyattes, king of Lydia (c. 610–560 BCE), was the great-grandson of Gyges—the monarch who is said to have sent hoplite troops to help Psammetichus I of Egypt.

THE CONQUEST OF BETHEL

There is a clue in the postscript to the Bible's David and Solomon story that King Josiah was believed to be the descendant of David who would fully revive the glories of the united monarchy. It is reported that soon after the death of Solomon, at the time of the division of the kingdoms of Israel and Judah, the renegade northern king Jeroboam set up an altar at the ancient shrine of Bethel— thereby establishing a symbol of north Israelite independence and committing Israel's original religious sin. We have suggested that the idea of the centrality of the Jerusalem Temple did not predate the reforms of Hezekiah and was certainly not codified before the compilation of the Deuteronomistic History in the late seventh century BCE. But what is important in the biblical account is not its lack of historical accuracy, but rather the retrospective prophecy that it makes. An unnamed Judahite prophet reacts to Jeroboam's heretical declaration of independence from the Jerusalem Temple and the true religion of Israel by uttering the following oracle, in direct address to the idolatrous altar at Bethel:

> *O altar, altar, thus says the Lord: "Behold, a son shall be born to the house of David, Josiah by name; and he shall sacrifice upon you the priests of the high places who burn incense upon you, and men's bones shall be burned upon you." (1 Kings 13:2)*

Bethel was not merely an isolated cult place; it was one of the central shrines of Judah's great rival, the kingdom of Israel. As a center of north Israelite ritual and tradition, located only ten miles north of Jerusalem,* it was an obvious place of pilgrimage and devotion that potentially competed with the Jerusalem Temple. The repeated, hostile references to Bethel in the Deuteronomistic History suggest

---

* Identified with the mound of Beitin, the ancient site lies under modern village structures and has not been systematically excavated. Investigations carried out there beginning in the 1930s revealed extensive Bronze and Iron Age remains.

that it remained an important and active cult place even after the Assyrian conquest of Israel.

An odd story in the second book of Kings relates to the period when foreign settlers were brought to the area of Bethel and worshipped there:

And the king of Assyria brought people from Babylon, Cuthah, Avva, Hamath, and Sepharvaim, and placed them in the cities of Samaria instead of the people of Israel; and they took possession of Samaria, and dwelt in its cities. And at the beginning of their dwelling there, they did not fear the LORD; therefore the LORD sent lions among them, which killed some of them. So the king of Assyria was told, "The nations which you have carried away and placed in the cities of Samaria do not know the law of the god of the land; therefore he has sent lions among them, and behold, they are killing them, because they do not know the law of the god of the land." Then the king of Assyria commanded, "Send there one of the priests whom you carried away thence; and let him go and dwell there, and teach them the law of the god of the land." So one of the priests whom they had carried away from Samaria came and dwelt in Bethel, and taught them how they should fear the LORD. (2 Kings 17:24–28)

We have already mentioned how Hezekiah's reform of the Jerusalem Temple, at a time of significant Israelite immigration from the area around Bethel, may have been intended to discourage pilgrimage to the rival shrine and to unify a diverse population by creating a single national cult. But as long as the Assyrians ruled the territory of the former northern kingdom—and as long as Judah remained an Assyrian vassal—the opposition to the Bethel shrine had to remain merely ideological.

After the withdrawal of the Assyrians during the reign of Josiah, the situation changed dramatically. On the one hand, the population of the area would have been free to develop their own traditions and perhaps even dream of renewed independence under a resurrected northern kingdom of Israel. But at the same time, with no threat of Assyrian retaliation, Judah could begin to look northward and put its own dreams of a vast, "resurrected" Davidic kingdom into action. The account of Josiah's reform describes his brutal takeover of Bethel and his desecration of the tombs around it as the fulfillment of prophecy:

> *Moreover the altar at Bethel, the high place erected by Jeroboam the son of Nebat, who made Israel to sin, that altar with the high place he pulled down and he broke in pieces its stones, crushing them to dust; also he burned the Asherah. And as Josiah turned, he saw the tombs there on the mount; and he sent and took the bones out of the tombs, and burned them upon the altar, and defiled it, according to the word of the LORD which the man of God proclaimed, who had predicted these things. (2 Kings 23:15–16)*

To destroy the shrine at Bethel and restore the true faith of the Jerusalem Temple to that ancient place of infamy was the first, highly symbolic step toward undoing the centuries of northern apostasy and to resurrecting the vast, divinely protected united monarchy.

In the absence of clear archaeological evidence from the site of Bethel, we cannot possibly tell if this story in all its details is true. But as we have mentioned, characteristic seventh-century BCE Judahite artifacts, such as inscribed weights, pillar-shaped figurines, and distinctive types of ceramic vessels, have been found as far north as the area of Bethel, suggesting a spread of southern influence there during Josiah's reign. And two details in the Deuteronomistic History suggest that the conquest of Bethel was indeed closely connected in contemporary consciousness with Josiah's fulfillment of his Davidic legacy. The only monument Josiah is reported to have left standing at Bethel was the tomb of the prophet who had "predicted" his destruction of the shrine. The second detail is no less telling: Bethel is mentioned as one of the places to which David distributed booty after his raid on the southern Amekelites (1 Samuel 30:27). Josiah seems to have been self-consciously acting the role of a new David. By his time, the elaborate Davidic tradition no longer was merely for internal Judahite consumption but had become the guiding doctrine of a holy war to bring all of the land of Israel under his rule.

The Deuteronomistic History thus can be read as a political program, from the conquest of Joshua to the days of the judges, to the rise of David, through the united monarchy and its breakdown to the days of the two separate states, and to the climax of the story with the reign of Josiah, the most pious of all the Davidic kings. The Assyrian empire had crumbled, Egypt was seemingly interested only in its coastal possessions, and Judah was free to fulfill its pan-Israelite dreams. It was evidently a time of great exhilaration and expectation. Under the righteous rule of the new David and under the auspices of the Temple of Solomon, all Israelite territories and people would soon live in one state, worship one God in one Temple in Jerusalem, and inherit all the eternal blessings of God.

RESHAPING DAVID AND SOLOMON

The book of Deuteronomy and the Deuteronomistic History, which contains the David and Solomon epic, were written to serve Josiah's cult reform strategy and territorial (or state) ideology. Who were the people responsible for this essential contribution to the biblical tradition? Though there is no scholarly agreement on the identity of the leaders of this movement, the basic coalition of forces is relatively clear. The deep concern for the sanctity of the Jerusalem Temple suggests that its priests played an important role in formulating and promoting the Deuteronomic ideology. The concern for equitable social relations between rich and poor expressed in the laws of Deuteronomy suggests that a popular resistance against the excesses of the Assyrian period and those who profited from them was also involved. But at the core was a deep veneration for the Davidic dynasty that could only have been expressed by those with wholehearted sympathy for the welfare of the royal court. And the stories of David and Solomon—which describe the days of the pious founder of the dynasty, the establishment of Jerusalem as his capital, his great conquests, the glamour of the united monarchy, and the building of the Temple by his son—were put in the heart of the Deuteronomistic History.

The earlier stories of the founding fathers of the kingdom of Judah were largely taken over and accepted. Yet the vivid accounts of the personal flaws of David—which would have doomed any other leader by Deuteronomy's own strict standards—could not simply be discarded in the compilation of the traditions, myths, tales, memories, and historical accounts of ancient Israel, south and north alike, into a single definitive history. The Deuteronomistic editors seem to have kept all or much of the previous material, which was first put in writing in the late eighth and early seventh century BCE, only adding formulaic speeches (such as David's challenge to Goliath in 1 Samuel 17:45–47), editorial comments, details of contemporary culture, and, of course, plotting the stories to serve their theological goals.

The new, composite epic drew in a wide range of traditions as a proven way to continue cultivating a national consensus among formerly separate circles—and to further Josiah's plan of expanding into territories that formerly belonged to the northern kingdom, a plan that actually materialized in the case of the plateau of Benjamin and the area of Bethel. Hence the northern traditions about Saul—even if containing a negative tone about David—were retained in the story, though in comparison to David, tarnishing and diminishing the stature of Saul.

The Deuteronomistic historians also retained the earlier stories of the wealth, wisdom, and greatness of Solomon drawn from the high age of Assyrian imperialism. Those elaborate descriptions of unimaginable riches and power could be used to show what the future might again hold for Judah, if the law was obeyed and a united monarchy of all Israel could be constructed "again." But the Solomon story (1 Kings 11:1–10) also provided a lesson that global trade and internationalism could breed apostasy—and endanger Judah's age-old tradition and identity.

In accordance with this ideology, the author of Deuteronomy's "Law of the King" seems to have used Solomon's greatness and opulence to express a message of condemnation about kings who sought majesty above righteousness:

> *When you come to the land which the LORD your God gives you, and you possess it and dwell in it, and then say, "I will set a king over me, like all the nations that are round about me"; you may indeed set as king over you him whom the LORD your God will choose. One from among your brethren you shall set as king over you; you may not put a foreigner over you, who is not your brother. Only he must not multiply horses for himself, or cause the people to return to Egypt in order to multiply horses, since the LORD has said to you, "You shall never return that way again." And he shall not multiply wives for himself, lest his heart turn away; nor shall he greatly multiply for himself silver and gold. (Deuteronomy 17:14–17)*

The lesson was clear and unambiguous: only Solomon's wisdom and his Temple were important. All the other trappings of worldly power that he cherished so greatly—horses, wives, and wealth—were sinful diversions from observing the true will of God, past and present.

The long and complex description of the construction and inner layout of the Temple, which—as we hinted in the previous chapter—could have dated a bit earlier than the days of Josiah, may have served to bolster his thorough cleansing of all idolatrous objects by showing that the current, purified Temple resembled Solomon's original, divinely inspired sanctuary in every way. And indeed it is noted, in the characteristic phrase of the Deuteronomistic historian, that the poles of the Ark of the Covenant in Solomon's Temple "were so long that the ends of the poles were seen from the holy place before the inner sanctuary; but they could not be seen from outside; and they are there to this day" (1 Kings 8:8).

This layer of Deuteronomistic revision substantially completed the biblical story of David and Solomon in the books of Samuel and 1 Kings that is so familiar to us today. Minor elements were inserted later, but the spirit and general tone of the story—as well as the traces of all its previous layers of creative mythmaking, storytelling, memory collection, ideological development, and literary activity—remained intact.

THE MESSIANIC LEGACY

As things turned out, the original Deuteronomistic dream came to nothing, at least on the earthly plane. In 609 BCE, Pharaoh Necho, the son and successor of Psammetichus I, embarked on a massive military expedition to assist the dying remnant of the Assyrian empire in recapturing the city of Harran, far to the north. The second book of Kings offers a laconic account of an event that would have enormous implications, not only for Judah and its Davidic legacy, but for the subsequent religious history of the western world:

> *In his days Pharaoh Neco king of Egypt went up to the king of Assyria to the river Euphrates. King Josiah went to meet him; and Pharaoh Neco slew him at Megiddo, when he saw him. And his servants carried him dead in a chariot from Megiddo, and brought him to Jerusalem, and buried him in his own tomb. (2 Kings 23:29–30)*

We can only speculate on the reasons for this execution, for the event is not reported outside the Bible.* Whether it was the boldness of

---

* The second book of Chronicles reports that Josiah was killed at Megiddo in a *battle* against Necho, but one should prefer the close-to-contemporary testimony of the book of Kings over the much later, fourth-century BCE account of Chronicles.

Josiah's manner toward the pharaoh—who must have expected the king of Judah to declare his vassal oath—or possible reports of unauthorized and threatening Judahite expansion in the Shephelah and the highlands, we do not know. But one thing is clear: even though Josiah's son Jehoahaz was duly anointed as the legitimate successor in the line of David, the Hebrew term for "anointed one," *mashiach* (messiah) would henceforth bear a new significance. So much hope had been invested in the destiny of Josiah, the new David, and so sure were his supporters of the inevitability of their divinely promised triumph that his death at the hands of the pharaoh caused a national trauma that would never be healed. Even the name of the place of his assassination—Megiddo—has never been forgotten. Har Megiddo ("the mound of Megiddo"), translated from the Hebrew into Greek centuries later as "Armageddon," would always be remembered as the fateful spot where the forces of good and evil would someday do battle to determine the fate of the world. A righteous king of the lineage of David would someday return to the place where the last righteous Davidic king perished. With the death of Josiah in 609 BCE, the tradition of Judeo-Christian eschatology and Davidic messianism was born.

The days of the kingdom of Judah were numbered. In 597 BCE, a Babylonian army laid siege to Jerusalem and carried off King Jehoiachin, along with an entourage of priests and nobles. Eleven years later Jerusalem and its Temple were put to the torch and the rule of the Davidic dynasty came to an end. But despite its destruction and the exile of its ruling classes, the story of the kingdom of Judah lived on in the narrative artistry of the biblical epic that had now reached its definitive—if still not completed—form. The legend of David and Solomon, as the centerpiece of the saga and model for Israel's eventual redemption, would be told and retold for centuries, gradually losing its link with history and assuming increasingly cosmic proportions and spiritual meaning, from which it would never retreat.

PART III

HOW THE LEGEND SHAPED HISTORY

PERIOD	STAGES IN DEVELOPMENT OF BIBLICAL MATERIAL
6th—4th Centuries BCE	Second, Exilic Deuteronomistic redaction, bringing the story up-to-date and explaining the exile. Exilic-period prophecies (e.g., Haggai and Zechariah). Use of David and Solomon as religious symbols in Chronicles.

HISTORICAL BACKGROUND	ARCHAEOLOGICAL FINDS
Judah and Jerusalem devastated by Nebuchadnezzar. Judahite deportees in Babylonia. King Cyrus of Persia allows some of the deportees return to Yehud. Construction of the Second Temple. End of hopes for political restoration of Davidic Dynasty.	Jerusalem devastated. Mizpah survives. Seal impressions of Yehud. Jerusalem slowly recovers. Construction of Samaritan Temple on Mt. Gerizim.

CHAPTER 7

Patron Saints of the Temple

From Royal Propaganda to Religious Ideal

— SIXTH TO FOURTH CENTURIES BCE —

WHY DOES THE TRADITION OF DAVID AND SOLOMON still move us, if their legend was born and shaped by the political concerns of a long-extinct Iron Age dynasty? The answer lies in its gradual transformation from a down-to-earth political program into the symbolic embodiment of a religious faith that would spread throughout the world. For the death of Josiah at Megiddo and the destruction of Jerusalem twenty-three years later in 586 BCE not only put an irreversibly tragic twist on the myth of the Davidic dynasty; it also ended its practical political usefulness. Never again would a Davidic king reign in Jerusalem; much less ever possess durable political power. From now on, the Near East would be ruled by great empires. The resurrection of a Davidic kingdom—of the kind envisioned by Josiah and the Deuteronomists—would be unthinkable. Mighty empires would succeed one another in ruling and controlling the region's lands and peoples: the Babylonians would give way to the Persians, and the Persians would give way to the great Hellenistic kingdoms in Egypt and Syria.

Cities would grow, new economies would develop, and new ethnic identities and historical understandings would emerge. Yet the David and Solomon story would never be forgotten. It offered a timeless image of founding fathers, of a golden age, and of a divine promise that would serve powerful new ideological functions undreamt of by the courtly bards of ninth century BCE Jerusalem, by the followers of Kings Hezekiah and Manasseh, or by the Deuteronomistic editors of Josiah's day. This would happen when its emphasis was permanently shifted from the political and dynastic concerns of the present to a more sweeping vision of redemption—linked not to earthly kingship but to a code of religious belief.

For a few generations after the destruction of Jerusalem, hopes for the imminent restoration of the house of David still flickered brightly, at least in some circles, despite their increasing futility. Jerusalem lay in ruins. The kingdom's elite was exiled, joining earlier groups of Judahite deportees (including the retinue of Josiah's grandson King Jehoiachin) who had been resettled in the heartland of Babylonia.* Yet among the communities of the exiles in Babylon and the survivors in ruined Judah, scribal creativity continued—based partly on the traditional texts of the kingdom, and partly on new visions and prophetic oracles—serving to keep alive the traditions of the now-deposed Davidic dynasty. At least among the exiles in Babylonia, Josiah's grandson Jehoiachin was still apparently considered the legitimate heir of David,† and hopes for his eventual return to Judah endured. This persistence of belief in the face of triumphant (and seemingly unshakable) Babylonian imper-

---

* For an estimate of the numbers of exiles, see Appendix 7.

† The prophet Ezekiel, who belonged to the exiled community, reckoned the dates of his oracles by the years of Jehoiachin's exile (1:2; 33:21; 40:1)—apparently an alternative royal dating formula that suggests continuing allegiance to the exiled king.

ial power required an increasingly metaphysical justification. And the David and Solomon tradition, embodying the core of Judahite royal ideology, began to undergo a series of changes that would eventually transform it from a political platform into a unifying religious ideal.

The first step was an urgently needed revision of the Deuteronomistic History. Several decades ago, the American biblical scholar Frank Moore Cross noted two main strata in its composition that reflect this literary process. The earlier layer, which he called Dtr[1], represents the original compilation, expressing the ideology and historical understandings of late monarchic Judah. As we suggested in the last chapter—offering archaeological data that essentially confirms Cross's original theory—this version of the David and Solomon tradition crystallized during the reign of Josiah as a validation and impetus for an ambitious political program. But with his death and the subsequent Babylonian conquest of Judah, Josiah's grand strategy came to nothing. If the Deuteronomistic History were to maintain its authority, certain explanations would have to be made. Why did Josiah *not* succeed in uniting all of the land of Israel under his kingship? How could such a pious Judahite king be killed by a foreign monarch? Why had the God of Israel later allowed the Babylonians to plunder and burn the Temple and destroy the holy city of Jerusalem? A revision of the Deuteronomistic History was needed. This expanded version, written during the exile, has been called by Cross and other scholars Dtr[2].

With a few deft editorial touches and additions, the story was continued to include Josiah's death and the catastrophe of 586 BCE. The overall message of the Deuteronomistic History was thereby reshaped. In place of the expectations of Josiah as the long-awaited successor of David, the destruction of the kingdom and the Babylonian exile now assumed an essential place in the history of Israel. Passages foretelling the exile were inserted throughout the Deuteronomistic History; the failure of Josiah's reforms and the eventual destruction of the kingdom of Judah was blamed on the

irredeemable wickedness of Manasseh, for which all Israel had to
atone, despite Josiah's righteousness:

> And the LORD said by his servants the prophets, "Because Manasseh
> king of Judah has committed these abominations, and has done
> things more wicked than all that the Amorites did, who were before
> him, and has made Judah also to sin with his idols; therefore thus
> says the LORD, the God of Israel, Behold, I am bringing upon
> Jerusalem and Judah such evil that the ears of every one who hears
> of it will tingle. And I will stretch over Jerusalem the measuring line
> of Samaria, and the plummet of the house of Ahab; and I will wipe
> Jerusalem as one wipes a dish, wiping it and turning it upside down.
> And I will cast off the remnant of my heritage, and give them into
> the hand of their enemies. (2 Kings 21:10–14)

Indeed, the story of Israel and the ultimate fate of the house of
David—as told in the Deuteronomistic History—was brought to a
conclusion not in Jerusalem but in distant Babylonia, with a subdued
yet hopeful notice of the release of King Jehoiachin from prison in
the thirty-seventh year of his exile, equivalent to 561 BCE (2 Kings
25:27–30).

A PROPHETIC REVIVAL

The Davidic dynasty remained central in literary expressions of
Judahite self-definition, but with the collapse of the kingdom and
the dynasty's fall from earthly power, those expressions became
increasingly poetic and metaphorical. Some of the most eloquent
and moving biblical evocations of faith in Davidic restoration were
expressed in works of sixth-century BCE prophecy, which begin to
shift the emphasis to national regeneration and away from purely
dynastic legitimation or short-term political strategy. The book of
Isaiah, though ascribed to the late-eighth-century prophet, also

includes material that expresses the hopes of later generations, down to at least the end of the sixth century BCE. Its image of the return of the Davidic redeemer is cosmic in scope and global in reach—no longer restricted to the political fate of the lineal heirs of Jesse's son, the shepherd from Bethlehem:

> *There shall come forth a shoot from the stump of Jesse, and a branch shall grow out of his roots. And the Spirit of the LORD shall rest upon him, the spirit of wisdom and understanding, the spirit of counsel and might, the spirit of knowledge and the fear of the LORD. And his delight shall be in the fear of the LORD. He shall not judge by what his eyes see, or decide by what his ears hear; but with righteousness he shall judge the poor, and decide with equity for the meek of the earth; and he shall smite the earth with the rod of his mouth, and with the breath of his lips he shall slay the wicked. Righteousness shall be the girdle of his waist, and faithfulness the girdle of his loins. The wolf shall dwell with the lamb, and the leopard shall lie down with the kid, and the calf and the lion and the fatling together; and a little child shall lead them. The cow and the bear shall feed; their young shall lie down together; and the lion shall eat straw like the ox. The sucking child shall play over the hole of the asp, and the weaned child shall put his hand on the adder's den. They shall not hurt or destroy in all my holy mountain; for the earth shall be full of the knowledge of the LORD as the waters cover the sea. In that day the root of Jesse shall stand as an ensign to the peoples; him shall the nations seek, and his dwellings shall be glorious. (Isaiah 11:1–10)*

An oracle in the book of Jeremiah is no less stunning in its vision of a Davidic restoration as a complete moral transformation of Judahite society, living securely in its land:

> *Behold, the days are coming, says the LORD, when I will raise up for David a righteous Branch, and he shall reign as king and deal wisely, and shall execute justice and righteousness in the land. In his*

days Judah will be saved, and Israel will dwell securely. And this is
the name by which he will be called: "The LORD is our righteous-
ness." (Jeremiah 23:5–6)

In a famous oracle of Ezekiel, the shepherd motif—historically founded in Judah's highland pastoralist background—becomes a metaphor of beneficent moral leadership:

And I will set up over them one shepherd, my servant David, and he
shall feed them: he shall feed them and be their shepherd. And I, the
LORD, will be their God, and my servant David shall be prince among
them; I, the LORD, have spoken. I will make with them a covenant of
peace and banish wild beasts from the land, so that they may dwell
securely in the wilderness and sleep in the woods. (Ezekiel 34:23–24)

These verses all reflect a generalized hope of redemption that went far beyond the earlier territorial and strategic goals of the earthly Davidic dynasty. By the sixth century BCE the era of the small independent kingdoms had given way to a contest of grand empires. Babylonia's rule over the Near East did not remain unchallenged for long. The Medes of western Persia rose to wrest control over the upper Tigris and Euphrates Valleys. They were, in turn, conquered by the southern Persian Achaemenids, led by Cyrus the Great (559–530 BCE), who swept eastward and westward to construct a great empire for himself. These developments were watched closely by the Judahite community in Babylonia, Egypt, and Judah, who saw them as evidence of God's plan on a scale vaster than ever before. Some, like the author of the oracle in Isaiah 45:1, declared the Persian king—rather than a descendant of David—to be God's anointed savior in the redemption of the world. But with Cyrus's conquest of Babylon in 539 BCE, the political fortunes of the Davidic dynasty suddenly rose again.

In establishing a new basis for his empire, Cyrus reversed the old Babylonian policy of deportation and exile. The Persians tolerated and even promoted local cults in their vast empire, and granted autonomy to loyal local elites. Indeed, Cyrus issued an edict giving permission to the exiled Judahites to return to Jerusalem and rebuild the Temple. We have only the later testimony of the book of Ezra (1; 6:3–5) for the developments in this period, but they mesh well with contemporary Persian policy concerning the restoration of other regional shrines. The Temple vessels were handed over to "Sheshbazzar, the prince of Judah," who was appointed governor of the newly formed Persian province of *Yehud*, as Judah was now called (Ezra 1:8; 5:14). Also returning to Jerusalem were prominent members of the exiled community (Ezra 2:2; 3:2), including a priest named Jeshua son of Jozadak and a Davidic prince Zerubbabel, grandson of Jehoiachin.* Hopes were apparently high that the national life of Judah under the leadership of the Davidic dynasty could be restored. Yet what occurred was a series of far-reaching developments that would put a final end to the earthly pretensions of the Davidic dynasty and begin the transformation of Judah's national cult into the religion we now know as Judaism.

DAVIDIC ROYALTY'S LAST FLICKER

At the time of the arrival of successive waves of Judahite exiles from Babylonia, the province of Yehud was a pale shadow of its former existence as the kingdom of Judah.† Its borders were shrunken, its population significantly diminished, and Jerusalem remained in ruins, the official center of neither state nor cult, nor a developed and diversified economy. Production was—perhaps with the exception of village handcrafts—entirely devoted to agriculture.

---

* His Davidic lineage is noted in 1 Chronicles 3:19. His name, meaning "seed of Babylon" in Akkadian, is an indication of how assimilated to Babylonian society the Judahite elite—and even the Davidic aristocracy—had become in just a few decades of exile.

† See Appendix 7 for more details on the numbers of returning Judahite exiles and the size and status of the province of Yehud in the post-exilic period.

Comprehensive archaeological surveys of recent years have produced a reasonable picture of the demographic situation in this period. They largely confirm the sketchy details to be found in the biblical texts. The second book of Kings and the book of Jeremiah tell us that after the destruction of Jerusalem in 586 BCE, the leadership of the remaining population was centered in the town of Mizpah, about eight miles to the north of Jerusalem. Excavations at Tell en-Nasbeh—the location of biblical Mizpah, near modern Ramallah—have shown that the site was not destroyed in the Babylonian campaign and that it became the central and most important urban center in this region. Indeed, other sites in the same area north of Jerusalem, including Bethel and Gibeon, continued to be inhabited in the early sixth century BCE with no evidence of destruction during the Babylonian campaign.

The area around Jerusalem, on the other hand, was thoroughly devastated. Intensive excavations in Jerusalem have shown that the city was systematically destroyed by the Babylonians and its immediate vicinity remained sparsely settled for decades. To the south, around Bethlehem, rural life seems to have continued without interruption, mainly in the form of small villages that extended no farther southward than the vicinity of Beth-zur. The population of the whole province was considerably sparser than it had been in the previous century. The Israeli biblical historian Oded Lipschits analyzed the archaeological data from this period and has estimated the total built-up area in all of Yehud as no more than around 350 acres (140 hectares). Multiplying this number by a density factor of about two hundred people per hectare (the accepted estimate of average village population in premodern Middle Eastern societies), we arrive at an overall figure of about thirty thousand people—around 40 percent of the population of late monarchic Judah. In short, the province of Yehud to which the Babylonian exiles returned was a rural landscape of scattered communities of survivors, with a ruined city where a Temple and royal capital had once stood.

The books of Ezra and Nehemiah, combined with the prophecies of Haggai and Zechariah, offer a fragmentary picture of the early attempts at the restoration of the Jerusalem Temple—a start-and-stop process conducted under the watchful eyes of the Persian administration, the hostility of neighboring peoples, and the suspicions of the remaining local population, who feared dispossession or domination by the returning exiles. Nevertheless, it was in this small community that a major development in the western religious tradition occurred.

Zerubbabel, the Davidic heir, participated in the first act of restoration, when the foundations of the new Temple were laid. Yet some years later, when revolts were raging throughout the Persian empire, the house of David took center stage. The distress of King Darius in the face of rebellions in Media, Babylonia, Egypt, and Asia Minor brought hopes to Judahite prophets that the world order was about to be shaken again. Perhaps the moment had arrived for the long-awaited Davidic restoration. Zerubbabel, who had in the meantime been officially appointed governor of Yehud, became the focus of renewed messianic hopes. The prophet Haggai explicitly identifies him as the long-expected Davidic savior who would usher in a new era:

> *Speak to Zerubbabel, governor of Judah, saying, I am about to shake the heavens and the earth, and to overthrow the throne of kingdoms; I am about to destroy the strength of the kingdoms of the nations, and overthrow the chariots and their riders; and the horses and their riders shall go down, every one by the sword of his fellow. On that day, says the LORD of hosts, I will take you, O Zerubbabel my servant, the son of Shealtiel, says the LORD, and make you like a signet ring; for I have chosen you, says the LORD of hosts. (Haggai 2:21–23)*

The prophet Zechariah links Zerubbabel with the successful completion of the Temple, using Jeremiah's poetic metaphor "righteous Branch" to refer to the Davidic heir:

Behold, the man whose name is the Branch: for he shall grow up in his place, and he shall build the temple of the LORD. It is he who shall build the temple of the LORD, and shall bear royal honor, and shall sit and rule upon his throne. And there shall be a priest by his throne, and peaceful understanding shall be between them both. (Zechariah 6:12–13)

It is noteworthy that Zechariah sees the leadership of restored Jerusalem as shared by king and priest. The Jerusalem Temple was completed and dedicated by about 516 BCE, after which Zerubbabel disappears from history. Whether his disappearance was due to unrest caused by these messianic expectations, or the fear of the Persian authorities (or hostile neighbors) that the growing prestige of a Davidic leader might endanger imperial interests, or some other forgotten reason, we cannot be sure. What is clear is that after the end of the sixth century BCE, the earthly house of David vanished as an element in Yehud's contemporary political life. Never again would a lineal descendant of David seek to rule Jerusalem. And never again would the David and Solomon tradition serve the political aims of a family dynasty whose continuous existence could be traced back for five hundred years. David and Solomon now belonged to the ages. And a dramatically different vision of these founding fathers would be born.

FROM KINGS TO PRIESTS

Throughout the fifth century BCE, Jerusalem slowly revived as Temple city and capital of a small, remote imperial province. The archaeological remains of this period are modest: they are limited mainly to the ridge of the City of David, where the Early Iron Age settlement had stood. It is reasonable to assume, as suggested by archaeologist David Ussishkin, that the rebuilding of the walls of Jerusalem described in the book of Nehemiah (3:1–32) refers to the renovation of fortifications first established by Hezekiah, though the population of the city had dwindled greatly. From a relatively large city of about sixty hectares before the Babylonian destruction, Jerusalem shrank in the Persian period to a settlement less than one-tenth that size.

At its center—its main reason for existence—was the restored Temple and the cultic activities carried out in its sacred precincts. With no king to lead the nation, a dual system of rule was established in the province of Yehud. The Persian-appointed governor dealt with secular matters such as collection of tax and imperial administration, while the Temple priesthood, led by a high priest, supervised ritual sacrifice and oversaw the collection of offerings. This duality is already evident in the division of power between the governor Zerubbabel and the high priest Joshua in the late sixth century BCE (Haggai 1:1). The priests' religious activities included responsibility for the sacred writings of the community, editing and revising them over the course of generations—but also producing new works as well. Among the most important of the new historical works are the books of Chronicles, in which—despite the disappearance of the Davidic dynasty—David and Solomon play central roles.

Most biblical scholars agree that Chronicles (a single work of two books) was written in Jerusalem Temple circles, but the precise time of its composition is less clear. Since it mentions the edict of Cyrus about the rebuilding of the Jerusalem Temple in its closing verses, it must have been written after 539 BCE. Another clue places it still later: a reference to the Persian coin called the *daric* in connection with contributions to the Temple (1 Chronicles 29:7) could not have been written before the initial minting of that coin during the reign of Darius, in 515 BCE. Estimated dates for its composition range from the very late sixth century BCE all the way up to the early Hellenistic period, around 300 BCE. Yet Chronicles does not show any influence of Greek culture or Greek language, so it likely dates from before the Hellenistic period. Unlike the books of Ezra and

Nehemiah, Chronicles does not show much concern for the characteristic institutions of the Persian empire, which disappeared from Yehud with its conquest by Alexander the Great in 332 BCE.* Considering these and other clues, most scholars opt for a mid-to-late-fourth-century BCE date, with the possibility that Chronicles includes somewhat earlier materials.

In any event, the books of Chronicles were written in Jerusalem, a long time—possibly three centuries—after the compilation of the Deuteronomistic History. These books were written under very different circumstances: there were no more Davidic kings in power; Yehud was part of a world empire; and the Jerusalem community was led by priests. No wonder these literary works express different goals and ideals than those of the earlier books of Samuel and Kings. With no Davidic king to lead the community, and no hope of independence in an era of world empires, the Temple became the center of community identity. Its priests took over Yehud's spiritual and social leadership. Yet despite all these changes, David and Solomon remained central to the Chronicles narrative. Why?

THE CHRONICLES VERSION

The books of Chronicles present an entirely different David and Solomon, shorn of complex personality traits and stripped of all human frailties. At a superficial glance, one may think that the description in Chronicles repeats the account of the books of Samuel and Kings in different words, merely omitting some original material and elaborating certain other themes. Yet the story of

---

* Biblical scholars, such as Hugh Williamson of Oxford University, noted that on many central issues the author of Chronicles presents a different view from that expressed in the books of Ezra and Nehemiah. It seems that Chronicles and Ezra-Nehemiah—though written roughly in the same period—promote different ideologies, though they are not in total opposition to each other. Their authors belonged to the same community of postexilic Jerusalem, but they express different outlooks on Israelite history and on the needs of their own community.

the founders of the Jerusalem dynasty as portrayed in Chronicles is far from being a dutiful repetition. Major parts of the story that appear in Samuel and Kings—such as the description of David's rise to power, the succession of Solomon to the throne of David, and the apostasy of the aged Solomon—simply do not appear in Chronicles. There is no mention of David's service as a Philistine vassal; not a word about all the murders and conflicts in the course of his rise to power; no reference to his adulterous affair with Bathsheba and its tragic aftermath, or to Absalom's rebellion. There is no discussion of Solomon's pagan ways or his foreign wives. This is not simply a matter of abridgment. All critical or unflattering stories about David and Solomon have been intentionally and selectively omitted. Every story that could have shed negative light on David and Solomon is carefully excised in order to depict them as flawless, almost saintly monarchs. The material *added* by Chronicles—which does not appear in the Deuteronomistic History—deals almost exclusively with the Temple and its personnel.

In the books of Chronicles, the Temple is the fulfillment of God's promise to David, not a distant hope but a living reality. Over half of the historical chapters of the two books of Chronicles (if one excludes the genealogies in the beginning of 1 Chronicles) are devoted to the time of the united monarchy. The account is almost entirely preoccupied with the construction of the Temple, its furnishings, and its rituals. This is not merely a matter of elaborated detail. The significance of David's election and Solomon's reign is shifted from earthly power and territorial conquest to the establishment of the Temple cult. David and Solomon's dynastic prestige is now placed entirely in the service of ecclesiastical legitimation: showing the people of the province of Yehud and the communities of their kinsmen scattered throughout the Near East—now increasingly known as "Yehudim," or Jews—that the long-awaited redemption should be sought not in dynastic restoration but in the rituals and laws of the Temple of Jerusalem.

For the authors of Chronicles, the Temple was the very heart of Israelite existence, an essential fulfillment of God's eternal plan. David plays a far more significant role in the building of the Temple and the activities of its personnel than he had done in the earlier Deuteronomistic History. The story of his bringing the holy Ark to Jerusalem (1 Chronicles 15–16) is filled with detailed instructions about the proper roles of priest and levites in ritual activities of music making, sacrifices, and psalm singing, which are utterly lacking in the account of the same event in 2 Samuel 6. Moreover, David takes a far more active role in the building of the Temple. While the earlier scriptural version had disqualified him from this action "because of the warfare with which his enemies surrounded him" (1 Kings 5:3), the David of Chronicles dedicates himself wholeheartedly to the project, as organizer, architect, and master engineer. In short, he is depicted as the founder of the Temple cult.

David summons a great assembly to announce the beginning of the project and to hand over a detailed blueprint:

Then David gave Solomon his son the plan of the vestibule of the temple, and of its houses, its treasuries, its upper rooms, and its inner chambers, and of the room for the mercy seat; and the plan of all that he had in mind for the courts of the house of the LORD, all the surrounding chambers, the treasuries of the house of God, and the treasuries for dedicated gifts. . . . All this he made clear by the writing from the hand of the LORD concerning it, all the work to be done according to the plan. (1 Chronicles 28:11–19)

All these elaborated elements were part of the Temple ground plan and ritual as it was carried out in postexilic Jerusalem. The account of David's central role in its construction directly linked the authority of the priesthood and the sanctity of the cult with the actions of the founding father. Its effect was to substantially elevate and empower the priesthood as the true bearers of the Davidic promise—in place of the now-discontinued monarchy.

Solomon, too, serves as a founding patron for later Temple practice, even more than in the earlier scriptural account. In Chronicles, Solomon's wealth, power, and wisdom are almost entirely directed to his involvement with the Temple. The intrigue surrounding his succession to the throne is omitted. He reigns with one overarching mission: to complete the building of the Temple and initiate the complex plan for its operation in much the same way that Joshua inherited the leadership over the children of Israel to put into action the laws that Moses had received at Sinai. For the authors of Chronicles, the Temple and the Dynasty are inseparably intertwined; the promise to David is conditional on the completion of the Temple and its proper functioning according to law. The inheritance of the people of Israel is no longer just an earthly Davidic kingdom but—through the laws and rituals of the Jerusalem Temple—a kingdom of God.

Thus by the time of the writing of the books of Chronicles in the fourth century BCE, we see a fundamental reversal of the significance of the David and Solomon tradition. Whereas the Temple and its cult had served to boost the political prestige of the Davidic dynasty during its rule of the kingdom of Judah, nostalgic memories of independent kingship now served as support for the centrality of the Temple and its rituals in the life of postexilic Yehud and in the spiritual imagination of communities of *Yehudim*—Jews—all over the ancient world.

SAMARIA, AGAIN

Many biblical scholars have suggested that the transformation of the image of David and Solomon in the books of Chronicles is based not only on the efforts of the Jerusalem priesthood to secure their position within Yehud, but also to overcome political and religious rivalry from the north. The Persian kings retained the administrative division established by their predecessors the Baby-

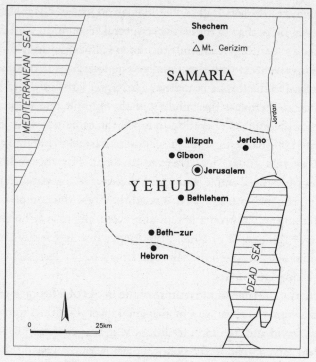

The Persian provinces of Yehud and Samaria

lonians and Assyrians and they organized the territory immediately to the north of the province of Yehud, the core of the former northern kingdom of Israel, as the province of Samaria. Its mixed population of former Israelites who did not go into exile and of foreign groups resettled in the area by the Assyrians were now known as Samaritans.

In the books of Ezra and Nehemiah, we hear of continual Samaritan hostility to the rebuilding of Jerusalem and the establishment of the Temple. That hostility was abundantly returned. The inhabitants of Samaria saw themselves as the successors of the northern kingdom—specifically as members of the tribes of Manasseh and Ephraim who had not been deported by the Assyrians. The Jerusalem priesthood, by contrast, saw them as aliens and pagans, descendants of the foreign peoples who had been brought in and resettled in this area by the Assyrian kings.

The historical truth undoubtedly lies somewhere between these opposing visions. Whatever their precise genealogical connection to the inhabitants of the northern kingdom of Israel, the people of the northern highlands maintained their attachment to the traditions of the people of Israel through the adoption of a distinctive and eventually sectarian version of the Five Books of Moses—the Samaritan Pentateuch. The biblical traditions connected with northern localities like Shechem and Bethel, and important biblical personalities like Jacob, Joseph, and Joshua, are explicitly connected with the north.

At the time of the writing of Chronicles, the northern kingdom was no more than a vague memory, having been destroyed by the Assyrians four centuries before. Yet the continuing political and religious power of Samaria was of great concern to the leaders of Yehud. Archaeological surveys in the highlands of Samaria have noted a substantial continuity of settlement from the end of the Assyrian period through the succeeding centuries. The discovery of an archive of inscribed fourth-century BCE papyri in a cave on the desert fringe of Samaria has revealed the complexity of political and social life and legal activity in the province during the later Persian period.

For centuries there had been a natural rivalry between the northern and southern highlands; this expressed itself in matters of religious practice and political strategy. The establishment of the province of Yehud and the rebuilding of the Jerusalem Temple brought those tensions once again into focus and resulted in a final schism between Jews and Samaritans. The construction of a single, central Samaritan temple on Mount Gerizim near Shechem posed a northern religious alternative—and a severe threat—to the Jerusalem ideology.

The date of the construction of the Mount Gerizim temple has long been a matter of debate. The first-century CE Jewish historian Flavius Josephus dated its foundation to the early Hellenistic era in the time of Alexander the Great, yet Samaritan tradition maintained that their temple was constructed closer to the time of the rebuilding of the Jerusalem Temple, in the Persian period. These arguments rested solely on historical texts, as the site of the Samaritan temple was not investigated archaeologically. Finally, in the 1980s, large-scale excavations were carried out at the site by the Israeli archaeologist Yitzhak Magen. It is now clear that the Samaritan Temple was built in the Persian period, probably as early as the first half of the fifth century BCE; that it was devoted to the cult of the God of Israel; and that its layout was strikingly similar to the descriptions of the Temple in Jerusalem. Indeed, the vision of David and Solomon in Chronicles represents a direct response to the Samaritan challenge by redefining the very notion of Israel.

According to the Deuteronomistic History, the religious practices of the northerners were sinful. The cultic missteps of Saul, the reported construction by the first northern king, Jeroboam, of the idolatrous shrines at Bethel and Dan, and the Baal worship of the Omrides at Samaria were violations of divine command for which they would dearly pay. Although the northern kingdom and the northern kings were considered illegitimate, the inhabitants of the north were nonetheless still part of the people and land of Israel over which David and Solomon had ruled and which a righteous successor of their dynasty would rule again someday. Chronicles, on the other hand, does not deal with the conflict between David and Saul over the kingship or with Judah's continuing conflict with the northern kings. The divine mission of David and Solomon is self-evident; in their version of history from Adam to Cyrus's edict to rebuild the Temple, the books of Chronicles argue that God's plan for his people centered on the giving of laws that could be fulfilled only in Jerusalem. Any other dynasty than the house of David and any other place of worship than the Jerusalem Temple was simply irrelevant—it was not part of the true history of the people of Israel.

The people of Israel must therefore be defined by religious allegiance rather than geography or political institutions. The unity of

Israel would not be achieved by territorial conquest or holy war but by a clear religious choice. Chronicles makes the reign of David and Solomon not merely a golden age that might someday be recaptured, but the standard of acceptable religious behavior that will last for all time. David and Solomon—and their united monarchy—became a model and symbol for the unity of the nation, an archetype for a holy community of all Israel. Chronicles thus points the way for individuals from the north to join the community of God. The speech in Chronicles of Abijah, Solomon's grandson, to the northern Israelites (which does not appear in Kings!) powerfully expresses this new vision:

> *And now you think to withstand the kingdom of the LORD in the hand of the sons of David, because you are a great multitude and have with you the golden calves which Jeroboam made you for gods. Have you not driven out the priests of the LORD, the sons of Aaron, and the Levites, and made priests for yourselves like the peoples of other lands? Whoever comes to consecrate himself with a young bull or seven rams becomes a priest of what are no gods. But as for us, the LORD is our God, and we have not forsaken him. We have priests ministering to the LORD who are sons of Aaron, and Levites for their service. They offer to the LORD every morning and every evening burnt offerings and incense of sweet spices, set out the showbread on the table of pure gold, and care for the golden lampstand that its lamps may burn every evening; for we keep the charge of the LORD our God, but you have forsaken him. Behold, God is with us at our head, and his priests with their battle trumpets to sound the call to battle against you. O sons of Israel, do not fight against the LORD, the God of your fathers; for you cannot succeed. (2 Chronicles 13:8–12)*

Chronicles not only stresses that this standard of religious behavior was established by David and Solomon; it emphasizes the invitation of two later pious Davidic kings, Hezekiah and Josiah, to the northerners to come and worship in Jerusalem and become part of God's people. In short, the books of Chronicles put the emphasis on the most Judahite figure, David; the most Judahite city, Jerusalem; and the most Judahite institution, the Temple, in order to show that the Samaritans' attempts to usurp the traditions of Israel are folly. No kingdom, no people, and no individual can claim to be a part of Israel without Jerusalem and without following the righteous religious foundations established by David and Solomon. The Jerusalem Temple community of the time of Chronicles is presented as the only legitimate successor of the ideal, great Israel of the time of David and Solomon.

DAVID AND SOLOMON AS THEOLOGY

With David and Solomon established as the touchstones of religious authority in the Jerusalem Temple, important literary collections of cultic poetry, prose, and songs of thanksgiving were gradually ascribed to them. Although Chronicles was the crystallized expression of their place in religious tradition, the earlier narrative in the Deuteronomistic History proved a rich source of allusions and associations that provided links with other cultic practices and beliefs. The tradition of David's skill with the harp in stilling the tortured soul of King Saul—mentioned in 1 Samuel 16:14–23—became the basis for ascribing to him the establishment of ritual music in the Temple as well as the authorship of dozens of psalms probably regularly sung there. Likewise the fabled wisdom of Solomon—"He also uttered three thousand proverbs; and his songs were a thousand and five" (1 Kings 4:32)—suggested that he was the source for the collections of traditional wisdom contained in "the proverbs of Solomon, son of David, king of Israel" (Proverbs 1:1). And his reputation as a great lover linked him forever with the erotic verses of yet another composition retained in the Hebrew Bible: "The Song of Songs, which is Solomon's" (Song of Solomon 1:1).

Scholars disagree on the date of composition of these books of the Bible. The book of Psalms contains hymns of praise, lament, and celebration that may have been sung in the Temple in monarchic times. Yet its present form is postexilic. The origins of Proverbs and the Song of Songs are even harder to pin down, but they are generally believed to be postexilic. All of them were preserved, edited, and elaborated in the scribal circles of the Temple; their ascription to David and Solomon is hardly surprising in view of their theological centrality. One might also mention the book of Ruth—placed by its author in the period of the Judges, but most likely compiled in postexilic times. Its romantic story of the Moabite maidservant who chooses to stay with her Judahite in-laws ("for where you go I will go, and where you lodge I will lodge; your people shall be my people, and your God my God"—Ruth 1:16) not only embodies the principle of religious choice as the basis for membership in the house of Israel; it explicitly identifies Ruth as the grandmother of David himself.

Thus, by the end of the postexilic period, and certainly in the Hellenistic era, David and Solomon had become icons: distant, dreamlike embodiments of the official cult and theology of the Jerusalem Temple—and through the Temple, to communities of Jews everywhere. With the translation of the Hebrew Bible into Greek during the Hellenistic period, the images of David and Solomon reached an even wider audience, tied neither to the political fate of the long-vanished Davidic dynasty nor to Judah's territorial conquest of the highland towns and villages of the north. David and Solomon had been transformed from Iron Age kings into models of religious virtue. They had become a focus for personal religious allegiance that would be maintained both by Rabbinic Judaism and—as we will see—by Christianity. That central fact alone explains why their tradition is still so powerful.

PERIOD	STAGES IN DEVELOPMENT OF BIBLICAL MATERIAL
3rd Century BCE to **5th Century** CE	Greek Translation of Kings and Chronicles; developed versions of Psalms, Proverbs, Song of Songs; Extra and post-Hebrew Bible material with messianic overtones: Psalms of Solomon, Flavius Josephus, Dead Sea Scrolls. New Testament links Jesus to Davidic tradition, Rabbinic literature and Church Fathers expand and elaborate religious associations and metaphors.

HISTORICAL BACKGROUND	ARCHAEOLOGICAL FINDS
Hellenistic period: Rule by Ptolemies and Seleucids; Hasmonean Dynasty. Roman period: Herod the Great, the Jewish revolts fueled by messianic ideologies. Early Christianity and its official establishment in the Byzantine period.	Increasing Hellenistic influence in culture and economy; Hasmonean building activity in Jerusalem and desert areas. Destruction of the Samaritan Temple on Mt. Gerizim. Herod the Great expands Jerusalem and builds a new Temple; builds other cities and forts, such as Masada. Dead Sea Scrolls. Jerusalem devastated by the Romans. Roman and Byzantine period synagogues. Byzantine churches.

CHAPTER 8

Messianic Visions

David and Solomon, from Judaism to Christianity

— SECOND CENTURY BCE TO FIFTH CENTURY CE —

IF THE AUTHORS OF CHRONICLES BELIEVED THAT DAVID and Solomon would forever remain just patron saints of the rebuilt Temple and its cultic rituals, they were badly mistaken. Over time, as the region's political and economic landscape was gradually transformed, the powerful traditions of the founding fathers of Judah—and united Israel—offered a kaleidoscope of other stunning images that were useful in new ways. Sweeping victories over foreign invaders; miraculous election to the kingship; royal repentance and concern for the downtrodden; vast wealth, wisdom, and esoteric knowledge: all these stories would be put to uses far wider than the regulation of daily sacrifices and yearly festivals by the Jerusalem priestly establishment.

Our sources for the later history and development of the David and Solomon tradition are scattered. We cannot be sure that the various Hebrew, Aramaic, Syriac, Greek, and Latin documents from the following centuries that we still possess actually express all of the uses to which the David and Solomon tradition was eventually put. Yet it is obvious that the great ideological switch that occurred in the postexilic period—namely, the use of David and Solomon as the avatars of later religious belief, rather than dynastic fortune—gave rise to a wide range of interpretations that would be influential among the new religious variations that gradually evolved within Judaism, and later in Christianity.

By the Hellenistic period, the prestige of David and Solomon had become pervasive among communities of Jews throughout the Near East and the Mediterranean. And as adherence to some form of the biblical tradition began to spread beyond the people of Israel, David and Solomon would be seen as the ancient embodiments of the true faith and harbingers of future redemption, in whatever form a particular interpreter—or community of interpreters—believed that faith and that redemption would take.

DAVID AND SOLOMON: THE ROYAL HELLENISTIC VERSION

In Hellenistic times the Jerusalem Temple continued to be the focal point of Jewish practice. David and Solomon's paramount role as its founders continued to be elaborated in priestly circles and celebrated in a growing body of wisdom literature. In addition to the final forms of the book of Psalms (largely ascribed to David) and of Proverbs and the Song of Songs (ascribed to Solomon), various other works of worldly wisdom and personal guidance drew their authority from their supposed connection to David and Solomon themselves. Thus, for example, the book of Qoheleth, "the Preacher," known as Ecclesiastes in its Greek version and probably written in the late third century BCE, offered the insights and observations of a world-weary Jewish sage under the pen name of "the son of David, king in Jerusalem" (1:1). In the apocryphal book of Ben Sira, also known as Ecclesiasticus, which was composed in the early second century BCE, both David and Solomon are likewise described as paragons of religious virtue and righteousness.

Yet the meaning of kingship was changing even as these works were being written or elaborated in their final forms. The David and Solomon tradition had grown out of the ancient Near Eastern milieu in which Egyptian, and especially Assyrian, models of divine royalty were the dominant forms. By the Hellenistic period new concepts of kingship were emerging, deeply influenced by Greek conceptions of the ideal ruler as a philosopher king. They can be seen clearly in the images of David and Solomon in the Greek translation of the Bible, the Septuagint, the first parts of which were compiled in the third century BCE, probably in Ptolemaic Egypt. In its description of David's righteousness and Solomon's wisdom, the semidivine qualities of the Hellenistic king are apparent: in addition to piety, the two kings are endowed with philosophical insight and extraordinary practical knowledge of the sciences most prized in Hellenistic circles. A Hellenistic Jewish composition entitled the Wisdom of Solomon places in the mouth of the ancient Judahite king a lengthy paean to Sophia, the feminine emanation of God's wisdom, with whom he seeks mystical union, with a philosophical intention that is unmistakably Greek.

We lose the trail of written commemoration of the David and Solomon tradition in Judea* during most of the rule of the Hasmonean dynasty, extending from 165 to 37 BCE. The reason is quite simple. Although the Hasmoneans (or the Maccabees, as they were originally called after their first great leader, Judah Maccabeus) rose to power at the head of a national revolt and established the first

---

* The name changes again in the Hellenistic period, with the Greek "Ioudaia" and the Latinized "Judea" of the Roman period. These replace the Aramaic "Yehud" of the Persian period, which in turn had replaced the original Hebrew "Yehudah," or Judah.

independent state in Judea after more than four centuries of imperial subjection, and although their capital was Jerusalem and its focus was the Temple, they were not themselves of Davidic ancestry. To make matters worse they ousted the priestly Zadokite line (which traced its origins back to the time of David) from succession to the high priesthood, thus earning for themselves bitter religious opposition within Judea and—as we will see—sparking among their opponents a renewed interest in David and Solomon. Yet even the Hasmoneans could not completely ignore the power of the Davidic tradition. The ancient core of Jerusalem was still known as the City of David, and local legend ascribed the inner line of the Hellenistic fortifications to the building projects of David and Solomon. (Flavius Josephus, *The Jewish War* 5.137–43.) Indeed when Simon the Hasmonean assumed the titles of national leader and high priest, his appointment was conditional—"until a trustworthy prophet shall arise" (1 Maccabees 14:41)—that is to say, when Davidic rule in Jerusalem would presumably resume.

The grandest impresario of Hellenistic-style commemoration of David and Solomon was Herod the Great, the notorious client of Rome and iron-fisted tyrant of Judea from 37 to 4 BCE. Though not of Jewish ancestry, Herod gained Roman support for his assumption of kingship over Judea, ousting the last of the Hasmonean rulers in a bloody civil war. Yet once in power he demonstrated his respect for the national traditions by erecting a great new Temple and palace in Jerusalem, on the model—if not in quite the same style and size—as the biblical Solomon. Clearing the summit of the Temple Mount, where the earlier Jerusalem Temples had stood, Herod conscripted thousands of workmen to erect a massive platform on which elaborate colonnades and courtyards and the great Herodian sanctuary would be built.

There are other indications that Herod self-consciously modeled himself as a symbolic successor to David, as ruler of nearly the entire biblical land of Israel, and to Solomon, as the Temple's great patron and master architect. Yet as a king imposed by distant Rome, he could not force anyone to venerate him, since his rule over Judea was brutal and his fawning subservience to his Roman overlords angered local Jewish sensibilities. In the end, Herod reinforced the religious iconography of the Davidic tradition without doing much to quell political unrest. He thus ironically ensured that David and Solomon would become even more potent symbols of political and eschatological hope.

MESSIANIC VISIONS

The rule of non-Davidic kings in Judea and the dispossession of the Zadokite priesthood in the second century BCE gave rise to persistent countercurrents that would once more energize the David and Solomon tradition. During the rule of the Hasmoneans, when various sectarian groups split off from the religious mainstream, a new vision of David and Solomon emerged—not as establishment founding fathers, but as models of righteous behavior to be followed in order to *regain* control of the Temple from a wicked, illegitimate priesthood and to lead the people of Israel piously.

The Dead Sea Scrolls, for example, are filled with allusions to David as the standard of righteousness that would ultimately triumph. Composed in the second and first centuries BCE, the collection of more than eight hundred texts discovered in caves near the western shore of the Dead Sea between 1947 and 1956 includes many previously unknown works of poetry, religious instruction, and prophecy in which an uncompromising veneration for David can be seen. At a time when the authors believed the Temple to be in the hands of an evil and impious priesthood, one text (known to scholars as 4Q505) sees David as the eternally elected leader, with whom God had established a covenant "so that he would be like a shepherd, a prince over Your people, and would sit upon the throne of Israel forever." Others more pointedly anticipate that a Branch of David would arise to destroy Israel's internal oppressors and external enemies.

These messianic allusions closely follow phrases of earlier prophets, but they place them in a decidedly contemporary context. Other groups had equally vivid visions and began to see the return of the Davidic savior as a moral guide as much as a military leader, who would destroy foreign domination and impiety at a single stroke. In a collection of hymns titled by later editors *The Psalms of Solomon*, the tribulations of the first century BCE were described in moving, quasi-biblical verses—in particular, they focused on the wickedness of the Jerusalem elite and the unspeakable horror of the ransacking of the Temple by the Roman general Pompey in 63 BCE. They nevertheless had great faith that a change was coming in the person of a Davidic heir, as predicted by the earlier prophets:

> *See, Lord, and raise up for them their king, the son of David, to rule over your servant Israel in the time known to you, O God. Undergird him with the strength to destroy the unrighteous rulers, to purge Jerusalem from the Gentiles who trample her to destruction; in wisdom and in righteousness to drive out the sinners from the inheritance; to smash the arrogance of sinners like a potter's jar; to shatter all their substance with an iron rod; to destroy the unlawful nations with the word of his mouth; at his warning the nations will flee from his presence; and he will condemn sinners by the thoughts of their hearts. (Psalms of Solomon 17:21–25)*

The longing for such a heavenly savior continued through the first century BCE, but with the death of Herod, in 4 BCE, at least for some, the time of waiting seemed to be over. A succession of rebel leaders arose in Judea over the following decades, many of them acting the part of the long-awaited savior, hoping to restore the glory of Judah and Israel not by righteous word or miracle, but by the sword.

In a description that is suggestively reminiscent of "David's Rise to Power," the first-century CE Jewish historian Flavius Josephus recounts the emergence of a particular bandit leader amidst the disturbances that followed Herod's death:

> *Now, too, a mere shepherd had the temerity to aspire to the throne. He was called Athrongaeus, and his sole recommendations to raise such hopes were vigor of body, a soul contemptuous of death, and four brothers resembling himself. To each of these he entrusted an armed band and employed them as generals and satraps for his raids, while he himself, like a king, handled matters of graver moment. It was now that he donned the diadem, but his raiding expeditions throughout the country with his brothers continued long afterwards. (Jewish War 2.60–62)*

Athrongaeus was eventually captured by the Roman forces, but new royal pretenders arose to take his place. Josephus describes the pervasive (and to his mind, mistaken) belief among the Jewish masses that "one from their country would become ruler of the world." And indeed, throughout the first century CE, as Judea became a Roman province, messianic visions and messianic leaders repeatedly arose to challenge Roman power and to take up the messianic quest.

We cannot tell to what extent all of them identified themselves as Davidic redeemers, for through the years of Roman rule a whole parade of biblical-like figures strutted on the revolutionary stage: In the forties, a would-be Joshua named Theudas drew crowds to accompany him down to the Jordan River, which he promised he would split asunder to permit a victorious reentry of the people of Israel into their Promised Land. Later, a mysterious Moses-like figure known only as "the Egyptian" led thousands of eager followers to the summit of the Mount of Olives with the promise that he would cause Jerusalem's walls to collapse miraculously and then lead them into the city as conquerors rather than slaves. These would-be saviors were all killed or expelled by Roman forces. In time, however, these messianic hopes spun out of control.

In 66 CE, despite the pleading of its Hellenized aristocracy, Judea exploded in open revolt against Roman rule. Sacrifices for the health of the emperor (which had been instituted in the time of Herod) were abruptly discontinued; the Roman garrison in Jerusalem was slaughtered; and the people of Judea prepared to meet the might of Rome—presumably with the divine protection that the oracles of the coming of the "last days" and the Davidic savior had foretold.

As battles raged and the Roman general (and later emperor) Vespasian gradually regained the upper hand, the various revolutionary factions within Judea fought among each other, with several of the rival leaders conspicuously assuming a kingly manner. Menachem, the leader of the violent rebel group who had seized Herod's fortress at Masada, appeared in the Jerusalem Temple "adorned with royal clothing," according to Josephus, only to be killed by members of a rival gang. Simon bar Giora, one of the last surviving rebel commanders in the final Roman siege of Jerusalem—led by Vespasian's son Titus—attempted to stage a dramatic, if desperate, miracle even after the Temple itself had been destroyed. According to Josephus, "imagining that he could cheat the Romans by creating a scare, [he] dressed himself in white tunics and buckling over them a purple mantle, arose out of the ground at the very spot on which the temple had formerly stood." This attempt at simulating the supernatural materialization of the long-expected messiah failed miserably. Stripped of his royal purple, Simon was thrown in chains and shipped off to Rome, where he was executed for public amusement during Vespasian and Titus's victory parade.

The destruction of Jerusalem and the final razing of the Temple in 70 CE put an end to the resuscitated belief that God would protect the city and its divinely elected kings from all earthly enemies. But the lingering hope that a Davidic messiah would someday rise to save the people of Israel was still perceived as a dangerous threat to Roman security. Indeed, the efforts the Romans made to snuff out this messianic hope reveal how literally they accepted it. From the writings of the fourth-century CE church historian Eusebius, we learn that after the fall of Jerusalem the Romans made at least two attempts to exterminate all those who claimed to be of the Davidic line. Eusebius quotes an earlier Christian writer, Hegesippus, in describing how the emperor Vespasian (69–79 CE) "gave orders that all that belonged to the lineage of David should be sought out, in order that none of the royal race might be left among the Jews" (III. xii), and how his son the emperor Domitian (81–96 CE) "commanded that the descendants of David should be slain" (III. xix).

It is highly unlikely that any of the victims were actually genealogically descended from the house of David, which had died out centuries before. But the power of the David and Solomon tradition would not be dimmed even by these liquidations. Jewish messianic rebellions would flare up again in 117 and 132 CE. More important, the veneration for David and Solomon now lay primarily in the religious imagination, where—invulnerable to Roman arrows, swords, or even the pain of public crucifixion—it would continue to flourish and take on new forms.

EXORCISING THE DEMONS

During the first century BCE, when Herod was building his great Temple and the stirrings of radical messianism arose among the underclasses of Judea, another fascinating development in the parallel and competing traditions of David and Solomon occurred. Drawing on the biblical hint that David's skill with the harp was effective in stilling Saul's tortured spirit (1 Samuel 16:14–23) and that such exorcistic powers were inherited by Solomon (who also, according to 1 Kings 4:33, possessed an extraordinary knowledge of nature), the belief began to spread that the "Son of David" was a unique protector against demons and evil spirits of all kinds. This belief would, much later, be expressed in Jewish folk traditions in amulets, magic bowls, incantations, and in the protective power of

Solomon's magic ring and the symbolic Shield of Solomon—also known as the Star of David. These beliefs and symbols would eventually descend into the secret lore of mystical brotherhoods and esoteric Judeo-Christian legends, but their origins lay very much in the mainstream of popular Jewish veneration for David and Solomon in the Hellenistic and Roman periods.

These traditions originated in the gradual transformation of the image of David—and especially Solomon—into figures of Hellenistic royalty. The Greek traditions of philosopher-kings as men of extraordinary power, combined with the biblical tradition of Solomon's wisdom and the rich postbiblical Jewish speculation about angels and demons, produced the image of Solomon as a figure to be summoned and appealed to by individual supplicants who sought relief from misfortune, disease, or insanity. Perhaps the earliest example of this vision, as the Spanish scholar Pablo Torijanos has pointed out, comes from an otherwise obscure document among the Dead Sea Scrolls, known to scholars as 11QPsAp^a. This small fragmentary text is one of several exorcistic compositions that demonstrate interest in rituals of what might be called black magic in Judea in the Roman period.

This document contains four psalms of exorcism, the last being the biblical Psalm 91, which is explicitly credited to David. In the second composition, the names of David and Solomon are mentioned, with Solomon, in a reconstructed portion, given the power of invoking God's name to deliver sufferers from "any plague of the spirits and the demons and the Liliths, the owls, and the jackals." The figure of Solomon addresses the attacking demons directly with the question "Who are you?" This question seems to be the beginning of a ceremony of exorcism. It appears in a later esoteric text called the Testament of Solomon that may include materials composed as early as the first century CE. In it, Solomon describes the secrets of controlling demons and explains that he had succeeded in forcing them to work for him in the construction of the Temple of Jerusalem! The similarity of the expressions indicates a shared popular tradition of Solomon, the "Son of David," as the patron saint of exorcists—a very practical and powerful application of the wisdom that God had granted to him.

Flavius Josephus reflects this widespread belief in the occult powers of Solomon in his report that "God granted him knowledge of the art used against demons for the benefit and healing of men. He also composed incantations by which illnesses are relieved, and left behind forms of exorcisms with which those possessed by demons drive them out, never to return. And this cure is of very great power among us to this day" (*Jewish Antiquities* VIII. 45).

What makes this image of Solomon as exorcist especially intriguing is its connection to New Testament literature. The gospel of Mark reports that when Jesus and his disciples were leaving Jericho in the course of their ministry,

> *Bartimaeus, a blind beggar, the son of Timaeus, was sitting by the roadside. And when he heard that it was Jesus of Nazareth, he began to cry out and say, "Jesus, Son of David, have mercy on me!" And many rebuked him, telling him to be silent; but he cried out all the more, "Son of David, have mercy on me!" And Jesus stopped and said, "Call him." And they called the blind man, saying to him, "Take heart; rise, he is calling you." And throwing off his mantle he sprang up and came to Jesus. And Jesus said to him, "What do you want me to do for you?" And the blind man said to him, "Master, let me receive my sight." And Jesus said to him, "Go your way; your faith has made you well." And immediately he received his sight and followed him on the way. (Mark 10:46–52)*

The close correspondence between the title "Son of David" and the act of healing suggests an original identification of Jesus of Nazareth as an embodiment of Solomon's exorcistic personality. This is quite distinct from the earlier belief in David and Solomon as the founders of the Temple or the long-awaited liberators of Israel.

244   DAVID AND SOLOMON

Eventually, however, all the earlier strains of the Davidic tradition were powerfully merged in the person of Jesus, to make him, in the eyes of his followers, the ultimate inheritor of God's promises to the Davidic dynasty and the long-awaited savior for all the people of Israel.

PROPHETS OF A NEW GOSPEL

Biblical scholars have wrestled for centuries with the meaning of Jesus' various messianic titles. Little agreement has been achieved about whether, in the course of his ministry in Galilee and Judea in the late twenties and thirties CE, Jesus of Nazareth explicitly identified himself as the Son of David, as other figures of the time surely did. What is obvious is that the authors of the gospels and other early Christian literature, writing shortly after the fall of Jerusalem, went to great lengths to cement this identification. They did it with a major distinction from contemporary Jewish tradition: they stressed that although Jesus was born of the earthly line of David, his messianic legacy was much greater than that of Israel's founding king.

In the gospel of Matthew, Jesus perfectly fulfills contemporary Davidic expectations. The genealogy with which it begins traces Jesus' lineage from Abraham through David, Solomon, and all the subsequent kings and postexilic heirs of the house of David—all the way down to Joseph, "the husband of Mary, of whom Jesus was born" (1:1–16). Later in the gospel, in its description of Jesus' preparations for his triumphal entry into Jerusalem, he bids his disciples to bring him a donkey and a colt, in order to fulfill an ancient Davidic prophecy of Zechariah:*

* The identity and date of the author of Zechariah 9–14 (Deutero-Zechariah) is debated. Dates for its various chapters range between the seventh and fourth centuries BCE.

*Lo, your king comes to you; triumphant and victorious is he, humble
and riding on an ass, on a colt the foal of an ass. (Zechariah 9:9)*

According to Matthew, the crowds who lined the route of his procession understood this prophetic message, proclaiming, "Hosanna
to the Son of David! Blessed is he who comes in the name of the
Lord!" (21:9). His subsequent cleansing of traders and money
changers from the courtyards of the Temple (the place most closely
associated with the postexilic Davidic tradition) is likewise greeted
by the onlookers with a messianic acclamation that the Son of David
had finally arrived (21:15).

The gospel of Luke also repeatedly stresses Jesus' Davidic lineage
through both his genealogical connections and the circumstances of
his birth in David's hometown of Bethlehem. Indeed, Luke's quota-
tion of the words of the angel Gabriel, announcing Jesus' impend-
ing birth to Mary, makes the messianic destiny explicit:

*And behold, you will conceive in your womb and bear a son, and you
shall call his name Jesus. He will be great, and will be called the Son
of the Most High; and the Lord God will give to him the throne of
his father David, and he will reign over the house of Jacob for ever;
and of his kingdom there will be no end. (Luke 1:31–33)*

For the early Christian community, Jesus was far different from any
other messianic contender for the Davidic mantle. In his resurrection from death on the third day after his crucifixion, Jesus had
shown himself to be greater even than David, who died and "slept
with his fathers, and was buried in the City of David," according to
1 Kings 2:10. This difference sparked a revolutionary reinterpretation; for Psalm 16, attributed by that time to David himself, seemed
to predict that bodily resurrection was a clear prophetic sign of the
Davidic legacy:

For thou dost not give me up to Sheol, or let thy godly one see the Pit. Thou dost show me the path of life; in thy presence there is fullness of joy, in thy right hand are pleasures for evermore. (Psalm 16:10–11)

In the Acts of the Apostles, Peter explains the new gospel succinctly as he addresses the assembled crowds in the courtyard of the Temple of Jerusalem:

Brethren, I may say to you confidently of the patriarch David that he both died and was buried, and his tomb is with us to this day. Being therefore a prophet, and knowing that God had sworn with an oath to him that he would set one of his descendants upon his throne, he foresaw and spoke of the resurrection of the Christ, that he was not abandoned to Hades, nor did his flesh see corruption. This Jesus God raised up, and of that we all are witnesses. Being therefore exalted at the right hand of God, and having received from the Father the promise of the Holy Spirit, he has poured out this which you see and hear. For David did not ascend into the heavens; but he himself says, "The Lord said to my Lord, Sit at my right hand, till I make thy enemies a stool for thy feet." Let all the house of Israel therefore know assuredly that God has made him both Lord and Christ, this Jesus whom you crucified. (Acts 2:29–36)

Just as the significance of David had been shifted to the Temple and its rituals in the era after the Babylonian exile and to Hellenistic kingship in succeeding centuries, early Christians shifted the focus of Davidic expectations to become the foundation of their own faith. The reputation of David as the fulcrum of the history of Israel was now beyond dispute. But for Christians, the context was no longer just the history of Judah or even Israel. They now saw the figures of David, Solomon, and all other heirs of the Davidic dynasty as forerunners and prophets of the universal savior born in David's hometown Bethlehem and crucified and resurrected in his capital city of Jerusalem.

Although the ministry, passion, and resurrection of Jesus were now seen as the ultimate fulfillment of the biblical story, David and Solomon remained, in the eyes of all believing Christians, supremely important religious personalities. As the ancient embodiments of true righteousness, wisdom, and repentance, they foreshadowed Jesus' message. Given their role as eloquent prophets of his messianic mission, the psalms ascribed to them, their biblical legend, and the vivid images of sacred kingship they represented lived on powerfully, at the very core of Christian consciousness.

SCHOLARS OF THE LAW

Rabbinic tradition remained unfazed by Christian identification of Jesus as the true heir of the divine promise to David. Yet the Jewish David and Solomon tradition also underwent a dramatic transformation after the fall of Jerusalem. As the Jews gradually recovered from the shock and the trauma of the destruction of their Temple and holy city, David and Solomon continued to be seen as the definitive model for religious emulation. After 70 CE, however, the focus of Jewish spiritual life had changed. With the destruction of the Jerusalem Temple sacrifice had given way to study and observance of the biblical ordinances, as they were progressively elaborated and reinterpreted in homiletic commentaries known as midrashim and extensively analyzed and interpreted in the Mishnah and Talmud. David and Solomon's religious role now shifted: in the traditions and literature of Rabbinic Judaism both were revered, each in his own way, to provide a guiding example for reverence and study of the law.

The American biblical scholar Jouette Bassler has collected a series of representative examples in which David can be seen as the archetype of the pious rabbinic scholar. David's skill in playing the harp, for example, was seen as necessary for a specific purpose: to rouse King Saul from his slumbers and to encourage him to study the law. In the rabbinic midrash on the book of Leviticus, David himself was seen as a Torah scholar of unparalleled insight, who encouraged his contemporaries to do the same (Leviticus Rabbah 34.16). Indeed David's devotion to the Torah and its observance, according to rabbinic commentators, caused God to bestow the kingdom on him. Even Solomon—who grew increasingly prominent in medieval Jewish tradition as a miraculous healer and exorcist—was likewise praised for his adherence to the legal tradition, and for his deep understanding of the reasons for the various laws.

The great variety of depictions and moral contradictions embedded in the scriptural David and Solomon tradition proved a fertile source of discussion and debate on the nature of humanity. The sometimes sketchy, puzzling, or contradictory descriptions of events narrated in the Bible became subjects for speculation and themes for often-contentious discussion about family relations, legal observance, and conduct in the community. In the midrash and the commentaries on the Bible, David becomes yet another indulgent father, chided for spoiling Absalom and Adonijah—and thus being at least partially to blame for their misdeeds. In a midrash on Samuel, the rabbis declared that Bathsheba was at least partially to blame for David's act of adultery and all its consequences, since she knowingly undressed for her bath in a place where she knew she would be seen by the king. In such discussions, the founding fathers of the Davidic dynasty gradually are seen as objects for reflection and theological discussion rather than static ideals.

In the elaboration of this wide range of vivid personal anecdotes and events mentioned in the Bible, David and Solomon remained at the bedrock of Jewish tradition. The golden age they achieved and symbolized was central to understanding God's intentions and Israel's history. To deny or ignore the importance of David and Solomon was to demean one of Judaism's central traditions. As one particularly colorful expression in the Talmud put it: "Whoever contends against the sovereignty of the House of David deserves to be bitten by a snake" (Sanhedrin 110a).

DAVID AND SOLOMON AS
CHRISTIAN METAPHORS

Even as the Jewish traditions and legends of David and Solomon were elaborated by the rabbis, the church fathers brought the image of David and Solomon to a far wider audience. The earlier Christological interpretations of Jesus as the true inheritor of God's promise—and the contents of David and Solomon's psalms as explicitly referring to Jesus—were taken one important step further. David and Solomon, examined from a purely Christian perspective, were increasingly seen not as independent biblical personalities, but as powerful metaphors for the history of Christ and the church, in every anecdote and episode.

In his commentary on the book of Samuel in *The City of God*, Saint Augustine wrote with faith-filled conviction "of the promises made to David in his son, which are in no wise fulfilled in Solomon, but most fully in Christ." The religious scholar Jan Wojcik has highlighted some of the most vivid patristic metaphorical interpretations of the David and Solomon tradition, noting, for example, how Augustine suggested that David's betrayal by Achitophel during Absalom's revolt actually concealed a veiled reference to Jesus' betrayal by Judas. Indeed Augustine's interpretations of the psalms can be read as a fascinating exercise in metaphorical theology, seeing every act and expression of David and Solomon related in an illuminating way to the many lessons of Christian doctrine. In Augustine's view, the narrative of David and Solomon should be split into a sequence of thematic religious examples, completely detached from their original context in the biblical narrative.

Another church father, Eucherius, saw in David's marriage to Bathsheba, the former wife of Uriah, a metaphor of the church's wooing the community of true believers away from the grasp of the discredited Jewish faith. Many similar metaphors can be mentioned—David's battle with Goliath as a symbol of Christ's confrontation with Satan; David's speech to his followers during his flight from Absalom as a mere shadow of Jesus' farewell speech to his disciples; and the Song of Solomon (Song of Songs) being not the erotic verses of an ancient monarch, but an expression of God's love for his church.

By the fourth century CE, the Christian fathers were convinced that the psalms were really talking about Jesus and that David and Solomon's lives were intended by God to be inspired metaphors. This reading of the David and Solomon tradition had become a matter of faith. But as Christian missionaries wandered from the intellectual milieu of the Roman cities around the Mediterranean into more distant pagan lands, a more down-to-earth meaning reappeared. The Bible that served as a pattern book of Christological symbols soon found audiences who listened to the colorful stories of ancient Israel and its glorious kings and absorbed them—quite literally—as examples to be followed by their own earthly leaders and as expressions of their own identity. In a sense, the process that began in the highlands of Judah in the tenth century BCE came to life again among new peoples and in new lands.

NEW DAVIDS AND SOLOMONS

The legendary cycle was adopted with new energy and with distinctive new variations across the vast plain of northern Europe, as a new civilization emerged. With the gradual disintegration of the once great Roman Empire, peoples were on the move and patterns of society were changing—not only in the former provinces of Britannia, Gaul, Pannonia, Illyricum, Dacia, and Moesia, but also across the vast stretches of forest, mountains, and steppe land of northern Europe that had never come directly under Roman rule. The historian Patrick Geary has traced this complex process of splintering, migration, and integration, in which the modern nations of Europe first reached their recognizable form. As he suggests, Franks, Goths, Lombards, Saxons, Avars, and Vandals (among many others) were not initially distinct or even recognizable peoples. They only gradually assumed their identities as the result of the crystallization of societies that were once blurred together by the Romans as "barbarians."

In many ways this process repeated the story of imperial disintegration and the emergence of new peoples and states that had taken place many times in history before. As we have seen earlier, the collapse of New Kingdom Egypt at the end of the Late Bronze Age was also accompanied by the movements and crystallization of peoples on the historical stage.

The rise of David in the highlands of Judah was one such development that spawned a long-lasting tradition. Based on the memories of a unique leader who emerged in a time of political and social crisis, it would be expanded and altered to serve as the focus of identity for an ever-changing community as it developed through the stages of chiefdom, kingdom, imperial vassal, and religious community. And as Christian missionaries spread through the peoples of Europe, bringing the good news of salvation to the Roman imperial subjects at a time when the empire was in an advanced state of disintegration, the tradition of David and Solomon was prominent in their sermons and their biblical tales.

The images of the great king and warrior—and psalmist—and of the wise and wealthy king who built the great city and the Temple lay in the background of the gospel stories. Yet it came increasingly to the fore as the bold and sometimes bloody tales of biblical Israel had greater impact on pagan proselytes than the parables of the gospels and the metaphorical interpretations of early Christian literature. Here and there bandit leaders gathered their coteries of followers around them, slowly and gradually seeing the advantage of the conversion to Christianity. Jesus himself remained seated in heaven, replacing the protecting gods that they had all previously known. David and Solomon, however, emerged as more tangible models for the kingdoms that they were building themselves.

And so new Davids arose to battle their people's fearsome enemies and snatch divine anointment from other contenders. New Solomons built rustic towns and imposing castles and churches across Europe, in which the biblical images of Jerusalem's kings were attractive, if impossibly dreamlike ideals. The story of David and Solomon thus inherited a place at the very heart of the new civilization of European Christendom. As the very model of righteous kingship with its human frailties and complexities, visions of grandeur and forgiveness, apocalyptic hopes, and its vivid moments of struggle and triumph, the images of David and Solomon— painted, sculpted, and placed in soaring stained-glass windows— would become as much a part of medieval and modern western traditions as the heroic folktales and legends of Europe itself.

Symbols of Authority

Medieval and Modern Images of David and Solomon

THE IMAGES OF DAVID AND SOLOMON IN MEDIEVAL European art are countless. The scenes of their lives and imaginative portraits exist in illuminated manuscripts and on frescoes, stained glass, stone, ivory, enamel, mosaic, textiles, and metalwork. In 2002, *The Index of Christian Art* published a catalogue of 245 scenes in which David regularly appears, in over five thousand examples from all across Europe, spanning every episode of the biblical story from his birth to his death. A similar accounting of the medieval artistic representations of Solomon would certainly add thousands more to the list. What is it about these two ancient figures that captured the imagination of so many generations of medieval craftsmen and so transfixed their patrons, both royal and ecclesiastical? To put it most simply, David and Solomon had come to represent a shared vision of pious Christian rule.

The story of the spread of this vision can now be traced only in surviving artworks and scattered literary references. Each represents a moment of self-reflection and recognition, in which the biblical stories of anointment, conquest, wealth, judgment, lust, and regret struck a deeply familiar chord. As we have seen, the David and Solomon tradition is by no means an accurate chronicle of tenth-century BCE Judah, but in its accumulated layers and reinterpretations it encompassed the collective wisdom and experience of centuries of observation and reflection about the nature of kingly power and national identity.

Carried to Europe in the stories and biblical manuscripts that accompanied Christian missionaries, and preserved by the scribes of monasteries and builders of cathedrals, the legend of David and Solomon beckoned to kings and prelates as a guidebook of church-crown relations. Great monarchs like Charlemagne could revel in David's stunning military achievements and in Solomon's incomparably wealthy and wisely ruled realm. The bejeweled crown of the Holy Roman Emperor Conrad II bore the cloisonné images of both David and Solomon. Bishops and prelates could call princes and monarchs all over Europe to repentance and contrition for impious behavior by evoking the lessons of David's adulterous affair with Bathsheba and Solomon's apostasy. In a delicate balance of earthly grandeur and spiritual submission, the David and Solomon saga both reflected and shaped a uniquely complex vision of the world.

That vision was not restricted to Europe. As Islam spread through the Near East, North Africa, and the Balkans, the image of David and Solomon also exerted a lasting impact in the consciousness of caliphs, sultans, and imams. The Quran had adopted a great deal from the biblical tradition, and both Daoud and Suleiman appear in the Islamic lore as noble kings and judges who precociously expressed the will of Allah. Suleiman, in particular, was regarded as one of the four greatest leaders in history, along with Nimrod, Nebuchadnezzar, and Alexander the Great. His magical powers and his encounter with the queen of Sheba (known in Arabic as Bilqis) were celebrated from Persia to Morocco in elaborate artworks, extensive literature, and popular folklore. As in their Jewish and Christian incarnations, Daoud and Suleiman personified the larger-than-life standards by which contemporary leaders would be judged.

By the high middle ages in Europe, the lineage of David and Solomon—depicted in the spidery "Trees of Jesse" ascending upward and entwining generations of biblical monarchs, Christian saints, and medieval princes on façades of soaring Gothic cathedrals and rising luminously in stained-glass windows—had come to express the divine right of kings and universalize the principle of hereditary rule. As in every stage of the evolution of the David and Solomon tradition, and in every place where it developed, the present was seen as the culmination of God's eternal plan and the defining models for European kingship itself.

Yet the story continued. In the Renaissance, a new vision of individual action and destiny changed the image of David from pious king to the muscular, aspiring youth, so familiar in Michelangelo's *David*. Still later, in the somber biblical paintings of Rembrandt and the other Old Masters, David and Saul become embodiments of personal conflict and introspection, whose virtues and vices would be left for final assessment by the viewer, rather than by the dogma of an established church. The images of David and Solomon have, in fact, never ceased evolving; they remain enigmatic but ever-present founding fathers for every generation's dreams of a golden age. Their story's power lies, ultimately, in its anticipation of a utopian future, whose meaning and form has been deeply shaped by the particular historical situation in which the David and Solomon story was ever sung, painted, or read.

Our challenge in this book has been to search for the historical David and Solomon and to utilize the tools of archaeology and history to trace the evolution of their biblical images through the millennia. Step by step we have suggested a reconstruction of complex historical processes by which the figures of David and Solomon became the focus of a complex and adaptable foundation legend that began in ancient Judah and ultimately spread throughout the western world. We have shown how the memories of the founders of Judah's Iron Age dynasty were reshaped to serve changing economic and social conditions. And we have described the centuries-long process in which the David and Solomon tradition was used to bolster the authority of Jewish and Christian religious ideologies—with David and Solomon ultimately becoming deeply ingrained western models for royal leadership and paradigms of the nation and the individual.

Archaeology's new vision of David and Solomon has allowed us to separate historical fact from its continuous reconstruction. History is full of accidents, and insistent quests for survival in the face of external threats and domestic upheavals. The accessibility and fluidity of the narrative elements in the David and Solomon tradition allowed it to be passed on and freely reinterpreted again and again. And there is no sign of an end to this process of veneration and transformation of their images.

We all live in a world of clashing nationalisms and global empire—the very themes that brought about the rise of the Davidic legend in eighth- and seventh-century BCE Judah, and two of the most important themes on which the David and Solomon story has been developed and reshaped time and again. Our perspective on those themes is uniquely modern. We no longer honestly hope for the resurrection of an Iron Age kingdom. We can no longer rely on messianic dreams to overcome our shared nightmares. And we can no longer rely on the divine right of kings as the justification for the acts of our leaders. And yet—because of our need for historical identity and our continuing quest to believe that noble leadership is possible—the David and Solomon story retains its power.

Understanding the process of the mythmaking about David and Solomon in no way questions the value of the tradition. On the contrary, it is of vital importance to appreciating our shared history and its role in shaping the biblical tradition of Judaism and Christianity. The figures of David and Solomon embody the foundation of the evolving civilization we live in, in its attempt to reconcile dreams of golden ages and ideal leaders with ever-changing political, social, and religious realities. In that sense—and in light of all the discoveries we have presented—archaeology has not destroyed or even dimmed the value of the ancient David and Solomon tradition. It has merely reshaped it once again.

APPENDIXES

Appendix 1

Did David Exist?

THE MINIMALISTS AND THE
TEL DAN INSCRIPTION

According to a certain school of thought within biblical studies—sometimes described as historical minimalism—the various David and Solomon stories, as well as the wider Deuteronomistic History, are late and largely fictional compositions motivated entirely by theology and containing only vague and quite unreliable historical information about the origins and early history of Israel.

Opinions differ among the minimalists about when ancient scribes wrote the Bible—from the Persian to the Hellenistic period (sometime between the fifth and the second centuries BCE)—but in any case they are confident that it took place many centuries after the kingdom of Judah ceased to exist.

The British scholar Philip Davies put the composition of the story into a clear political context. In his book *In Search of Ancient Israel* (1992), he sees the creation and compilation of the Deuteronomistic History as a long process, with the final form of the narrative probably being created in Hasmonean Judea during the second century BCE. "As an historical and literary creation," writes Davies, "the Bible . . . is a Hasmonaean concept." Davies depicted the authors of the biblical text as ideologues in service of the Temple establishment. Other minimalist scholars traced their ideology back to the political goals of the Judean priests and nobles who had returned from the Babylonian exile in the late sixth and fifth centuries BCE. These new leaders, the theory suggested, were loyal agents of the imperial power but they were also eager to bolster their position among the population that had remained in the land during the exile. As an imposed elite that had ousted the local leadership of Judah, they needed to create a history to legitimate their role. The Jerusalem scribes of the postexilic period thus supposedly collected folktales and vague memories and skillfully wove them into a wholly imaginary history that stressed the centrality of Jerusalem, its Temple, its cult, and its priests. It was a complete innovation, designed to establish a "national" myth of origin where none existed before. According to this premise, the Bible's story is not only historically baseless, but powerful, focused propaganda that sold an essentially made-up narrative of patriarchs, exodus, conquest, and the glorious golden age of David and Solomon to a credulous public in the Persian and Hellenistic periods.

What is the minimalist reconstruction of the history of the land of the Bible *before* the Bible? In his book *The Mythic Past* (2000), the American biblical scholar Thomas Thompson not only accepted the idea of a very late and almost entirely fictional history of Israel but also reinterpreted the archaeological evidence to reconstruct a multi-ethnic society in Iron Age Palestine with no distinctive religion or ethnic identity at all. It was a heterogeneous population split between regional centers at Jerusalem, Samaria, Megiddo, Lachish, and other cities. Its people cherished their own local heroes and worshiped a wide panoply of ancient Near Eastern deities. The Bible falsified that reality with its uncompromising theology of national sin and redemption. That was why, the minimalists argue, there can be no archaeological evidence of the united monarchy, much less evidence of a historical personality like David, because they were part of a religious mythology wholly made up by Judean scribes in the Persian and Hellenistic periods.

This revisionist theory has both logical and archaeological inconsistencies. First of all, the evidence of literacy and extensive scribal activity in Jerusalem in the Persian and early Hellenistic periods was hardly greater—in fact much smaller—than that relating to the eighth and seventh centuries BCE. To assume, as the minimalists do, that in the fifth or fourth or even second century BCE, the scribes of a small, out-of-the-way temple town in the Judean mountains compiled an extraordinarily long and detailed composition about the history, personalities, and events of an imaginary Iron Age "Israel" without using ancient sources was itself taking an enormous leap of faith.

The sheer number of name lists and details of royal administrative organization of the kingdom of Judah that are included in the Deuteronomistic History seem excessive or even unnecessary for a purely mythic history. Yet if they were all contrived or artificial, their coincidence with earlier realities is striking. Archaeological surveys have confirmed that many of the Bible's geographical listings—of the towns and villages of the tribes, of the districts of the kingdom—closely match settlement patterns and historical realities in the eighth and seventh centuries BCE.

Equally important, a relatively large number of extrabiblical historical records—mainly Assyrian—verify ninth-to-seventh-century BCE events described in the Bible. And no less significant, much of the Deuteronomistic History is written in late monarchic Hebrew, different from the Hebrew of postexilic times.

Can archaeology show that David and Solomon are historical figures? Even as the scholarly debate raged on, a discovery at the excavations of the ancient site of Tel Dan in northern Israel, near one of the sources of the Jordan River, altered the nature of the debate over the historical existence of David and Solomon.

A STONE FROM TEL DAN

Tel Dan is a biblical site excavated for many years by the veteran Israeli archaeologist Avraham Biran and has been conclusively identified with Dan, the northernmost city of the kingdom of Israel. The excavations there revealed extensive sections of the Middle Bronze and Iron Age cities and uncovered a massive platform on which, it was supposed, sacrifices had been offered by Israelite priests and kings. Located far from Jerusalem, Dan would not be expected to offer much new evidence for an increasingly acrimonious debate over the historical existence of David and Solomon. But on July 21, 1993, Gila Cook, the surveyor for the Dan project, was working in a large open plaza outside the outer city gate of the Israelite city. A wall built of cracked and tumbled stones taken from earlier buildings marked the edge of the plaza. In the late afternoon sun, as she glanced at the wall's rough construction, she spotted ancient writing on the smooth surface of one of the reused building stones.

It was a fragment of a triumphal inscription written in Aramaic, its ancient letters chiseled in black basalt. In the following year, two more fragments of the stele were discovered, altogether preserving thirteen lines of a longer royal declaration that had been set up in a public square. The king it commemorates was most probably Hazael, ruler of Aram Damascus, who was known both from the Bible and Assyrian records as an important international player in the late ninth century BCE. His battles against Israel are recorded in the book of Kings, yet here in a contemporary inscription, translated according to the epigrapher Joseph Naveh and Avraham Biran, the voice of King Hazael himself was heard once again:

1. [. . .   . . .] and cut [. . .   ]
2. [. . .] my father went up [against him when] he fought at [. . .]
3. And my father lay down, he went to his [ancestors]. And the king of I[s-]

4. rael entered previously in my father's land. [And] Hadad made me king.

5. And Hadad went in front of me, [and] I departed from [the] seven [. . . -]

6. s of my kingdom, and I slew [seve]nty kin[gs], who harnessed thou[sands of cha-]

7. riots and thousands of horsemen (*or* horses). [I killed Jeho]ram son of [Ahab]

8. king of Israel, and [I] killed [Ahaz]iahu son of [Jehoram kin-]

9. g of the **House of David.** And I set [their towns into ruins and turned]

10. their land into [desolation . . .   ]

11. other [. . .   and Jehu ru-]

12. led over Is[rael . . .   and I laid]

13. siege upon [. . .   ]

Though highly fragmentary and heavily reconstructed by Naveh and Biran, this inscription offers a unique perspective on the turbulent politics of the region in the ninth century BCE. It records, from the Aramean side, the territorial conflict between Israel and Damascus that led to frequent attacks and devastation. It tells how Hazael (described as the "son of a nobody" in an Assyrian source) launched a punishing offensive against his southern enemies.

In words chiseled into the stone around 835 BCE, Hazael claimed to have killed the king of Israel and his ally, the king of the "House of David." It is the first use of the name David in any source outside the Bible, in this case only about a century after David's own time. It most probably refers to the deaths of King Jehoram of Israel and Ahaziah of the "House of David." The minimalists' contention that biblical history was a late and wholly creative composition and that David was a fictional figure was dealt a serious blow.

The "House of David" inscription, as it has come to be called, testifies to the existence of a line of kings who as early as the ninth century BCE traced their legitimacy back to David. Hazael used the common genre of his period, of referring to a state after the name of the founder of its ruling dynasty. But the mention of the royal name—though confirming the existence of a dynastic founder named David, offers no new information about the man himself. There is also a conflict with the narrative in the Bible. The biblical authors report in 2 Kings 9:14–27 that Jehoram and Ahaziah had indeed died at the same time, but they ascribed their deaths to an entirely different cause—not Hazael, but a violent coup d'etat by the Israelite general (and later king) Jehu. Biblical historians rationalized the discrepancy by suggesting that Jehu was merely a vassal of Hazael. But something far more complex seems to be involved here—and once again it concerns the tension between historical reality and biblical myth.

A faded memory of a shocking historical event—the sudden, almost simultaneous deaths of Jehoram and Ahaziah—survived through the centuries even as its specific historical context in ninth-century politics became vague and eventually forgotten. The survival of the memory, though transformed into a somewhat different scenario in the Bible, testifies to a continuing collective memory of ancient Israel, later incorporated into the text of the Deuteronomistic History. In short, the Tel Dan inscription provides an independent witness to the historical existence of a dynasty founded by a ruler named David, from just a few generations after the era in which he presumably lived.

Appendix 2

The Search for David and Solomon's Jerusalem

EXCAVATIONS, THE BIBLE, AND THE ARCHAEOLOGICAL EVIDENCE

Jerusalem has always been a primary focus for the archaeological search for David and Solomon. For centuries, pilgrims, explorers, and antiquarians had been drawn to the city of Jerusalem to visit the traditional religious shrines and to search for authentic traces of David's citadel and Solomon's fabled monuments. Throughout the biblical narrative, Jerusalem is the place where David and Solomon's most glorious achievements were celebrated and where their most memorable acts occurred. From the time of David's conquest of the city in a daring assault in an underground water tunnel (2 Samuel 5:6–8), through his residence in the city's "stronghold" and his bringing the Ark of the Covenant to Jerusalem (2 Samuel 6), to Solomon's massive project to build there a great palace and a holy Temple (1 Kings 7–8), Jerusalem was the sacred stage on which their biblical drama was played out.

Some sites in Jerusalem have been connected with David as the result of folktales—and have no historical basis. The traditional

Tomb of David on Mount Zion is a medieval structure. The famous Tower of David near the Jaffa Gate, long an icon for Jewish aspirations to return to the city, was actually built in the sixteenth century, by Sultan Suleiman the Magnificent, as a minaret for the city's Ottoman garrison. But with its wealth of ancient remains, buried or obscured by modern buildings, Jerusalem has never lacked explorers intent on discovering authentic, if hidden, evidence of David and Solomon's glorious reigns.

Dominating the ruins, bazaars, and clustered domes of the Old City of Jerusalem is the massive Temple platform constructed in the first century BCE by Herod the Great on the site of earlier Jewish Temples. The first of these, according to the Bible, was the Temple of Solomon. Yet the holiness of the site both to Jews and to Muslims (as the location of the Dome of the Rock and the el-Aqsa mosque) and the sheer extent and size of the remains of the later Herodian Temple have posed a nearly insurmountable obstacle to the hope of locating remains here from the time of David and Solomon.

One of the first modern excavators in Jerusalem, Captain Charles Warren of the British Royal Engineers, led an expedition for the Palestine Exploration Fund in 1867–70, risking his life and the lives of his men by excavating deep shafts alongside the massive walls of the Herodian enclosure, to search for traces of the earlier Solomonic sanctuary. Warren thoroughly examined the substructures and complex of ancient buildings attached to the Herodian platform to produce the first detailed plan of the area, but it became clear that the later remains had completely covered and probably obliterated any earlier structures built on this sacred site. So here on the Temple Mount, at least, the archaeological search for David and Solomon reached a dead end.

DIGGING IN THE CITY OF DAVID

As archaeological research in Jerusalem continued and expanded, it became clear that the best location for finding archaeological remains from the time of David and Solomon was not on the Temple Mount or among the close-packed buildings within the walled Ottoman city, but on a narrow, steep ridge that extended South of the Temple Mount, beyond the walls. This area was identified as early as the nineteenth century as the "Ophel," or the "City of David" mentioned repeatedly in the biblical text. Indeed, this is the tell, or ancient mound, containing layers of accumulation and structures from Bronze and Iron Age Jerusalem. This ridge became the scene of large-scale excavations throughout the twentieth century.

The ancient remains uncovered here have always been quite fragmentary. Each of the major excavators in this part of Jerusalem— Raymond Weill (1913–14; 1923–25), Robert Alexander Stewart Macalister and Garrow Duncan (1923–25), John Winter Crowfoot and Gerald M. Fitzgerald (1925–27), Kathleen Kenyon (1961–67), and Yigal Shiloh (1978–84)—argued that because of the steepness of the slope and the destructive force of continuous erosion, the full extent of the Davidic city had been lost. Still, here and there among the various excavation areas, they found deposits of pottery or isolated architectural elements that they connected to the time of David, in the tenth century BCE: the possible podium of David's royal stronghold; the underground water shaft through which he and his men conquered the city; and the supposed tombs of David, Solomon, and other Judahite monarchs. However, these claims were based on a kind of circular reasoning. Beginning with the assumption that the biblical narratives were reliable historical sources, the researchers identified these ruins as features mentioned in the Bible. And they used the hypothetical identifications as archaeological "proof" that the biblical descriptions were true.

A prime example is the so-called "Stepped Stone Structure," first uncovered in the 1920s. It is an imposing rampart of fifty-eight courses of limestone boulders, extending for more than fifty feet, like a protective sheath or reinforcement over the upper end of the eastern slope of the City of David. Later excavations by Kenyon and by Shiloh discovered a network of stone terraces beneath it, probably constructed in order to stabilize and expand the narrow flat surface on the spine of the ridge, and perhaps to support a large structure built there. The early excavators suggested that the Stepped Stone Structure was part of the fortification of the Jebusite city that David conquered. Kenyon and Shiloh believed that it was evidence of substantial building activity in the tenth century, at the time of David and Solomon—perhaps even part of the enigmatic feature described in the Bible as the Millo (2 Samuel 5:9).

Yet the pottery retrieved from within the courses of the Stepped Stone Structure included types from the Early Iron Age to the ninth or even early eighth centuries BCE. It seems therefore that this monument was constructed at least a century later than the days of David and Solomon. Who used it, when exactly, and for what purpose still remains—archaeologically, at least—a mystery. The most that can be said, and even this is not absolutely clear, is that some of the terraces beneath it were in use in the tenth century.

Another important discovery in this area has been related to David's cunning conquest of Jerusalem via an underground water shaft, mentioned in an enigmatic biblical passage:

> *And the king and his men went to Jerusalem against the Jebusites, the inhabitants of the land, who said to David, "You will not come in here, but the blind and the lame will ward you off"—thinking, "David cannot come in here." Nevertheless David took the stronghold of Zion, that is, the city of David. And David said on that day, "Whoever would smite the Jebusites, let him get up the water shaft to attack the lame and the blind, who are hated by David's soul." Therefore it is said, "The blind and the lame shall not come into the house." (2 Samuel 5:6–8)*

In 1867, the British explorer Charles Warren investigated an underground water system on the upper, eastern slope of the City of
David, not far from the Stepped Stone Structure. He found that it
led through a system of two shafts and a horizontal tunnel, over fifty
meters long and around thirty meters deep, to the area of
Jerusalem's only permanent source of freshwater, the Gihon spring,
located in the Valley of Kidron at the foot of the slope. Such an
underground water system is by no means unique in the ancient
Near East, since one of the most severe problems that faced the
inhabitants of even modest-sized cities was how to protect access to
springs outside the fortifications during times of siege. The most
sophisticated solution was to create a covered passage from the city
to the spring, usually by cutting an underground tunnel.

Many biblical scholars have proposed that this was the very water
shaft that David used to conquer the city in an act of heroic surprise.
But the dating of "Warren's shaft" has proved extremely difficult.
Recent research on the eastern slope of the City of David by the
Israeli archaeologists Ronnie Reich and Eli Shukron has indicated
that Warren's shaft was cut and extended over hundreds of years. It
was first hewn in the Middle Bronze Age (2000–1550 BCE) and then
expanded in late monarchic times, in the eighth century BCE. With
such a long history, this find cannot prove that the biblical story of
David's conquest of Jerusalem reflects a historical reality, but rather
could be a folktale that developed in later periods to explain the origin of the system of shafts and tunnels on the eastern slope of the
ridge. The ending of the biblical story with the words "Therefore it
is said" seems to support this explanation of a folk etiology.

THE TOMB OF THE EARLY
DAVIDIC KINGS?

Another questionable relic was a half-destroyed feature cut from the
bedrock that has been identified by some scholars with the resting

place of many members of the Davidic dynasty. The original tomb of David—as distinguished from the medieval shrine on Mount Zion—is indirectly mentioned in the biblical narrative, in the repeated reports about David, Solomon, and later kings of Judah, that each "was buried with his fathers in the City of David." In the early twentieth century, the French scholar Raymond Weill uncovered a series of artificial caves cut in the bedrock near the southern tip of the City of David and found two unusual barrel-shaped chambers, whose front portions had been quarried away. Weill interpreted these structures as remains of the tombs of the kings of Judah. Several other scholars, including the Israeli biblical historian and archaeologist Benjamin Mazar, specifically related them to David and Solomon.

This interpretation has been questioned in light of a growing archaeological familiarity with the characteristic tomb types of the noble Jerusalem families in the Iron Age, some of which are known from the Siloam cemetery facing the City of David on the east. The rock-cut features excavated by Weill bear no similarity to the single- or multiple-chamber family tombs of Judahite nobility in various phases of the Iron Age. Of course, the royal tombs of Judah may have been unique, but at present, the empty rock-cut chambers in the City of David are more a mystery than conclusive proof of anything.

ABSENCE OF EVIDENCE, OR EVIDENCE OF ABSENCE?

As we noted earlier, both early and modern scholars proposed that the main archaeological remains of David and Solomon's Jerusalem were located at the very summit of the ridge, in the area now covered by the Temple Mount, and that the massive construction activities undertaken there by King Herod the Great in Roman times covered or obliterated every trace of this settlement. Yet if this was a bustling royal capital with intense daily activity, at least some of its refuse would have been preserved. The slopes of every ancient city mound in the Near East served as dumps for the garbage of the ancient inhabitants, and thick layers of bones, building material, and broken potsherds are found outside the walls. Yet thorough, large-scale excavations on the slope to the south and southwest of the Temple Mount have failed to find more than a scatter of potsherds from the tenth century BCE.

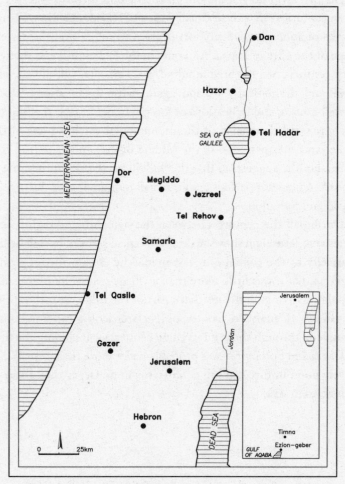

Sites connected to the debate over the archaeology of the united monarchy

The archaeological results in this part of Jerusalem have been impressive, but they do not mesh with the chronology of the biblical narrative. Although the site was occupied continuously from the Chalcolithic period (in the fourth millennium BCE) to the present, there were only two periods of major building and expansion before Roman times—and neither could possibly be identified with the reigns of David and Solomon. In the Middle Bronze Age, six or seven centuries *before* the estimated time of David, massive walls and towers of an impressive city fortification were built on the eastern slope of the City of David. And only in the late eighth and the seventh century, two to three hundred years *after* David, did the city grow and dramatically expand again, with fortifications, close-packed houses, and indications of foreign trade. In fact, the impressively preserved remains of the monumental fortifications of the earlier and later periods—of the Middle Bronze and Late Iron II—contradict the suggestion that the building activities in the time of Herod and in later periods eradicated all monuments of the time of David and Solomon.

During all the centuries between the sixteenth and eighth centuries BCE, Jerusalem shows no archaeological signs of having been a great city or the capital of a vast monarchy. The evidence clearly suggests that it was little more than a village—inhabited by a small population living on the northern part of the ridge, near the spring of Gihon. If analyzed from a purely archaeological standpoint, Jerusalem, through those intervening centuries—including the time of David and Solomon—was probably never more than a small, relatively poor, unfortified hill country town, no larger than three or four acres in size.

Appendix 3

Solomon's Fabled Kingdom

THE ARCHAEOLOGY OF MEGIDDO, HAZOR, AND GEZER

THE CLUE OF THE CITY GATES

The difficulty of excavating in Jerusalem for archaeological evidence of the united monarchy eventually turned scholarly attention to the sites of three important ancient cities—Hazor, Megiddo, and Gezer—that are specifically mentioned in the Bible in connection with King Solomon's ambitious building activities (I Kings 9:15).

Megiddo was the first of these cities to become the scene of intensive archaeological excavations. Located at the edge of the Jezreel Valley, on the international highway from Egypt to Anatolia and Mesopotamia, Megiddo was an important strategic spot throughout all of its history. Uncovering the city levels from Solomon's time has always been high on the agenda of its excavators. In the 1920s, in the course of excavations by the Oriental Institute of the University of Chicago, remains were indeed identified as representing the time of Solomon.

Close to the surface of the mound, the University of Chicago team uncovered two sets of large public buildings sharing a characteristic plan. Each was composed of a series of long, rectangular

275

structures attached to one another in a row. Each of the individual structures featured three long aisles separated by rows of alternating stone pillars and stone basins. (See figure on p. 165.) The expedition director Philip Langstaffe Orde Guy identified these buildings as stables and dated them to the time of Solomon. His interpretation was based on the connection that he made between the pillared buildings, the reference to the building activity of Solomon at Megiddo in 1 Kings 9:15, and the mention of Solomon's cities for chariots and horsemen in 1 Kings 9:19.

In the mid-1950s, Yigael Yadin of the Hebrew University began excavations at Hazor, another of the cities mentioned in the account of Solomon's reign. Hazor is the largest ancient mound in Israel, located north of the Sea of Galilee, with layers of occupation stretching back to the Early Bronze Age. In one of the excavation areas Yadin and his team uncovered a large city gate dating to the Iron Age. On each side of the gateway were three chambers arranged in a row, fronted by a tower. Yadin immediately recognized the similarity of this gate—in both layout and size—to a gate that had been uncovered at Megiddo (see figure on p. 160) and saw this similarity as a possible confirmation of the biblical verse mentioning Solomon's activities at "Hazor and Megiddo and Gezer."

What was the situation at Gezer, the third city mentioned, which is a large site strategically located in the Valley of Aijalon, guarding the road from the coast to Jerusalem? Yadin went to dig Gezer—not in the field, but in the library—in the excavation reports of the early-twentieth-century British archaeologist R. A. S. Macalister, who published three thick volumes describing his finds. Yadin paged through the excavation plans in the Macalister report and was stunned to see a plan of what Macalister (incorrectly) described as a "Maccabean Castle." Within it was a pattern of walls that seemed identical to one side of the Megiddo and Hazor gates. Yadin was now fully convinced that 1 Kings 9:15 was a reliable description of Solomonic building activities. He theorized that a royal architect from Jerusalem drew a master plan for the Solomonic city gates, and this master plan was followed by the builders of the provincial centers of Hazor, Megiddo, and Gezer—as demonstrated by the archaeological finds.

FORTIFICATION WALLS AND PALACES

Yadin's ingenious theory was haunted by a major problem: the gates were attached to different kinds of fortifications. Two types of city walls were constructed at various times in the Iron Age. One type is a solid stone or brick wall with insets and offsets; the other is composed of a linked series of chambers and is known as a casemate wall. The problem was that at Hazor and Gezer the six-chambered gates were connected to a casemate wall, while the Megiddo gate was connected to a solid wall—thus calling into question the theory of a single Solomonic master plan. Convinced that the earlier Megiddo excavators had missed an underlying casemate wall (presumably the original fortification built with the gate), Yadin decided to go to Megiddo with a new excavation team in order to recheck the archaeological stratigraphy.

Yadin chose an area to the east of the gate where the University of Chicago team had uncovered one of the sets of "stables" linked to the solid city wall, which was in turn connected to the gate. Under the stables and solid wall, he discovered a beautiful palace built of large ashlar blocks, with a row of rooms on both sides. It was built on the edge of the mound and although the outer row of rooms was much different in shape from the typical casemate walls of the Iron Age, he interpreted it as the "missing" casemate wall that was originally (at least according to his theory) built with the six-chambered gate.

With the discovery of this edifice, Yadin turned his attention to a roughly similar palace, also built of beautiful dressed blocks, uncovered by the earlier Oriental Institute team on the southern side of the mound. This palace too lay under the city of the "stables" and thus Yadin believed that he had identified yet another of Solomon's magnificent palaces at Megiddo—an apparent manifestation of the grandeur of the Solomonic state.

This city of palaces was destroyed in a conflagration, which Yadin attempted to link with a specific historical event: the military campaign of Pharaoh Shishak in Palestine in the fifth year of King Rehoboam—the son of King Solomon (supposedly 926 BCE). This campaign (which we analyzed in chapter 2) is mentioned in the Bible (1 Kings 14:25–26) and recorded on one of the walls of the temple of Amun at Karnak in Upper Egypt. Megiddo is specifically mentioned in the Karnak list, and indeed, a fragment of a stele that was erected by Shishak at Megiddo was discovered at the site (unfortunately not in a stratified or dated context).

So archaeology seemed to fit the biblical testimony perfectly. The Bible recounts the building activities of Solomon at Hazor, Megiddo, and Gezer; surely, the similar gates discovered at the three cities revealed that they were built together, on a unified plan. The Bible says that Solomon was an ally of King Hiram of Tyre and that he was a great builder; indeed, the layout and masonry of the magnificent Megiddo palaces seemed to show northern influence, and were among the most beautiful edifices discovered in the Iron Age strata in Israel. The Bible says that Pharaoh Shishak campaigned in Israel and Judah right after the death of King Solomon; and lo and behold, Solomon's city at Megiddo was destroyed in an intense conflagration and a stele of Shishak was found at the site. From that moment on, the entire reconstruction of the history and material culture of the Solomonic state rested on these finds.

Yet this harmonized archaeological image of a golden age of the united monarchy did not last long. Two decades after Yadin demonstrated an apparently perfect match between Bible and archaeology, the various elements of the theory started to crumble, one by one.

A QUESTION OF DATING

The first to go down were the gates. A detailed study of the Megiddo gate by David Ussishkin showed that it was built later than the gates of Hazor and Gezer. In addition, similar gates were found in much later periods and at clearly non-Israelite sites, among them Philistine Ashdod. Even the basis for the dating of the Solomonic levels was shown to be the result of circular logic: the pottery and other artifacts found in the gate levels were dated to the tenth century BCE *because* of the association of the gates with the biblical verse about the building project of King Solomon. Later ardent defenders of the "Solomonic grandeur" theory simply forgot about this circular reasoning when they argued that the biblical verse (and the great Solomonic kingdom) *must* be historical, since the gates and other impressive structures were found in levels dating from the tenth century BCE!

New data from ongoing excavations in Israel and a reanalysis of old finds undermined the rest of Yadin's basis for "Solomonic" archaeology. Less than ten miles to the east of Megiddo is the site of Jezreel, the location of a palace of the Omride dynasty, described in the Bible as the scene of the bloody coup that brought this dynasty down (2 Kings 9). The historical existence of the Omrides is supported by Assyrian records and the evidence of the Mesha and Tel Dan stelae. Jezreel was excavated in the 1990s by David Ussishkin and John Woodhead, who uncovered a large fortified enclosure that they readily identified as an Omride royal compound, strikingly similar in conception to the royal acropolis of Samaria, the capital of the Omride dynasty. The Jezreel compound was destroyed and abandoned soon after its construction—either due to internal political changes in the kingdom or as a result of a military attack by the Arameans on northern Israel, both of which took place, according to historical records, around the middle of the ninth century BCE.

Surprisingly, the pottery types found in the Jezreel compound are identical to the pottery of the city of the ashlar palaces at

Megiddo, which was supposed to have been destroyed by Pharaoh Shishak almost a century *before* the fall of the Omrides. Could it be that Yadin's "Solomonic" city at Megiddo was in fact an Omride city, built and destroyed in the ninth century BCE, like Jezreel, long after the time of Solomon?

Other, clear evidence points to that conclusion. The first clue comes from Samaria, the capital of the Omride kingdom, located in the highlands about twenty miles to the south of Megiddo. We have already mentioned the similarity of the Jezreel and Samaria royal compounds, but there is another architectural link. The excavations at Samaria, initially carried out in the early twentieth century by an expedition from Harvard University, uncovered the foundations of a large palace built of ashlar blocks in the center of the elevated royal acropolis. The excavators identified it as the royal palace of the Omride dynasty, constructed in the first half of the ninth century BCE.*

There are unmistakable similarities in the building methods between the Samaria palace and at least one of the two Megiddo palaces. These similarities were first noted by the early excavators Clarence Fisher (at Samaria and Megiddo) and John Crowfoot (at Samaria) but were subsequently forgotten after the wide acceptance of Yadin's Solomonic theory. However, Norma Franklin of Tel Aviv University has recently revived the comparison with important new evidence: the ashlar blocks in the palace at Samaria and the southern palace at Megiddo bear similar masons' marks unknown at any other Iron Age sites in Israel. It is likely that they were built at the same time, probably by the same team of masons—working under the auspices of the Omride dynasty, *not* Solomon.

Finally, in the last few years, radiocarbon dating has hammered the final nail into the coffin of the Solomonic mirage. Carbon 14

---

* The Bible specifically attributes the building of the capital Samaria to Omri, Ahab's father (1 Kings 16:24). This is supported by extrabiblical evidence: the Assyrians referred to the northern kingdom as the house of Omri, acknowledging the fact that he was the founder of the capital of Israel.

samples from major sites involved in the united monarchy debate (including Dor on the coast, Tel Rehov in the Jordan Valley south of Beth-shean, Tel Hadar on the eastern shore of the Sea of Galilee, and Rosh Zayit near Akko, Hazor, and Megiddo) have been submitted for testing and analysis. The samples came from numerous grain seeds and olive stones found in levels that were traditionally linked with the Davidic conquests and the Solomonic kingdom of the tenth century BCE.

The results were stunning. Almost all of the samples produced dates lower, that is, later, than the widely accepted dates of the conquests of David and the united monarchy of King Solomon. Destruction layers that had previously been dated to around 1000 BCE and linked to the conquests of King David provided dates in the mid–tenth century BCE—the supposed time of King Solomon if not a bit later. And the destruction layers that had traditionally been dated to the late tenth century BCE and linked to the campaign of Pharaoh Shishak after the breakdown of the united monarchy provided dates in the mid–ninth century BCE—almost a century later.

Thus the conventional view on the archaeology of the united monarchy was wrong by almost a century. In historical terms, this means that the cities assumed to have been conquered by David were still centers of Canaanite culture throughout the time of his presumed reign in Jerusalem. And the monuments that have traditionally been attributed to Solomon and seen as symbols of the greatness of his state were in fact built by the kings of the Omride dynasty of the northern kingdom of Israel, who ruled in the first half of the ninth century BCE. Archaeology, therefore, far from proving the historical reliability of the biblical narratives, has forced us to undertake a far-reaching reevaluation of the nature of tenth-century society in Judah and Israel.

Appendix 4

King Solomon's Copper Industry?

ARCHAEOLOGY AND THE PROSPERITY OF THE UNITED MONARCHY

Between the 1930s and the 1950s the biblical references to copper smelting and production of copper vessels for the Temple led to a major effort in the search for the historical Solomon. Archaeologists who accepted the biblical description at face value tried to locate the precise sources of Solomon's copper ores and sites connected with his smelting industry. This quest was localized around Timna, in the south of modern Israel.

The first investigations on this subject were undertaken by the American archaeologist Nelson Glueck, who conducted large-scale surveys and excavations in Transjordan and the Negev desert. Considering that Solomon's port of Ezion-geber (mentioned in the Bible as a major trade emporium of the united monarchy) was located at the northern tip of the Gulf of Aqaba, Glueck focused his search for Solomon's copper mines at Timna, only fifteen miles to the north.

Fieldwork conducted at Timna by Glueck, and later by the Israeli archaeologist Beno Rothenberg, showed that it was indeed a major source of copper in antiquity. Copper mines and smelting sites dating to different periods, from the Chalcolithic period in the fourth millennium BCE to the early Islamic period, were discovered in the Timna Valley and its immediate surroundings. Glueck was convinced that many of these mines and installations dated to the time of Solomon.

Glueck then examined the possible relationship to the nearby site of Tell el-Kheleifeh, a few miles to the west of the modern port of Aqaba, which was identified in the 1930s with the biblical Ezion-geber. Indeed this is the only possibility, as no other Iron Age site is known in this region and decades of intensive explorations around Aqaba in Jordan and south of Eilat in Israel have failed to yield any pre-Roman remains.

Glueck excavated Tell el-Kheleifeh between 1938 and 1940 and uncovered much of the site. He separated the remains into five periods of activity and dated them from the tenth to the fifth century BCE, identifying each according to biblical references to Ezion-geber and Elath. Every monarch who was mentioned in relation to activities in the Gulf of Aqaba was granted a stratum. And Glueck interpreted the remains of the first period—including what he described as flue holes, air channels, hand bellows, clay crucibles, and furnace rooms—as evidence for a huge copper smelting industry in the days of King Solomon. Glueck even went so far as to dub Ezion-geber the "Pittsburgh of Palestine" and King Solomon "a copper king, a shipping magnate, a merchant prince, and a great builder."

This romantic image later proved to be baseless—a wishful illusion based more on the biblical text than on any real archaeological evidence. The intensive research in the Timna Valley conducted by Beno Rothenberg in the 1960s, which included surveys and excavations of smelting sites, failed to reveal any evidence for tenth-century BCE activity. There was a strong phase of mining in the time of the Egyptian New Kingdom, until the twelfth century BCE, then a gap and renewal of activity during Roman times. Nothing was found from the days of King Solomon.

Tell el-Kheleifeh's relation to Solomon's copper industry also proved to be a fantasy. A thorough study of the finds for their final publication by the American scholar Garry Pratico and investigation by other scholars have found no evidence whatsoever for smelting activity at the site. The "crucibles" found at the site proved to be sherds of locally produced handmade pottery vessels; the "flue holes" were no more than holes for wooden beams that had rotted away; and there were only a few metal finds—certainly not evidence of an active smelting industry. No less important, it became clear that the site was established only in the late eighth or early seventh century BCE. The elaborate stratigraphy of successive copper kings and their industrial center simply did not exist. At the time of the historical Solomon in the tenth century BCE, this place near the shore of the Gulf of Aqaba was no more than a sand dune.

Appendix 5

Dismantling the Shrines

ARCHAEOLOGICAL EVIDENCE OF CULT
CENTRALIZATION IN THE TIME OF HEZEKIAH

Biblical scholars have long debated the historicity of the Bible's description of the reform of the Temple cult that took place during the reign of Hezekiah (2 Kings 18:3–4; 2 Chronicles 29–31). Literary studies of the texts—especially regarding the relationship between the differing narratives in Kings and Chronicles, their similarity to descriptions of the later cult reform of Josiah, and to the Deuteronomic laws requiring the eradication of pagan Canaanite cult objects—have not led to a decisive answer about the historical nature of the reported religious reform. Yet important archaeological evidence about possible changes in cultic practice during the monarchic period has come from the two southern sites of Arad and Beer-sheba and from the site of Lachish in the Shephelah (all three excavated by Yohanan Aharoni), where evidence for regional Judahite cult activity has been found.

A Judahite sanctuary with altar and open courtyard was discovered in the Iron Age fortress of Arad, yet its dating has long been a matter of dispute. Aharoni dated its construction to the tenth century BCE and suggested that it went out of use in two stages: the large altar was removed in the late eighth century BCE, in the course of Hezekiah's cult reform (Stratum VIII), and the shrine was closed and dismantled a century later, in the time of Josiah (Stratum VI), thus closely fitting the biblical description of the two most famous cult reforms in the history of Judah. The Arad excavation team later revised this historical reconstruction, suggesting that while the complex was built in the tenth century BCE, both the altar and the shrine were removed in the days of Hezekiah. The historian Nadav Na'aman proposed that the shrine continued to be in use throughout the time of Hezekiah.

In the course of the preparation of the Arad finds for final publication, one of the expedition members, Zeev Herzog, revised the stratigraphy and chronology of the Arad sanctuary. In his opinion the sanctuary had *not* been founded in the tenth century BCE and continued in use over three centuries, but had functioned only for a short period of time in the eighth century BCE (Strata X–IX). According to Herzog, both altar and shrine were dismantled at the same time—in the late eighth century—and buried under a one-meter fill. Thus the fort of the very late eighth century BCE (Stratum VIII)—the one conquered by Sennacherib in 701 BCE—did not have a sanctuary. It had presumably been removed in the course of Hezekiah's cult reforms.

Herzog presented clear evidence for his interpretation: walls and floors of Stratum VIII of the late eighth century were built over the sanctuary after it had gone out of use; the pottery on the floors dates to the eighth, rather than the seventh century BCE, and the Strata VII—VI floors in the vicinity of the sanctuary are two meters higher than the floor of the sanctuary of the shrine. Without ignoring the methodological problems related to the dig at Arad and the immense difficulties in interpreting the stratigraphy of the site, it seems to us that Herzog's reconstruction is the most convincing and suggests an intentional change in cultic ritual at Arad during the reign of Hezekiah, in the years before Sennacherib's attack in 701 BCE.

The finds from Beer-sheba and Lachish seem to support this

interpretation. At Beer-sheba, a large horned altar built of ashlar blocks was dismantled, with its stones buried in the city's fortification ramparts and reused in the pillared storehouses built in the late eighth century BCE (Stratum II). Aharoni suggested that the altar originally stood in a sanctuary. Since no such building was discovered at the site, he proposed that it had been completely and intentionally eradicated during the construction of the buildings of Stratum II. Thus Aharoni interpreted this evidence as supporting the biblical description of Hezekiah's cult reform, since the Beer-sheba sanctuary was supposedly destroyed and the stones of its altar buried and reused early in Hezekiah's reign.

The biblical historian Nadav Na'aman raised objections against Aharoni's interpretation, mainly concerning the original place of the altar. Yet regardless of the question of the location of the sanctuary, the finds at Beer-sheba seem to parallel those at Arad. An altar that had functioned in the eighth century (Stratum III) was dismantled at the very end of the century (Stratum II). This would have taken place during Hezekiah's reign, since Stratum II was destroyed during the campaign of Sennacherib in 701 BCE.

Lachish also provided evidence of changes of cult practice in the late eighth century BCE. Although Aharoni interpreted a stone altar and cult vessels as evidence of a Judahite sanctuary from the tenth century BCE, David Ussishkin recently reexamined the results of Aharoni's excavations and came to utterly different conclusions. According to his analysis, the cult objects linked by Aharoni to a hypothesized tenth-century sanctuary were actually deposited in a pit that was sealed by the construction of a vast late-eighth-century courtyard (Level III). He dated the vessels themselves to the ninth and early eighth centuries BCE (Level IV) and suggested that the sanctuary from which they had come went out of use sometime in the eighth century BCE and the pit into which they were dumped was covered by structures built during Hezekiah's reign.

The finds at Arad, Beer-sheba, and Lachish thus seem to point to a similar picture: all three sites show evidence for the existence of

Judahite sanctuaries in the eighth century BCE, but in all three the sanctuaries fell into disuse before the end of the eighth century. In other words, in all three the city that was destroyed by Sennacherib in 701 did not have a shrine, which suggests that a cult reform did indeed occur throughout Judah in the time of Hezekiah.

Tyrants, City Leagues, and Mercenary Bodyguards

ADDITIONAL SEVENTH-CENTURY BCE GREEK
CULTURAL TRAITS IN THE BIBLICAL STORIES
OF THE PHILISTINES

In addition to the seventh-century BCE Greek realities hidden in the story of the duel between David and Goliath, other details in the depiction of the Philistines in the Deuteronomistic History point to the same historical and cultural context.

THE LORDS OF THE PHILISTINES

The first is the use of the term *seranim* for the leaders of the Philistines (for example, 1 Samuel 5:8, 11; 6:4, 12, 16; 7:7)—an unusual term that is translated as "rulers" or "lords." In some cases the Bible speaks about five *seranim*, and in one place (Joshua 13:3), it specifically refers to a league of five Philistine cities, which scholars have labeled as the "Philistine Pentapolis." The term *seren/seranim* does not have a Semitic derivation and therefore is presumed to have been a Philistine word that was adopted into Hebrew. Scholars have usually connected it etymologically with the Greek word *tyrannos*, meaning "tyrant," which first appears in the seventh century BCE. *Tyrannos* was probably derived from the older Anatolian word, *tarwanis*, meaning "governor," which was later introduced into Greek.

However, there is a problem in this presumed chain of transmission since the biblical term *seren* has traditionally been dated to the Iron I period, several centuries *before* the appearance of the Greek *tyrannos*. Yet if we date the biblical use of the word *seren* in the seventh century BCE when the Deuteronomistic History was compiled, the problem is resolved: the title *tyrannos* developed in western Asia Minor in the seventh century BCE and the Hebrew form *seren* was derived from it and was incorporated into the Deuteronomistic History. It may not be a coincidence that the first ruler to be referred to as *tyrannos* in Greek literature was Gyges king of Lydia, who, according to Assyrian texts, sent mercenaries to Egypt.

The Philistines' city league also poses a problem. "Early" Philistine accounts in the Bible (for instance Joshua 13:3 and 1 Samuel 6:17) refer to a political organization of five Philistine cities: Ashdod, Gaza, Ashkelon, Gath, and Ekron. While this manner of organization is not typical in the ancient Near East, federations—or leagues of tribes or cities—are fairly common in the Aegean world, beginning in the archaic period (c. 700–480 BCE). By the seventh century BCE, they had already become a widespread phenomenon in Greece and western Asia Minor.

CHERETHITES AND PELETHITES

The Bible mentions the Cherethites and Pelethites as special mercenary units in the time of David—units that were distinct from the regular army corps and that were totally loyal to the king, even in times of crisis (1 Samuel 30:14; 2 Samuel 8:18; 2 Samuel 15:18). Some scholars have identified the Cherethites as a group of Sea People and associated them with Crete, since, according to a verse in Amos (9:7), the Philistines came from Caphtor, or Crete. The Pelethites have usually been identified with the Philistines, with the Hebrew *peleti* seen as a corruption of *pelisti*—Philistine.

But Cherethites and Pelethites do not appear among the groups of Sea People in the Egyptian sources, and in light of the modest nature of the tenth-century highland polity of Judah, it is highly unlikely that the stories about Aegean mercenary troops in the service of David can be accepted as reliable historical testimony.

However, in contrast to the situation in David's time, the phenomenon of Greek mercenaries was well known in the region, especially in Philistia and possibly also in the Judahite Negev, in the seventh century BCE. Crete—the probable land of origin of the Cherethites—was a major source of mercenaries in the Hellenistic world. The demographic and economic realities lying behind this phenomenon must have been quite similar in the archaic period. Therefore, the biblical description of Cherethites as mercenary troops in the time of David may have been an anachronistic feature drawn from firsthand experience with Cretan mercenaries in the seventh century BCE.

For the Pelethites, we should go back to the suggestion of the American scholar William Foxwell Albright, who noted the similarity of this name to the "later" Greek term *pelte*, meaning "light shield." But instead of understanding this term in an Iron I context, we should once again turn to the realities of the seventh century BCE. The word may indeed have originated from the Greek *pelte*, or perhaps from the medium-armed Greek warriors known as *peltastai*. The peltasts are mentioned for the first time by the Greek historian Thucydides, in the fifth century BCE, and are shown in Greek vase paintings as early as the sixth century BCE. They may well have appeared somewhat earlier.

So how can we explain the appearance of these archaic Greek elements in the David story? As we have indicated in Chapter 6, the Deuteronomistic historian must have had a clear ideological motivation to depict Goliath as a heavily armed Greek warrior. The same seems to hold true for the Cherethites and Pelethites. In this case, the biblical author may have sought to glorify the figure of David by showing that he—like the great kings of contemporary (seventh-century BCE) times—had Greek mercenary troops at his service. This would also have served to legitimize Judah's political or economic cooperation with Twenty-sixth Dynasty Egypt and its Greek mercenary troops. This was done by "reminding" the people of Judah that foreign mercenaries were the closest military allies of the pious David, the founder of their ruling dynasty.

Appendix 7

Deportees, Returnees, and the Borders of Yehud

THE ARCHAEOLOGY OF THE EXILIC AND EARLY POSTEXILIC PERIODS

In the early days of historical research, the notion was common among scholars that the Babylonian exile was almost total and that much of the population of Judah was carried away. According to this idea, Judah was emptied of its population and the countryside was left desolate throughout the exilic period (586–538 BCE). Moreover, many scholars accepted the biblical description: that the whole aristocracy of Judah—the royal family, the Temple priests, ministers, and high-profile merchants—was carried away, and that the few remaining inhabitants in Judah were poor peasants. It now seems that this was not the case.

The biblical reports on the number of exiles are frankly contradictory. The second book of Kings (24:14) gives the number of exiles in the days of King Jehoiachin (the first Babylonian campaign in 597 BCE) as ten thousand, while verse 16 in the same chapter counts eight thousand people. The book of Kings does not provide us with the number of exiles after the destruction of Jerusalem in

586 BCE but it states that following the murder of Gedaliah and the massacre of the Babylonian garrison at Mizpah, "all the people" ran away to Egypt (2 Kings 25:26). Jeremiah recounts a process of three deportations totaling forty-six hundred people (52:28–30). Scholars tended to prefer his numbers because they seem to be less rounded and therefore more precise. We do not know, of course, whether this figure represents the total number of deportees or the heads of the families; in the latter case, the total number of exiles would rise to about twenty thousand. In any event, there is no way to reach an accurate number. We are probably dealing with a total ranging between a few thousand and fifteen or twenty thousand people. The exiles (who probably came mainly from the capital and its surrounding area) comprised between 5 and 20 percent of the population of the Judahite state before the destruction—mainly the aristocracy. These figures indicate that most of the population of Judah, which was largely rural, did not go to exile. This community included not only poor villagers but also artisans, scribes, priests, and prophets. It is noteworthy that an important part of the prophetic work of the time—Haggai and Zechariah—was compiled in Judah.

How many people returned from Babylonia to settle in Jerusalem and other parts of Yehud? What was the overall population of the province of Yehud in the time of the Chronicler? The lists of the returnees from Babylonia reported in Ezra 2:1–67 and Nehemiah 7:6–63, totaling almost fifty thousand people, are of questionable historical value. Some scholars suggest that they represent the several successive waves of exiles who returned to Yehud during the course of the Persian period. Others argue that they reflect the total population of the area, rather than the number of the repatriates alone. Even so, these numbers seem to be considerably inflated.

Where did they settle? The most detailed territorial data on the province of Yehud come from the list of exiles who returned from Babylonia (Ezra 2; Nehemiah 7) and from the list of the builders of the walls of Jerusalem (Nehemiah 3). The southern boundary of Yehud passed immediately to the south of Beth-zur, leaving

Hebron—the second most important town in the highlands in monarchic times, the place where David was supposedly crowned, and the location of the tombs of the patriarchs—outside the territory of the province of Yehud. In the north, the border conformed to the late seventh-century border of monarchic Judah, passing to the north of Mizpah and Bethel. In the east, Jericho was included in Yehud. In the west, Yehud may have included the northern Shephelah. Yehud was therefore a small province, which covered mainly the Judean hills, to a distance of about fifteen miles to the north and south of Jerusalem, a total area of less than eight hundred square miles. This was a much smaller territory than even the limited area of the kingdom of Judah in the late seventh century BCE, which also controlled the southern Hebron hills, the Beer-sheba Valley, and the Shephelah.

This reconstruction of the boundaries of the province of Yehud from biblical evidence is confirmed by archaeological finds—particularly, distinctive seal impressions found on pottery vessels from the Persian period, written in Aramaic or Hebrew and carrying the name of the province, Yehud. Several hundred examples of such impressed handles are known from excavations and chance finds.* In fact, almost all the impressions were found in Jerusalem and in the sites immediately to its north and south. Their overall geographical distribution closely parallels the boundaries of the province of Yehud as described above: from the area of Mizpah in the north to Beth-zur in the south, and from Jericho in the east to Gezer in the west.

---

* One type of these impressions carries, in addition to the name of the province, a personal name and the title "the governor." The personal names are identified by most scholars as governors of the province of Yehud on behalf of the Persian empire.

BIBLIOGRAPHY AND
SUGGESTED READING

Authors' Note: Although there is a rich scholarly literature on David and Solomon also in Hebrew, German, French, and other European languages, we have selected the main sources in English for this bibliography (including translations from German). In a very few cases Hebrew, German, or French sources are cited when they are the only relevant references to a particular subject.

GENERAL BACKGROUND

Encyclopedias

THE MAIN ARCHAEOLOGICAL SITES IN ISRAEL AND JORDAN

Stern, E., ed. 1993. *The New Encyclopedia of Archaeological Excavations in the Holy Land.* Jerusalem.

BIBLE ENTRIES

Freedman, D. N., ed. 1992. *The Anchor Bible Dictionary.* New York.

THE ANCIENT NEAR EAST

Meyers, E. M., ed. 1997. *The Oxford Encyclopedia of Archaeology in the Near East.* New York.
Sasson, J. M., ed. 1995. *Civilizations of the Ancient Near East.* London.

Archaeological method

Renfrew, C., and P. Bahn. 1991. *Archaeology: Theories, Methods and Practice.* London.

History of archaeological research in Palestine

Silberman, N. A. 1982. *Digging for God and Country: Exploration in the Holy Land 1799–1917.* New York.

Introductory books on the archaeology of the Levant

Ben-Tor, A., ed. 1992. *The Archaeology of Ancient Israel.* New Haven.
Levy, T. E., ed. 1995. *The Archaeology of Society in the Holy Land.* London.
Mazar, A. 1990. *Archaeology of the Land of the Bible 10,000–586 B.C.E.* New York.
Stern, E. 2001. *Archaeology of the Land of the Bible. Vol. II, The Assyrian, Babylonian, and Persian Periods 732–332 BCE.* New York.

Geographical history of the Land of Israel

Aharoni, Y. 1979. *The Land of the Bible: A Historical Geography.* Philadelphia.

Translation of ancient Near Eastern texts

Pritchard, J. B. 1969. *Ancient Near Eastern Texts Relating to the Old Testament.* Princeton.

History of ancient Israel

Alt, A. 1966. *Essays on Old Testament History and Religion.* Oxford.
Finkelstein, I., and N. Silberman. 2001. *The Bible Unearthed: Archaeology's New Vision of Ancient Israel and the Origin of Its Sacred Texts.* New York.
Liverani, M. Forthcoming 2005. *Israel's History and the History of Israel.*
Miller, M. J., and J. H. Hayes. 1986. *A History of Ancient Israel and Judah.* London.

Historiography in the Bible

Halpern, B. 1988. *The First Historians: The Hebrew Bible and History.* San Francisco.
Long, V. P., ed. 1999. *Israel's Past in Present Research: Essays on Ancient Israelite Historiography.* Winona Lake.
Van Seters, J. 1983. *In Search of History: Historiography in the Ancient World and the Origins of Biblical History.* New Haven.

Commentaries on 1 and 2 Samuel

McCarter, K. P. 1980. *I Samuel*. Garden City.
———. 1984. *II Samuel*. Garden City.

Commentaries on 1 and 2 Kings

Brueggemann, W. 2000. *1 & 2 Kings*. Macon.
Cogan, M., and H. Tadmor. 1988–2001. *Kings*. Garden City.
Gray, J. 1970. *I & II Kings: A Commentary*. London.

Commentaries on 1 and 2 Chronicles

Japhet, S. 1993. *I & II Chronicles: A Commentary*. Louisville.
Williamson, H. G. M. 1982. *1 and 2 Chronicles*. London.

General books on David

Alter, R. 1999. *The David Story: A Translation with Commentary of 1 and 2 Samuel*. New York.
Ash, P. S. 1999. *David, Solomon and Egypt: A Reassessment*. Sheffield.
Auld, G. 1994. *Kings Without Privilege: David and Moses in the Story of the Bible's Kings*. Edinburgh.
Brueggemann, W. 1985. *David's Truth in Israel's Imagination and Memory*. Philadelphia.
Fleminger, J. 2002. *Behind the Eyes of David*. Sussex.
Frontain, R.-J., and J. Wojcik, eds. 1981. *The David Myth in Western Literature*. West Lafayette.
Halpern, B. 2001. *David's Secret Demons: Messiah, Murderer, Traitor, King*. Grand Rapids.
Kirsh, J. 2000. *King David: The Real Life of the Man Who Ruled Israel*. New York.
Isser, S. 2003. *The Sword of Goliath: David in Heroic Literature*. Atlanta.
McKenzie, S. L. 2000. *King David: A Biography*. Oxford.
Mettinger, T. N. D. 1976. *King and Messiah: The Civil and Sacral Legitimation of the Israelite Kings*. Lund.
Noll, K. L. 1997. *The Faces of David*. Sheffield.
Schniedewind, W. M. 1999. *Society and the Promise to David: The Reception History of 2 Samuel 7:1–17*. Oxford.

Selected articles on David

Dietrich, W., and W. Naumann. 2000. The David-Saul Narrative. In G. N. Knoppers and J. G. McConville, eds., *Reconsidering Israel and Judah: Recent Studies on the Deuteronomistic History*, 276–318. Winona Lake.

Edelman, D. 2000. The Deuteronomistic David and the Chronicler's David: Competing and Contrasting Ideologies? In T. Römer, ed., *The Future of the Deuteronomistic History*, 67–83. Leuven.

Gordon, R. P. 1994. In Search of David: The David Tradition in Recent Study. In A. R. Millard, J. K. Hoffmeier, and D. W. Baker, eds., *Faith, Tradition, and History*, 285–98. Winona Lake.

Knoppers, G. N. 1998. David's Relation to Moses: The Contexts, Content and Conditions of the Davidic Promises. In J. Day, ed., *King and Messiah in Israel and the Ancient Near East*, 91–118. Sheffield.

Lohfink, N. 2000. Which Oracle Granted Perdurability to the Davidides? A Textual Problem in 2 Kings 8:19 and the Function of the Dynastic Oracle in the Deuteronomistic Work. In G. N. Knoppers and J. G. McConville, eds., *Reconsidering Israel and Judah: Recent Studies on the Deuteronomistic History*, 421–43. Winona Lake.

McKenzie, S. L. 1999. Why Didn't David Build the Temple? The History of a Biblical Tradition. In M. P. Graham, R. R. Marrs, and S. L. McKenzie, eds., *Worship and the Hebrew Bible*, 204–24. Sheffield.

———. 2001. The Typology of the Davidic Covenant. In A. J. Dearman and P. M. Graham, eds., *The Land That I Will Show You: Essays in History and Archaeology of the Ancient Near East in Honour of J. Maxwell Miller*, 152–78. Sheffield.

Na'aman, N. 1996. Sources and Composition in the History of David. In V. Fritz and Ph. Davies, eds., *The Origin of the Ancient Israelite States*, 170–86. Sheffield.

Peckham, B. 1985. The Deuteronomistic History of Saul and David. *Zeitschrift für die alttestamentliche Wissenschaft* 97:190–209.

Rofe, A. 2000. The Reliability of the Source About David's Reign: An Outlook from Political Theory. In E. Blum, ed., *Mincha: Festgabe für Rolf Rendtorff zum 75*, 217–27. Neukirchen-Vluyn.

Rudman, D. 2000. The Commissioning Stories of Saul and David as Theological Allegory. *Vetus Testamentum* 50:519–30.

Van der Toorn, K., and C. Houtman. 1994. David and the Ark. *Journal of Biblical Literature* 113:209–31.

General books on Solomon

Handy, L. K., ed. 1997. *The Age of Solomon: Scholarship at the Turn of the Millennium*. Leiden.

Torijano, P. A. 2002. *Solomon the Esoteric King: From King to Magus, Development of a Tradition*. Leiden.

Selected articles on Solomon

Brettler, M. 1991. The Structure of 1 Kings 1–11. *Journal for the Study of the Old Testament* 49:87–97.

Frisch, A. 1991. Structure and Its Significance: The Narrative of Solomon's Reign (1 Kings 1–12:24). *Journal for the Study of the Old Testament* 51:3–14.

———. 1997. A Literary and Theological Analysis of the Account of Solomon's Sins (1 Kings 11:1–8). *Shnaton* 11:167–79.

Knoppers, G. N. 1995. Prayer and Propaganda: Solomon's Dedication of the Temple and the Deuteronomistic Program. *Catholic Biblical Quarterly* 57:229–54.

Na'aman, N. 1997. Sources and Composition in the History of Solomon. In L. K. Handy, ed., *The Age of Solomon: Scholarship in the Turn of the Millennium*, 57–80. Leiden.

Sweeney, M. A. 1995. The Critique of Solomon in the Josianic Edition of the Deuteronomistic History. *Journal of Biblical Literature* 114:607–22.

Van Seters, J. 1997. Solomon's Temple: Fact and Ideology in Biblical and Near Eastern Historiography. *Catholic Biblical Quarterly* 59:45–57.

Veijola, T. 2000. Solomon: Bathsheba's Firstborn. In G. N. Knoppers and J. G. McConville, eds., *Reconsidering Israel and Judah: Recent Studies on the Deuteronomistic History*, 340–57. Winona Lake.

Traditional works on the archaeology of the united monarchy

Dever, W. G. 1997. Archaeology and the "Age of Solomon": A Case Study in Archaeology and Historiography. In L. K. Handy, ed., *The Age of Solomon: Scholarship at the Turn of the Millennium* 217–51. Leiden.

Stager, L. E. 2003. The Patrimonial Kingdom of Solomon. In W. G. Dever and S. Gitin, eds., *Symbiosis, Symbolism, and the Power of the Past: Canaan, Ancient Israel, and Their Neighbors from the Late Bronze Age Through Roman Palestine*, 63–74. Winona Lake.

Yadin, Y. 1970. Megiddo of the Kings of Israel. *Biblical Archaeologist* 33:66–96.

Problems with the traditional view on the archaeology of the united monarchy

Finkelstein, I. 1996. The Archaeology of the United Monarchy: An Alternative View. *Levant* 28:177–87.

———. 1999. Hazor and the North in the Iron Age: A Low Chronology Perspective. *Bulletin of the American Schools of Oriental Research* 314:55–70.

Finkelstein, I., and E. Piasetzky. 2003. Recent Radiocarbon Results and King Solomon. *Antiquity* 77:771–79.

Sass, B. *The Alphabet at the Turn of the Millennium.* Tel Aviv.

Problems with the historical reconstruction of the united monarchy

Knauf, E. A. 1997. Le roi est mort, vive le roi! A Biblical Argument for the Historicity of Solomon. In L. K. Handy, ed., *The Age of Solomon: Scholarship at the Turn of the Millennium,* 81–95. Leiden.

Miller, M. J. 1991. Solomon: International Potentate or Local King. *Palestine Exploration Quarterly* 123:28–31.

———. 1997. Separating the Solomon of History from the Solomon of Legend. In L. K. Handy, ed., *The Age of Solomon: Scholarship at the Turn of the Millennium,* 1–24. Leiden.

Niemann, H. M. 1997. The Socio-Political Shadow Cast by the Biblical Solomon. In L. K. Handy, ed., *The Age of Solomon: Scholarship at the Turn of the Millennium,* 252–99. Leiden.

———. 2000. Megiddo and Solomon—A Biblical Investigation in Relation to Archaeology. *Tel Aviv* 27:59–72.

Silberman, N. A. 2003. Archaeology, Ideology, and the Search for David and Solomon. In A. G. Vaughn and A. E. Killebrew, eds. *Jerusalem in the Bible and Archaeology: The First Temple Period,* 395–405. Atlanta.

The minimalist approach

Davies, P. 1992. *In Search of "Ancient Israel."* Sheffield.

Garbini, G. 2003. *Myth and History in the Bible.* London.

Lemche, N. P. 1998. *The Israelites in History and Tradition.* London.

Thompson, T. L. 1992. *Early History of the Israelite People.* Leiden.

———. 1999. *The Bible in History: How Writers Create a Past.* London.

Against the minimalist approach

Albertz, R. 2001. An End to the Confusion? Why the Old Testament Cannot Be a Hellenistic Book! In L. L. Grabbe, ed., *Did Moses Speak Attic?,* 30–46. Sheffield.

Dever, W. G. 2001. *What Did the Biblical Writers Know and When Did They Know It? What Archaeology Can Tell Us About the Reality of Ancient Israel.* Grand Rapids.

Halpern, B. 1995. Erasing History. *Bible Review:* 26–35, 47.

Schniedewind, W. 2003. Jerusalem, the Late Judaean Monarchy and the Composition of the Biblical Texts. In A. G. Vaughn and A. E. Killebrew, eds. *Jerusalem in the Bible and Archaeology: The First Temple Period,* 375–394. Atlanta.

Hurwitz, A. 1997. The Historical Quest for "Ancient Israel" and the Linguistic Evidence of the Hebrew Bible: Some Methodological Observations. *Vetus Testamentum* 47:301–15.

CHAPTER 1. TALES OF THE BANDIT

Archaeological surveys in the highlands of Judah

Finkelstein, I. 1995. The Great Transformation: The "Conquest" of the Highlands Frontiers and the Rise of the Territorial States. In T. E. Levy, ed., *The Archaeology of Society in the Holy Land*, 349–65. London.

Lehmann, G. 2003. The United Monarchy in the Countryside: Jerusalem, Judah, and the Shephelah During the Tenth Century. In A. G. Vaughn and A. E. Killebrew, eds., *Jerusalem in the Bible and Archaeology: The First Temple Period*, 117–62. Atlanta.

Ofer, A. 1994. "All the Hill Country of Judah": From Settlement Fringe to a Prosperous Monarchy. In I. Finkelstein and N. Na'aman, eds., *From Nomadism to Monarchy: Archaeological and Historical Aspects of Early Israel*, 92–121. Jerusalem.

Settlement history of the Beer-sheba Valley

Herzog, Z. 1994. The Beer-Sheba Valley: From Nomadism to Monarchy. In I. Finkelstein and N. Na'aman, eds., *From Nomadism to Monarchy: Archaeological and Historical Aspects of Early Israel*, 122–49. Jerusalem.

———. 2002. The Fortress Mound at Tel Arad: An Interim Report. *Tel Aviv* 29:3–109, especially 84–102.

Settlement patterns in the Shephelah

Dagan, Y. 2004. Results of the Survey: Settlement Patterns in the Lachish Region. In D. Ussishkin, *The Renewed Archaeological Excavations at Lachish (1973–1994)*, vol. V, 2672–90. Tel Aviv.

Canaan in the Amarna period

Bunimovitz, S. 1994. The Problem of Human Resources in Late Bronze Age Palestine and Its Socioeconomic Implications. *Ugarit-Forschungen* 26:1–20.

Finkelstein, I. 1996. The Territorio-Political System of Canaan in the Late Bronze Age. *Ugarit-Forschungen* 28:221–55.

Na'aman, N. 1997. The Network of Canaanite Late Bronze Kingdoms and the City of Ashdod. *Ugarit-Forschungen* 29:599–626.

Late Bronze Age Jerusalem

Na'aman, N. 1996. The Contribution of the Amarna Letters to the Debate on Jerusalem's Political Position in the Tenth Century B.C.E. *Bulletin of the American Schools of Oriental Research* 304:17–27.

The Shosu and the Apiru

Giveon, R. 1971. *Les bédouin Shosou des documents égyptiens.* Leiden.

Greenberg, M. 1955. *The Hab/piru.* New Haven.

Na'aman, N. 1986. Habiru and Hebrews: The Transfer of a Social Term to the Literary Sphere. *Journal of Near Eastern Studies* 45:271–88.

Rainey, A. F. 1995. Unruly Elements in Late Bronze Canaanite Society. In D. P. Wright, D. N. Freedman, and A. Hurvitz, eds., *Pomegranates and Golden Bells,* 481–96. Winona Lake.

Rowton, M. B. 1976. Dimorphic Structure and the Problem of the *Apiru-Ibrim. Journal of Near Eastern Studies* 35:13–20.

Ward, W. A. 1972. The Shasu "Bedouin": Notes on a Recent Publication. *Journal of the Economy and Social History of the Orient* 15:35–60.

Banditry

Hobsbawm, E. J. 1985. *Bandits.* Harmondsworth.

Heroic tales in the second book of Samuel

Isser, S. 2003. *The Sword of Goliath.* Atlanta.

CHAPTER 2. THE MADNESS OF SAUL

Saul in biblical and historical studies

Edelman, D. 1988. Saul's Journey Through Mt. Ephraim and Samuel's Ramah (1 Sam. 9:4–5, 10:2–5). *Zeitschrift des Deutschen Palästina-Vereins* 104:44–58.

———. 1990. The Deuteronomist's Story of King Saul: Narrative Art or Editorial Product? In C. Brekelmans and J. Lust, eds., *Pentateuchal and Deuteronomistic Studies,* 207–20. Leuven.

———. 1991. *King Saul in the Historiography of Judah.* Sheffield.

———. 1996. Saul ben Kish in History and Tradition. In V. Fritz and Ph. R. Davies, eds., *The Origin of the Ancient Israelite States,* 142–59. Sheffield.

Gunn, D. 1981. A Man Given Over to Trouble: The Story of King Saul. In B. O. Long, ed. *Images of Man and God: Old Testament Short Stories in Literary Focus,* 89–112. Sheffield.

Humphreys, W. L. 1980. The Rise and Fall of King Saul: A Study of an Ancient Narrative Stratum in 1 Samuel. *Journal for the Study of the Old Testament* 18:74–90.

Long, V. P. 1989. *The Reign and Rejection of King Saul: A Case for Literary and Theological Coherence.* Atlanta.

———. 1994. How Did Saul Become King? Literary Reading and Historical Reconstruction. In A. R. Millard, J. K. Hoffmeier, and D. W. Baker, eds., *Faith, Tradition, and History,* 271–84. Winona Lake.

Na'aman, N. 1992. The Pre-Deuteronomistic Story of King Saul and Its Historical Significance. *Catholic Biblical Quarterly* 54:638–58.

Peckham, B. 1985. The Deuteronomistic History of Saul and David. *Zeitschrift für die alttestamentliche Wissenschaft* 97:190–209.

Scheffler, E. 2000. Saving Saul from the Deuteronomist. In J. C. de Moor and H. F. Van Rooy, eds., *Past, Present, Future: The Deuteronomistic History and the Prophets,* 263–71. Leiden.

Van der Toorn, K. 1993. Saul and the Rise of Israelite State Religion. *Vetus Testamentum* 43:519–42.

Walters, S. D. 1991. Saul of Gibeon. *Journal for the Study of the Old Testament* 52:61–76.

White, M. 2000. "The History of Saul's Rise": Saulide State Propaganda in 1 Samuel 1–14. In S. M. Olyan and R. C. Culley, eds., *"A Wise and Discerning Mind": Essays in Honor of Burke O. Long,* 271–92. Providence.

———. 2001. Searching for Saul. What We Really Know About Israel's First King. *Biblical Research* 17:22–29, 52–53.

The territory of Saul

Edelman, D. 1985. The "Ashurites" of Eshbaal's State (2 Sam. 2.9). *Palestine Exploration Quarterly* 117:85–91.

Na'aman, N. 1990. The Kingdom of Ishbaal. *Biblische Notizen* 54:33–37.

Archaeological surveys in the northern highlands

Finkelstein, I. 1995. The Great Transformation: The "Conquest" of the Highlands Frontiers and the Rise of the Territorial States. In T. E. Levy, ed., *The Archaeology of Society in the Holy Land,* 349–65. London.

Finkelstein, I., and Y. Magen, eds. 1993. *Archaeological Survey of the Hill Country of Benjamin.* Jerusalem. (Hebrew with English summaries.)

Zertal, A. 1994. "To the Land of the Perizzites and the Giants": On the Israelite Settlement in the Hill Country of Manasseh. In I. Finkelstein and N. Na'aman, eds., *From Nomadism to Monarchy: Archaeological and Historical Aspects of Early Israel,* 47–69. Jerusalem.

Settlement patterns in Jordan

Finkelstein, I. 1998. From Sherds to History: Review Article. *Israel Exploration Journal* 48:120–31.

Shiloh

Finkelstein, I., ed. 1993. *Shiloh: The Archaeology of a Biblical Site.* Tel Aviv.

Khirbet et-Tell and Khirbet Raddana

Callaway, J. A. 1976. Excavating Ai (et-Tell): 1964–1972. *Biblical Archaeologist* 39:18–30.

Callaway, J. A., and R. E. Cooley. 1971. A Salvage Excavation at Raddana, in Bireh. *Bulletin of the American Schools of Oriental Research* 201:9–19.

Lederman, Z. 1999. *An Early Iron Age Village at Khirbet Raddana: The Excavations of Joseph A. Callaway.* Ann Arbor.

The Shishak (Sheshonq I) campaign

Ahlstrom, G. W. 1993. Pharaoh Sheshonq's Campaign to Palestine. In A. Lemaire and B. Otzen, eds., *History and Traditions of Early Israel*, 1–16. Leiden.

Kitchen, K. A. 1986. *The Third Intermediate Period in Egypt (1100–650 B.C.)*, 432–47. Warminster.

Mazar, B. 1957. The Campaign of Pharaoh Shishak to Palestine. *Vetus Testamentum Supplement* 4:57–66.

Redford, D. B. 1992. *Egypt, Canaan and Israel in Ancient Times*, 312–15. Princeton.

The tenth century BCE, archaeology, and Shishak: a revised view

Finkelstein, I. 2002. The Campaign of Sheshonq I to Palestine: A Guide to the 10th Century BCE Polity. *Zeitschrift des Deutschen Palästina-Vereins* 118:109–35.

———. 2003. City-States to States: Polity Dynamics in the 10th–9th Centuries B.C.E. In W. G. Dever and S. Gitin, eds., *Symbiosis, Symbolism, and the Power of the Past: Canaan, Ancient Israel, and Their Neighbors from the Late Bronze Age Through Roman Palestine*, 75–84. Winona Lake.

Gibeon as the hub of the Saulides

Blenkinsopp, J. 1974. Did Saul Make Gibeon His Capital? *Vetus Testamentum* 24:1–7.

Walters, S. D. 1991. Saul of Gibeon. *Journal for the Study of the Old Testament* 52:61–76.

The apology of David

Dick, M. B. 2004. The "History of David's Rise to Power" and the Neo-Babylonian Succession Apologies. In B. F. Batto and K. L. Roberts, eds., *David and Zion: Biblical Studies in Honor of J. J. M. Roberts*, 3–19. Winona Lake.

Halpern, B. 2001. *David's Secret Demons: Messiah, Murderer, Traitor, King*, 73–103. Grand Rapids.

Ishida, T. 1991. The Succession Narrative and Esarhaddon's Apology. In M. Cogan and I. Ephal, eds., *Ah, Assyria . . . Studies in Assyrian History and Ancient Near Eastern Historiography Presented to Hayim Tadmor*, 166–73. Jerusalem.

McCarter, K. P. 1980. The Apology of David. *Journal of Biblical Literature* 99:489–504.

CHAPTER 3. MURDER, LUST, AND BETRAYAL

"The History of David's Rise" and the "Succession History"

de Pury, A., and T. Römer, eds. 2000. *Die sogenannte Thronfolgegeschichte Davids: Neue Einsichten und Anfragen*. Freiburg.

Keys, G. 1996. *The Wages of Sin: A Reappraisal of the "Succession Narrative."* Sheffield.

McKenzie, S. L. 2000. The So-Called Succession Narrative in the Deuteronomistic History. In A. de Pury and T. Römer, eds., *Die sogenannte Thronfolgegeschichte Davids: Neue Einsichten und Anfragen*, 123–35. Freiburg.

Rost, L. 1982. *The Succession to the Throne of David*. Sheffield.

Van Seters, J. 2000. The Court History and DtrH: Conflicting Perspectives on the House of David. In A. de Pury and T. Römer, eds., *Die sogenannte Thronfolgegeschichte Davids: Neue Einsichten und Anfragen*, 70–93. Freiburg.

Views on the question of the tenth century BCE in Jerusalem

Cahill, J. M. 2003. Jerusalem in the Time of the United Monarchy: The Archaeological Evidence. In A. G. Vaughn and A. E. Killebrew, eds., *Jerusalem in the Bible and Archaeology: The First Temple Period*, 13–80. Atlanta.

Finkelstein, I. 2003. The Rise of Jerusalem and Judah: The Missing Link. In A. G. Vaughn and A. E. Killebrew, eds., *Jerusalem in the Bible and Archaeology: The First Temple Period*, 81–101. Atlanta.

Steiner, M. 2003. The Evidence from Kenyon's Excavations in Jerusalem: A Response Essay. In A. G. Vaughn and A. E. Killebrew, eds., *Jerusalem in the Bible and Archaeology: The First Temple Period*, 347–63. Atlanta.

Ussishkin, D. 2003. Solomon's Jerusalem: The Text and the Facts on the Ground. In A. G. Vaughn and A. E. Killebrew, eds., *Jerusalem in the Bible and Archaeology: The First Temple Period*, 103–15. Atlanta.

State formation in Israel

Finkelstein, I. 1999. State Formation in Israel and Judah: A Contrast in Context, a Contrast in Trajectory. *Near Eastern Archaeology* 62:35–52.

Samaria, Jezreel, and other Omride cities

Finkelstein, I. 2000. Omride Architecture. *Zeitschrift des Deutschen Palästina-Vereins* 116:114–38.

Franklin, N. 2003. The Tombs of the Kings of Israel; Two Recently Identified 9th-Century Tombs from Omride Samaria. *Zeitschrift des Deutschen Palästina-Vereins* 119:1–11.

———. 2004. Samaria: From the Bedrock to the Omride Palace. *Levant* 36:89–202.

———. Forthcoming. Correlation and Chronology: Samaria and Megiddo Redux. In T. Levy and T. Higham, eds., *Radiocarbon Dating and the Iron Age of the Southern Levant: The Bible and Archaeology Today*. London.

Kenyon, K. 1973. *Royal Cities of the Old Testament*, 71–89. New York.

Ussishkin, D. 1997. Jezreel, Samaria and Megiddo; Royal Centres of Omri and Ahab. *Vetus Testamentum Supplement* 66:351–64.

Williamson, H. G. M. 1996. Tel Jezreel and the Dynasty of Omri. *Palestine Exploration Quarterly* 128:41–51.

Woodhead, J. 1998. Royal Cities in the Kingdom of Israel. In J. Goodnick Westenholz, ed., *Capital Cities: Urban Planning and Spiritual Dimensions*, 111–16. Jerusalem.

History of the Omride kingdom

Timm, S. 1982. *Die Dynastie Omri*. Göttingen.

The rise of urban centers in Judah in the ninth century

Bunimovitz, S., and Z. Lederman. 2001. Iron Age Fortifications of Tel Beth Shemesh: A 1990–2000 Perspective. *Israel Exploration Journal* 51:121–47.

Finkelstein, I. 2001. The Rise of Jerusalem and Judah: The Missing Link. *Levant* 33:105–15.

Herzog, Z., and L. Singer-Avitz. 2004. Redefining the Centre: The Emergence of State in Judah. *Tel Aviv* 31:209–44.
Ussishkin, D. 2004. *The Renewed Archaeological Excavations at Lachish (1973–1994)*, vol. I, 78–83. Tel Aviv.

The role of the queen mother

Knauf, E. A. 2002. The Queens' Story: Bathsheba, Maacah, Athaliah and the "Historia of Early Kings." *Lectio Difficilior: European Electronic Journal for Feminist Exegesis* 2 (http://www.lectio.unibe.ch/o2 2/axel.htm).

The Arameans and the kingdom of Damascus

Dion, P.-E. 1997. *Les Araméens à l'âge du fer.* Paris.
Lemaire, A. 1991. Hazaël de Damas, roi d'Aram. In D. Charpin and F. Joannès, eds., *Marchands, diplomates et empereurs*, 91–108. Paris.
Lipinski, E. 2000. *The Aramaeans: Their Ancient History, Culture, Religion.* Leuven.
Na'aman, N. 1997. Historical and Literary Notes on the Excavations of Tel Jezreel. *Tel Aviv* 24:122–28.

The Tel Dan inscription

Biran, A., and J. Naveh. 1995. The Tel Dan Inscription: A New Fragment. *Israel Exploration Journal* 45:1–18.
Halpern, B. 1994. The Stela from Dan: Epigraphic and Historical Considerations. *Bulletin of the American Schools of Oriental Research* 296:63–80.
Lemaire, A. 1998. The Tel Dan Stela as a Piece of Royal Historiography. *Journal for the Study of the Old Testament* 81:3–14.
Na'aman, N. 2000. Three Notes on the Aramaic Inscription from Tel Dan. *Israel Exploration Journal* 50:92–104.
Schniedewind, W. M. 1996. Tel Dan Stela: New Light on Aramaic and Jehu's Revolt. *Bulletin of the American Schools of Oriental Research* 302:75–90.

A revised view on the literary sources of the Davidic conquests

Na'aman, N. 2002. In Search of Reality Behind the Account of David's Wars with Israel's Neighbours. *Israel Exploration Journal* 52:200–224.

History and archaeology of Gath

Maeir, A., and C. S. Ehrlich. 2001. Excavating Philistine Gath: Have We Found Goliath's Hometown? *Biblical Archaeology Review* 27 (6):22–31.
Schniedewind, W. M. 1998. The Geopolitical History of Philistine Gath. *Bulletin of the American Schools of Oriental Research* 309:69–77.

Chapter 4. Temple and Dynasty

Assyrian military and economic activity

Finkelstein, I. 1992. Horvat Qitmit and the Southern Trade in the Late Iron Age II. *Zeitschrift des Deutschen Palästina-Vereins* 108:156–70.

Tadmor, H. 1966. Philistia Under Assyrian Rule. *Biblical Archaeologist* 29:86–102.

The assault of Israel and Damascus on Judah

Cazelles, H. 1991. La guerre syro-ephraimite dans le context de la politique internationale. In D. Garrone, ed., *Storia e tradizioni di Israele*, 31–48. Brescia.

Modern archaeological research in Jerusalem

Avigad, N. 1984. *Discovering Jerusalem*, 31–60. Oxford.

Geva, H., ed. 2000. *Ancient Jerusalem Revealed*. Jerusalem.

Steiner, M. L. 2001. *Excavations by Kathleen M. Kenyon in Jerusalem 1961–1967*, vol. III, *The Settlement in the Bronze and Iron Ages*. London.

Vaughn, A. G., and A. E. Killebrew, eds. *Jerusalem in the Bible and Archaeology: The First Temple Period*. Atlanta.

The expansion of Jerusalem

Broshi, M. 1974. The Expansion of Jerusalem in the Reigns of Hezekiah and Manasseh. *Israel Exploration Journal* 24:21–26.

Geva, H. 2003. Western Jerusalem at the End of the First Temple Period in Light of the Excavations in the Jewish Quarter. In A. G. Vaughn and A. E. Killebrew, eds., *Jerusalem in the Bible and Archaeology: The First Temple Period*, 183–208. Atlanta.

Reich, R., and E. Shukron. 2003. The Urban Development of Jerusalem in the Late Eight Century B.C.E. In A. G. Vaughn and A. E. Killebrew, eds., *Jerusalem in the Bible and Archaeology: The First Temple Period*, 209–18. Atlanta.

Iron Age cemeteries in Jerusalem

Barkay, G., A. Kloner, and A. Mazar. 1994. The Northern Necropolis of Jerusalem During the First Temple Period. In H. Geva, ed., *Ancient Jerusalem Revealed*, 119–27. Jerusalem.

Ussishkin, D. 1993. *The Village of Silwan: The Necropolis from the Period of the Judean Kingdom*. Jerusalem.

Olive oil economy in Judah

Finkelstein, I., and N. Na'aman. 2004. The Judahite Shephelah in the Late 8th and Early 7th Centuries BCE. *Tel Aviv* 31:60–79.

Lmlk *storage jars*

Na'aman, N. 1986. Hezekiah's Fortified Cities and the *LMLK* Stamps. *Bulletin of the American Schools of Oriental Research* 261:5–21.

Vaughn, A. G. 1999. *Theology, History, and Archaeology in the Chronicler's Account of Hezekiah*. Atlanta.

The expansion of writing and literacy in Judah

Jamieson-Drake, D. W. 1991. *Scribes and Schools in Monarchic Judah: A Socio-Archaeological Approach*. Sheffield.

Schniedewind, W. 2003. Jerusalem, the Late Judaean Monarchy and the Composition of the Biblical Texts. In A. G. Vaughn and A. E. Killebrew, eds., *Jerusalem in the Bible and Archaeology: The First Temple Period*, 375–94. Atlanta.

———. 2004. *How the Bible Became a Book: The Textualization of Ancient Israel*. Cambridge.

Data on population changes in the northern highlands (Iron II to Persian period)

Finkelstein, I., Z. Lederman, and S. Bunimovitz. 1997. *Highlands of Many Cultures: The Southern Samaria Survey: The Sites*, 898–906. Tel Aviv.

Zertal, A. 1989. The Pahwah of Samaria (Northern Israel) During the Persian Period. Types of Settlement, Economy, History and New Discoveries. *Transeuphratène* 2:9–30.

Deportees settled in the territories of the northern kingdom

Na'aman, N., and R. Zadok. 1988. Sargon II's Deportations to Israel and Philistia. *Journal of Cuneiform Studies* 40:36–46.

———. 2000. Assyrian Deportations to the Province of Samaria in the Light of the Two Cuneiform Tablets from Tel Hadid. *Tel Aviv* 27:159–88.

The cult reform of Hezekiah

ACCEPTING ITS HISTORICITY

Haran, M. 1978. *Temples and Temple-Service in Ancient Israel—An Inquiry into the Character of Cult Phenomena and the Historical Setting of the Priestly School*. Oxford.

Lowery, R. H. 1991. *The Reforming Kings: Cults and Society in First Temple Judah.* Sheffield.

McKay, J. 1973. *Religion in Judah Under the Assyrians.* Naperville.

Weinfeld, M. 1964. Cult Centralization in Israel in the Light of a Neo-Babylonian Analogy. *Journal of Near Eastern Studies* 23:202–12.

REJECTING ITS HISTORICITY

Fried, L. 2002. The High Places (Bamôt) and the Reforms of Hezekiah and Josiah: An Archaeological Investigation. *Journal of the American Oriental Society* 122:1–29.

Handy, L. 1988. Hezekiah's Unlikely Reform. *Zeitschrift für die altestamentliche Wissenschaft* 100:111–15.

Na'aman, N. 1995. The Debated Historicity of Hezekiah's Reform in the Light of Historical and Archaeological Research. *Zeitschrift für die altestamentliche Wissenschaft* 107:179–95.

Archaeological evidence for the abandonment of cult places in the late eighth century

Aharoni, Y. 1974. The Horned Altar at Beersheba. *Biblical Archaeologist* 37:2–23.

Herzog, Z. 2001. The Date of the Temple at Arad: Reassessment of the Stratigraphy and the Implications for the History of Religion in Judah. In A. Mazar, ed., *Studies in the Archaeology of the Iron Age in Israel and Jordan*, 156–78. Sheffield.

Ussishkin, D. 2003. The Level V "Sanctuary" and "High Place" at Lachish. In C. G. den Hertog, U. Hübner, and S. Münger, eds., *Saxa Loquentur: Studien zur Archäologie Palästinas/Israels, Festschrift für Volkmar Fritz*, 205–11. Münster.

Influence of Assyrian chronicles on biblical history writing

Van Seters, J. 1990. Joshua's Campaign of Canaan and Near Eastern Historiography. *Scandinavian Journal of the Old Testament* 4:1–12.

———. 1997. Solomon's Temple: Facts and Ideology in Biblical and Near Eastern Historiography. *Catholic Biblical Quarterly* 59:45–57.

Hezekiah's revolt

Grabbe, L. L., ed. 2003. *"Like a bird in a cage": The Invasion of Sennacherib in 701 BCE.* Sheffield.

Halpern, B. 1991. Jerusalem and the Lineages in the Seventh Century BCE: Kinship and the Rise of Individual Moral Liability. In B. Halpern and

D. W. Hobson, eds., *Law and Ideology in Monarchic Israel*, 11–107. Sheffield.

Lachish and its conquest by Sennacherib
Ussishkin, D. 1982. *The Conquest of Lachish by Sennacherib.* Tel Aviv.

CHAPTER 5. SOLOMON'S WISDOM?

The archaeology of the days of Manasseh
Finkelstein, I. 1994. The Archaeology of the Days of Manasseh. In M. D. Coogan, J. C. Exum, and L. E. Stager, eds., *Scripture and Other Artifacts: Essays on the Bible and Archaeology in Honor of Philip J. King,* 169–87. Louisville.

Settlement activity in the Judean Desert
Cross, F. M., and J. T. Milik. 1956. Explorations in the Judean Buqeah. *Bulletin of the American Schools of Oriental Research* 142:5–17.
Stager, L. E. 1976. Farming in the Judean Desert. *Bulletin of the American Schools of Oriental Research* 221:145–58.

The six-chambered "Solomonic" gates
Yadin, Y. 1970. Megiddo of the Kings of Israel. *Biblical Archaeologist* 33:66–96.

Evidence against the six-chambered gates theory
Ussishkin, D. 1980. Was the "Solomonic" City Gate at Megiddo Built by King Solomon? *Bulletin of the American Schools of Oriental Research* 239:1–18.
———. 1990. Notes on Megiddo, Gezer, Ashdod, and Tel Batash in the Tenth to Ninth Centuries B.C. *Bulletin of the American Schools of Oriental Research* 277/278:71–91.

Hazor in the ninth and eighth centuries
Finkelstein, I. 1999. Hazor and the North in the Iron Age: A Low Chronology Perspective. *Bulletin of the American Schools of Oriental Research* 314:55–70.

The debate over the dating of the Iron Age strata
Ben-Tor, A. 2000. Hazor and Chronology of Northern Israel: A Reply to Israel Finkelstein. *Bulletin of the American Schools of Oriental Research* 317:9–15.

Boaretto, E., A. J. T. Jull, A. Gilboa, and I. Sharon. 2005. Dating the Iron Age I/II Transition in Israel: First Intercomparison Results. *Radiocarbon* 47:39–55.

Bruins, H. J., J. van der Plicht, and A. Mazar. 2003. ¹⁴C Dates from Tel Rehov: Iron Age Chronology, Pharaohs, and Hebrew Kings. *Science* 300:315–18.

Finkelstein, I., and E. Piasetzky. 2003. Recent Radiocarbon Results and King Solomon. *Antiquity* 77:771–79.

———. 2003. Wrong and Right; High and Low—¹⁴C Dates from Tel Rehov and Iron Age Chronology. *Tel Aviv* 30:283–95.

———. 2003. Comment on "¹⁴C Dates from Tel Rehov: Iron-Age Chronology, Pharaohs, and Hebrew Kings." *Science* 302:568b.

Gilboa, A., and I. Sharon. 2003. An Archaeological Contribution to the Early Iron Age Chronological Debate: Alternative Chronologies for Phoenicia and Their Effects on the Levant, Cyprus, and Greece. *Bulletin of the American Schools of Oriental Research* 332:7–80.

Levy, T., and T. Higham, eds. 2005. *Radiocarbon Dating and the Iron Age of the Southern Levant: The Bible and Archaeology Today*. London.

Mazar, A. 1997. Iron Age Chronology: A Reply to I. Finkelstein. *Levant* 29:155–65.

The Solomonic districts

Na'aman, N. 2002. Solomon's District List (1 Kings 4:7–19) and the Assyrian Province System in Palestine. *Ugarit-Forschungen* 33:419–36.

Late monarchic realities behind the Solomon narrative

Knauf, E. A. 1991. King Solomon's Copper Supply. In E. Lipinski, ed., *Phoenicia and the Bible*, 167–86. Leuven.

The Megiddo stables

Cantrell, D. 2005. Stable Issues. In I. Finkelstein, D. Ussishkin, and B. Halpern, eds., *Megiddo IV: The 1998–2002 Seasons*. Tel Aviv.

Cantrell, D., and I. Finkelstein. 2005. A Kingdom for a Horse: The Megiddo Stables and Eighth Century Israel. In I. Finkelstein, D. Ussishkin, and B. Halpern, eds., *Megiddo IV: The 1998–2002 Seasons*. Tel Aviv.

Pritchard, J. B. 1970. The Megiddo Stables: A Reassessment. In J. A. Sanders, ed., *Near Eastern Archaeology in the Twentieth Century*, 268–75. Garden City.

Yadin, Y. 1976. The Megiddo Stables. In F. M. Cross, W. E. Lemke, and P. D. Miller, eds., *Magnalia Dei: The Mighty Acts of God. Essays on the Bible and Archaeology in Memory of G. E. Wright*, 249–52. Garden City.

Horses in Assyria and Israel

Dalley, S. 1985. Foreign Chariotry and Cavalry in the Armies of Tiglath-pileser III and Sargon II. *Iraq* 47:31–48.

Heidorn, L. A. 1997. The Horses of Kush. *Journal of Near Eastern Studies* 56:105–14.

The ancient Arabs

Ephal, I. 1982. *The Ancient Arabs.* Jerusalem.

The rise of Edom

Bienkowski, P., ed. 1992. *Early Edom and Moab: The Beginning of the Iron Age in Southern Jordan.* Sheffield.

———. 1994. The Origin and Development of Edom. In S. Mazzoni, ed., *Nuove fondazioni nel vicino oriente antico: Realtà e ideologia,* 263–68. Pisa.

Camels at Tell Jemmeh

Wapnish, P. 1984. The Dromedary and Bactrian Camel in Levantine Historical Settings: The Evidence from Tell Jemmeh. In J. Clutton-Brock and C. Grigson, eds., *Animals and Archaeology 3: Early Herders and their Flocks,* 171–200. BAR International Series 202. Oxford.

The kingdom of Sheba

Simpson, J., ed. 2002. *Queen of Sheba: Treasures from Ancient Yemen.* London.

King Hiram of Tyre

Green, A. R. 1983. David's Relations with Hiram: Biblical and Josephan Evidence for Tyrian Chronology. In C. L. Meyers and M. O'Connor, eds., *The Word of the Lord Shall Go Forth,* 373–97. Winona Lake.

Mendels, D. 1998. Hellenistic Writers of the Second Century BCE on the Hiram-Solomon Relationship. In *Identity, Religion and Historiography: Studies in Hellenistic History,* 379–93. Sheffield.

Glueck on Solomon's copper at Ezion-geber

Glueck, N. 1940. The Third Season of Excavation at Tell el-Kheleifeh. *Bulletin of the American Schools of Oriental Research* 79:2–18.

———. 1965. Ezion-geber. *Biblical Archaeologist* 28:70–87.

A reevaluation of the finds from Tell el-Kheleifeh

Pratico, G. D. 1993. *Nelson Glueck's 1938–1940 Excavations at Tell el-Kheleifeh: A Reappraisal.* Atlanta.

The Timna mines—a current view

Rothenberg, B. 1972. *Timna: Valley of the Biblical Copper Mines.* Aylesbury.

The copper mines at Wadi Feinan

Hauptmann, A., and G. Weisgerber. 1992. Periods of Ore Exploitation and Metal Production in the Area of Feinan, Wadi Arabah, Jordan. *Studies in the History and Archaeology of Jordan* 4:61–66.

Knauf, E. A., and C. J. Lenzen. 1987. Edomite Copper Industry. *Studies in the History and Archaeology of Jordan* 3:83–88.

CHAPTER 6. CHALLENGING GOLIATH

The figure of King Manasseh in the Deuteronomistic History

Ben-Zvi, E. 1991. The Account of the Reign of Manasseh in II Reg 21:1–18 and the Redactional History of the Book of Kings. *Zeitschrift für die alttestamentliche Wissenschaft* 103:355–74.

Eynikel, E. 1997. The Portrait of Manasseh and the Deuteronomistic History. In M. Vervene and J. Lust, eds., *Deuteronomy and Deuteronomic Literature,* 233–61. Leuven.

Halpern, B. 1998. Why Manasseh Was Blamed for the Babylonian Exile: The Revolution of a Biblical Tradition. *Vetus Testamentum* 48:473–514.

Schniedewind, W. M. 1991. The Source Citations of Manasseh: King Manasseh in History and Homily. *Vetus Testamentum* 41:450–61.

Van Keulen, P. 1996. *Manasseh Through the Eyes of the Deuteronomists.* Leiden.

The Deuteronomistic History

Cross, F. M. 1973. *Canaanite Myth and Hebrew Epic,* 274–88. Cambridge.

de Pury, A., T. Römer, and J.-D. Macchi, eds. 2000. *Israel Constructs Its History.* Sheffield.

Knoppers, G. N., and J. G. McConville, eds. 2000. *Reconsidering Israel and Judah: Recent Studies on the Deuteronomistic History.* Winona Lake.

McKenzie, S. L., and M. P. Graham, eds. 1994. *The History of Israel's Traditions: The Heritage of Martin Noth.* Sheffield.

Römer, T., ed. 2000. *The Future of the Deuteronomistic History.* Leuven.

Na'aman, N. Forthcoming. *The Past That Shapes the Present.*

Noth, M. 1981. *The Deuteronomistic History.* Sheffield.

King Josiah: the biblical text, history, and messianic expectations

Eynikel, E. 1996. *The Reform of King Josiah and the Composition of the Deuteronomistic History.* Leiden.

Laato, A. 1992. *Josiah and David Redivivus: The Historical Josiah and the Messianic Expectations of Exilic and Postexilic Times.* Stockholm.

Na'aman, N. 1991. The Kingdom of Judah Under Josiah. *Tel Aviv* 18:3–71.

Sweeney, M. 2002. *King Josiah of Judah: The Lost Messiah of Israel.* Oxford.

The geopolitical situation in the late seventh century

Malamat, A. 1988. The Kingdom of Judah Between Egypt and Babylon: A Small State Within a Great Power Confrontation. In W. Classen, ed., *Text and Context,* 117–29. Sheffield.

Redford, D. B. 1992. *Egypt, Canaan and Israel in Ancient Times,* 430–69. Princeton.

Distribution of late-seventh-century Judahite finds and the borders of Judah

Kletter, R. 1999. Pots and Polities: Material Remains of Late Iron Age Judah in Relation to Its Political Borders. *Bulletin of the American Schools of Oriental Research* 314:19–54.

Ekron: excavations, history, the Ekron inscription, and the oil industry

Eitam, D. 1996. The Olive Oil Industry at Tel Miqne-Ekron in the Late Iron Age. In D. Eitam and M. Heltzer, eds., *Olive Oil in Antiquity,* 167–96. Padova.

Gitin, S. 1995. Tel Miqne-Ekron in the 7th Century B.C.E.: The Impact of Economic Innovation and Foreign Cultural Influences on a Neo-Assyrian Vassal City-State. In S. Gitin, ed., *Recent Excavations in Israel: A View to the West,* 61–79. Dubuque.

———. 1996. Tel Miqne-Ekron in the 7th century B.C.: City Plan Development and the Oil Industry. In D. Eitam and M. Heltzer, eds., *Olive Oil in Antiquity,* 219–42. Padova.

Gitin, S., T. Dothan, and J. Naveh. 1997. A Royal Dedicatory Inscription from Ekron. *Israel Exploration Journal* 47:1–16.

Na'aman, N. 2003. Ekron Under the Assyrian and Egyptian Empires. *Bulletin of the American Schools of Oriental Research* 332:81–91.

Naveh, J. 1998. Achish-Ikausu in the Light of the Ekron Dedication. *Bulletin of the American Schools of Oriental Research* 310:35–37.

The Philistines in the Bible

Ehrlich, C. S. 1996. *The Philistines in Transition. A History from ca. 1000–730 B.C.E.* Leiden.

Machinist, P. 2000. Biblical Traditions: The Philistines and Israelite History. In E. Oren, ed., *The Sea Peoples and Their World: A Reassessment*, 53–83. Philadelphia.

Biblical Philistines and later Greek traditions

Finkelstein, I. 2002. The Philistine in the Bible: A Late-Monarchic Perspective. *Journal for the Study of the Old Testament* 27:131–67.
Yadin, A. 2004. Goliath's Armor and Israelite Collective Memory. *Vetus Testamentum* 54:373–95.

The biblical expression "until this day"

Geoghegan, J. C. 2003. "Until this Day" and the Preexilic Redaction of the Deuteronomistic History. *Journal of Biblical Literature* 122:201–27.

Greek arms and warfare

Hansen, V. D., ed. 1991. *Hoplites: The Classical Greek Battle Experience*. London.
Snodgrass, A. M. 1964. *Early Greek Armour and Weapons from the End of the Bronze Age to 600 B.C.* Edinburgh.
———. 1967. *Arms and Armour of the Greeks*. London.

Mesad Hashavyahu

Fantalkin, A. 2001. Mezad Hashavyahu: Its Material Culture and Historical Background. *Tel Aviv* 28:3–165.

The Kittim

Aharoni, Y. 1981. *Arad Inscriptions*, 12–13. Jerusalem.
Dion, P.-E. 1992. Les *KTYM* de Tel Arad: Grecs ou Phéniciens? *Revue Biblique* 99:70–97.
Heltzer, M. 1988. Kition According to the Biblical Prophets and Hebrew Ostraca from Arad. *Report of the Department of Antiquities, Cyprus*, 167–71. Nicosia.

Chapter 7. Patron Saints of the Temple

The Neo-Babylonian period

Lipschits, O. Forthcoming. *The Fall and Rise of Jerusalem—Judah Under Babylonian Rule*. Winona Lake.
Lipschits, O., and J. Blenkinsopp, eds. 2003. *Judah and the Judeans in the Neo-Babylonian Period*. Winona Lake.

Vanderhooft, D. S. 1999. *The Neo-Babylonian Empire and Babylon in the Latter Prophets*. Atlanta.

The Persian period: archaeology and history of Yehud

Berquist, J. L. 1995. *Judaism in Persia's Shadow*. Minneapolis.

Carter, C. E. 1999. *The Emergence of Yehud in the Persian Period*. Sheffield.

Davies, P. R., ed. 1991. *Second Temple Studies 1: The Persian Period*. Sheffield.

Eskenazi, T. C., and K. H. Richards, eds. 1994. *Second Temple Studies 2: Temple and Community in the Persian Period*. Sheffield.

Stern, E. 1982. *Material Culture of the Land of the Bible in the Persian Period, 538–332 B.C.* Warminster.

The Samaritans

Crown, A. D., ed. 1989. *The Samaritans*. Tübingen.

Pummer, R. 1987. *The Samaritans*. Leiden.

Purvis, J. 1968. *The Samaritan Pentateuch and the Origin of the Samaritan Sect*. Cambridge, Mass.

The Samaritan Temple on Mount Gerizim

Stern, E., and Y. Magen. 2002. Archaeological Evidence for the First Stage of the Samaritan Temple on Mount Gerizim. *Israel Exploration Journal* 52:49–57.

Messianic expectations in the exilic period

Collins, J. J. 2003. The Eschatology of Zechariah. In L. L. Grabbe and R. D. Haak, eds., *Knowing the End from the Beginning: The Prophetic, the Apocalyptic and Their Relationships*, 74–84. London.

Meyers, E. M. 1996. Messianism in First and Second Zechariah and the "End" of Biblical Prophecy. In J. E. Coleson and V. H. Matthews, eds., *"Go to the Land I Will Show You": Studies in Honor of Dwight W. Young*, 127–42. Winona Lake.

Rose, W. H. 2000. *Zemah and Zerubbabel*. Sheffield.

The books of Chronicles

Graham, M. P., K. G. Hoglund, and S. L. McKenzie, eds. 1997. *The Chronicler as Historian*. Sheffield.

Graham, M. P., and S. L. McKenzie, eds. 1999. *The Chronicler as Author: Studies in Text and Texture*. Sheffield.

Graham, M. P., S. L. McKenzie, and G. N. Knoppers, eds. 2003. *The Chronicler as Theologian: Essays in Honor of Ralph W. Klein*. Sheffield.

Japhet, S. 1997. *The Ideology of the Book of Chronicles and Its Place in Biblical Thought*. Frankfurt.

Noth, M. 1987. *The Chronicler's History*. Sheffield.

David and Solomon in Chronicles

Abadie, P. 1994. Le fonctionnement symbolique de la figure de David dans l'oeuvre du Chroniste. *Transeuphratène* 7:143–51.

Dillard, R. B. 1984. The Literary Structure of the Chronicler's Solomon. *Journal for the Study of the Old Testament* 30:85–93.

Edelman, D. 2001. Did Saulide-Davidic Rivalry Resurface in Early Persian Yehud? In A. J. Dearman and P. M. Graham, eds., *The Land That I Will Show You: Essays in History and Archaeology of the Ancient Near East in Honour of J. Maxwell Miller*, 69–91. Sheffield.

Knoppers, G. N. 1995. Images of David in Early Judaism: David as Repentant Sinner in Chronicles. *Biblica* 76:449–70.

———. 2003. "The City Yhwh Has Chosen": The Chronicler's Promotion of Jerusalem in the Light of Recent Archaeology. In A. G. Vaughn and A. E. Killebrew, eds., *Jerusalem in Bible and Archaeology: The First Temple Period*, 307–26. Atlanta.

Throntveit, M. A. 1997. The Idealization of Solomon as the Glorification of God in the Chronicler's Royal Speeches and Royal Prayers. In L. K. Handy, ed., *The Age of Solomon: Scholarship at the Turn of the Millennium*, 411–27. Leiden.

Van Seters, J. 1997. The Chronicler's Account of Solomon's Temple-Building: A Continuity Theme. In P. M. Graham, K. G. Hoglund, and S. L. McKenzie, eds., *The Chronicler as Historian*, 283–300. Sheffield.

Williamson, H. G. M. 1991. The Temple in the Books of Chronicles. In W. Horbury, ed., *Templum Amicitiae: Essays on the Second Temple Presented to Ernst Bammel*, 15–31. Sheffield.

Wright, J. W. 1998. The Founding Father: The Structure of the Chronicler's David Narrative. *Journal of Biblical Literature* 117:45–59.

David in the psalms

Cooper, A. M. 1983. The Life and Times of King David According to the Book of Psalms. In R. E. Friedman, ed., *The Poet and the Historian: Essays in Literary and Historical Biblical Criticism*, 117–31. Chico.

Mays, J. L. 1986. The David of the Psalms. *Interpretation* 40:143–55.

CHAPTER 8. MESSIANIC VISIONS

Messianic expectations in the Bible, Second Temple Judaism, and Christianity

Charlesworth, J. H., H. Lichtenberger, and G. S. Oegema, eds. 1998. *Qumran-Messianism*. Tübingen.

Collins, J. J. 1995. *The Scepter and the Star: The Messiahs of the Dead Sea Scrolls and Other Ancient Literature*. New York.

Evans, C. A., and P. W. Flint. 1997. *Eschatology, Messianism and the Dead Sea Scrolls*. Grand Rapids.

Green, D. E. 1980. *Messianic Expectations in the Old Testament*. Philadelphia.

Hess, R. S. and Carroll, M. D., eds. 2003. *Israel's Messiah in the Bible and the Dead Sea Scrolls*. Grand Rapids.

Neusner, J., W. S. Green, and E. S. Frerichs, eds. 1987. *Judaism and Their Messiah at the Turn of the Christian Era*. New York.

Oegema, G. S. 1998. *The Anointed and His People: Messianic Expectations from the Maccabees to Bar Kochba*. Sheffield.

Pompykala, K. E. 1995. *The Davidic Dynasty Tradition in Early Judaism: Its History and Significance for Messianism*. Atlanta.

Reventhrow, H. G., ed. 1997. *Eschatology in the Bible and in Jewish and Christian Tradition*. Sheffield.

The Wisdom of Solomon

Grabbe, L. L. 1997. *Wisdom of Solomon*. Sheffield.

The Psalms of Solomon

Atkinson, K. 2004. *I Cried to the Lord: A Study of the Psalms of Solomon's Historical Background and Social Setting*. Leiden.

Franklyn, P. N. 1987. The Cultic and Pious Climax of Eschatology in the Psalms of Solomon. *Journal for the Study of Judaism in the Persian, Hellenistic and Roman Periods* 18:1–17.

Jonge, M. de. 1991. The Expectation of the Future in the Psalms of Solomon. In *Jewish Eschatology, Early Christian Christology and the Testaments of the Twelve Patriarchs: Collected Essays*, 3–27. Leiden.

Trafton, J. L. 1994. The Psalms of Solomon in Recent Research. *Journal for the Study of the Pseudepigrapha* 12:3–19.

David in the Dead Sea Scrolls

Atkinson, K. 1998. On the Herodian Origin of Militant Davidic Messianism at Qumran: New Light from Psalm of Solomon 17. *Journal of Biblical Literature* 118:435–60.

De Roo, J. C. R. 1999. David's Deeds in the Dead Sea Scrolls. *Dead Sea Discoveries* 6:44–65.

Evans, C. A. 1997. David in the Dead Sea Scrolls. In S. E. Porter and C. A. Evans, eds., *The Scrolls and the Scriptures: Qumran Fifty Years After,* 183–97. Sheffield.

Messianic figures in Roman Judea

Hengel, M. 1989. *The Zealots: Investigations into the Jewish Freedom Movement in the Period from Herod I until 70 A.D.* Edinburgh.

Horsley, R. A. 1992. *Jesus and the Spiral of Violence.* Minneapolis.

Horsley, R. A., and P. S. Hanson. 1985. *Bandits, Prophets, and Messiahs: Popular Movements in the Time of Jesus.* Minneapolis.

Solomon as magician

Torijano, P. A. 2002. *Solomon the Esoteric King: From King to Magus, Development of a Tradition.* Leiden.

The Testament of Solomon

Duling, D. C. 1988. The Testament of Solomon: Retrospect and Prospect. *Journal for the Study of the Pseudepigrapha* 2:87–112.

David and Solomon in the works of Flavius Josephus

Feldman, L. H. 1989. Josephus' Portrait of David. *Hebrew Union College Annual* 60:129–74.

———. 1995. Josephus' Portrait of Solomon. *Hebrew Union College Annual* 66:103–67.

Jesus, David, and Solomon

Bowman, J. 1984–85. Solomon and Jesus. *Abr-Nahrain* 23:1–13.

Charlesworth, J. H. 1997. The Son of David: Solomon and Jesus (Mark 10:47). In P. Borgen and S. Giversen, eds., *The New Testament and Hellenistic Judaism,* 72–87. Peabody.

Chilton, B. 1982. Jesus ben David: Reflections on the Davidssohnfrage. *Journal for the Study of the New Testament* 14:88–112.

Paffenroth, K. 1999. Jesus as Anointed and Healing Son of David in the Gospel of Matthew. *Biblica* 80:547–54.

Smith, S. H. 1996. The Function of the Son of David Tradition in Mark's Gospel. *New Testament Studies* 42:523–39.

David and Solomon in rabbinic literature

Bassler, J. M. 1986. A Man for All Seasons. David in Rabbinic and New Testament Literature. *Interpretation* 40:156–69.

Shimoff, S. R. 1997. The Hellenization of Solomon in Rabbinic Texts. In L. K. Handy, ed., *The Age of Solomon: Scholarship at the Turn of the Millennium,* 457–69. Leiden.

David and Solomon in the literature of the church fathers

Wojcik, J. 1981. Discriminations Against David's Tragedy in Ancient Jewish and Christian Literature. In R.-J. Frontain and J. Wojcik, eds., *The David Myth in Western Literature,* 12–37. West Lafayette.

EPILOGUE. SYMBOLS OF AUTHORITY

David and Solomon in medieval and modern art and literature

Fleminger, J. 2002. *Behind the Eyes of David.* Sussex.

Frontain, R-J., and J. Wojcik, eds. 1981. *The David Myth in Western Literature.* West Lafayette.

Hourihane, C., ed. 2002. *King David in the Index of Christian Art.* Princeton.

ACKNOWLEDGMENTS

In researching and writing this analysis of the David and Solomon tradition in its archaeological and historical context, we owe thanks to many colleagues and friends who offered valuable assistance and welcome advice. Among those who discussed with us special historical problems or reviewed draft chapters, we are especially grateful to Professor Donald Redford of Penn State University, Professor Thomas Römer of the University of Lausanne, Dr. Oded Lipschits and Gidi Yahalom of Tel Aviv University, and Dr. Hanan Eshel of Bar Ilan University.

Our thanks also go to Yuri Smertenko of the Institute of Archaeology, Tel Aviv University for the maps and illustrations that appear in this book.

As always, our agent Carol Mann skillfully guided our concept from the very beginning. Bruce Nichols, our editor at the Free Press for both this book and our earlier book *The Bible Unearthed*, once again offered his unfailingly sage editorial insights and helped us enormously with his equally deft editorial pen.

Our families—Joëlle, Adar, and Sarai Finkelstein and Ellen and Maya Silberman—showed their patience and understanding through months of travel, research, writing, rewriting, and marathon phone calls between Belgium and Israel. We can only hope that the results of our work justify their continuing faith in us.

I.F.
N.A.S.
23 June 2005

INDEX

Page numbers in *italics* refer to illustrations.

Abdi-ashirta, 50
Abdi-Heba, 42–45, 48, 50, 51–52, 58, 69
Abigail, 49
Abijah, King of Judah, 229
Abijam, King of Israel, 101
Abner, 16, 93, 122*n*, 142
Abraham, 9, 244
Absalom, 8, 12, 16, 93, 109, 110, 116, 248, 249–50
Achaemenids, 216
Achilles, 198
Achish, King of Gath, 36, 39, 48, 84, 115, 189, 191–93
Achitophel, 249
"Acts of Solomon, The," 14–16
Acts of the Apostles, 246
Adam, 228
Adonijah, 16, 248
Adullam, cave of, 32, 35
Ahab, King of Judah, 19, 100–101, 103, 113, 115
Aharoni, Yohanan, 285, 287
Ahaz, King of Judah, 19, 126–27, 131, 138, 148, 154
Ahaziah, King of Judah, 105, 113, 265, 266

Akkadian language, 42, 217*n*
Albright, William Foxwell, 291
Alexander the Great, 222, 228, 254
Alyattes, King of Lydia, 199*n*
Amarna letters, 42–46, 48, 50, 51, 69, 80
Amel-Marduk (Evil-merodach), 17
Amenhotep III, Pharaoh, 42
Amenhotep IV (Akhenaten), Pharaoh, 42
Ammon, 107–8
Amnon, 8, 16, 109, 110
Amon, King of Judah, 182, 184
Amos, 39*n*, 166*n*, 190*n*, 291
Amun, temple of, at Karnak, 73, 75, 81, 84, 278
Amurru, 51
Anatolian language, 290
angels, 242
Apiru, 44–46, 50, 51, 52
apocrypha, 235
apologies, 86
Arabia, 8, 77, 131, 167–71
Arad, 285–86
Aramaic language, 128, 137, 234, 235*n*, 264, 295

Aram Damascus, Arameans, 96,
    101, 103, 109, 110, 111–12,
    115–16, 264
"Ark Narrative," 107n
Ark of the Covenant, 7, 61–62,
    107, 138, 205, 224, 267
Armageddon, 207
armor, 1, 196–97
Asa, King of Judah, 101
Ashurbanipal, King of Assyria,
    164, 191
Asia Minor, 219
Assyria, 100, 112, 123–28, 124, 135
    137, 142, 154, 175, 176, 180,
    193, 206, 226–27, 235
  chronicles of, 19, 39, 110, 142,
    186, 263, 264
  disintegration of, 186–87, 203
  horse trading and, 164–68
  imperial expansion of, 123–25,
    164
  Israel under control of, 125,
    136, 164, 186–88, 200–201
  Judah as vassal state of, 125–28,
    187–88, 201
  Judah's failed rebellion against,
    144–49
  Judah's yearly tribute owed to,
    155–56, 172
Assyrian Chronicle, 19, 39, 110,
    142, 186, 263, 264
Athaliah, Queen of Judah, 18, 103,
    105, 106, 113
Athrongaeus, 239
Augustine, Saint, 249
Avigad, Nahman, 129n
Aziru, 50

Baal, 228
Babylonia, 137, 145, 172, 211–12,
    219, 225–26

Cyrus's conquest of, 216
Israelites' exile in, 13, 212,
    293–94
Judah destroyed by, 9, 35n, 207,
    213, 218
Babylonian Chronicle, 19
Balkans, 254
"barbarians," 251
Bassler, Jouette, 247
Bastam, 163
Bathsheba, 106, 116, 223
  Christian metaphorical view of,
    249, 254
  David's seduction of, 8, 10, 93,
    107–8, 248
  midrash on, 248
  as mother of Solomon, 7, 108
  Uriah's death and, 8, 10, 93, 108
Belkin, Lawrence, 165
Benjamin:
  highlands of, 98, 137
  tribe of, 6, 61, 66
Ben Sira (Ecclesiasticus), 235
Bethel, 200–203, 218, 227, 228
Bethlehem, 14, 31, 35, 63, 84, 215,
    218, 245, 246
Bible, see Hebrew Bible; New Tes-
    tament; specific books
biblical minimalism, 261–63, 265
Bilqis, 254
Biran, Avraham, 264–65
Black Obelisk, 115, 125
"Book of the Law" ("Book of the
    Covenant"), 184–85
British Museum, 147
British Royal Engineers, 268
Bronze Age dates:
  Late, 20, 40
  Middle, 95, 271
Broshi, Magen, 135
Bunimovitz, Shlomo, 104

Canaan, *see* Israel, Kingdom of
Cantrell, Deborah, 163, *165*
caravans, 167–71
carbon 14 dating, 280–81
Chalcolithic period, 274, 283
Charlemagne, Emperor, 11, 254
Cherethites, 290–92
Chicago, University of, 163, 275, 277
chiefdoms, dimorphic, 41, 43, 52, 99
Christendom, *see* Europe
Christianity, 10, 231, 234
    David and Solomon story in, 246–47, 249–57
    early literature of, 244
    see also Judeo-Christian tradition
Christian missionaries, 250, 251, 254
Chronicles, First and Second
    books of, 190, 206*n*, 217*n*, 285
    books of Ezra and Nehemiah compared with, 222*n*
    David and Solomon story in, 222–25, 228–30, 233
    Israel redefined in, 228–30
    writing of, 206*n*, 221–22
City of David, 43, 52, 93, 95, 126, 129–31, 145, 170, 171, 220, 236, 245, 269–71, 274
City of God, The (Augustine), 249
Clovis, King of the Franks, 11
Conrad II, Emperor, 254
Constantine, Emperor, 11
Constantinople, 11
Cook, Gila, 264
copper, 77, 174–75, 282–84
"Court (Succession) History":
    dating and historicity of, 93–98,

105–6, 107–12, 116–17, 122–23
    description of, 14–16, 91–93, 122
    as literature, 16
    Omride dynasty and, 101, 106, 112
    political use of, 94, 106–10
courtly ballads, 122
covenant, between God and Israel, 185, 237–38
"creative historiographies," 174*n*
Crete, 290–91
Cross, Frank Moore, 213
Crowfoot, John Winter, 269, 280
cult worship, *see* idolatry
cuneiform inscriptions, 41–42, 115, 128, 137
Cyprus, 198–99
Cyrus the Great, 216–17, 221, 228

Damascus, 112, 126, 127, 265
    see also Aram Damascus, Arameans
daric, 221
Darius, King of Persia, 219, 221
David:
    bandit period of, 7, *30*, 31–32, 35–36, 46–50, 61, 63, 82, 86–87, 106, 121, 156
    Bathsheba seduced by, 8, 10, 93, 107–8, 248
    in Chronicles, 222–25, 230
    as collaborator with Philistines, 8, 36, 46, 48–49, 82, 84, 87, 122, 142, 193, 223
    death of, 15, 54, 93
    first nonbiblical use of name, 265
    flawed character of, 8, 86, 204
    God's choice of, 6, 7, 15, 88, 121, 143–44, 148

David (*continued*)
    God's promise to, 143–44,
        223–25, 237–38
    Goliath and, *see* Goliath
    historicity of, 58–59, 107–10,
        113, 116, 264–74, 281
    Jerusalem conquered by, 7, 14,
        32, 51, 93, 95, 267, 269–70
    Jerusalem court of, 91–117
    kingdom of, 7, 92, 111
    lineage of, 10, 11
    lyre (harp) playing of, 6, 10,
        230, 241, 247
    psalms and ritual music attrib-
        uted to, 230, 234
    rabbinic scholars and, 247–48
    Saul as enemy of, 7, 31–32, 36,
        39, 63, 67, 82, 85, 87, 121,
        122, 156
    Saul succeeded by, 6, 7, 15, 32,
        50, 63, 82, 91–93
    sons of, *see* Absalom; Amnon
    Tomb of, 268, 272
    Tower of, 268
    Uriah's death and, 8, 10, 93,
        108
    wars of, 92, 93, 94, 96, 111–12,
        254
    wives of, 106
David and Solomon story:
    artistic depictions of, 10–12, 66,
        253, 255
    biblical account of, 6–9; *see also*
        "Acts of Solomon, The";
        "Court History"; Deuteron-
        omistic History; "History of
        David's Rise, The"
    biblical minimalism and,
        261–63, 265
    Christianity and, 246–47,
        249–57

    in Chronicles, 222–25, 228–30,
        233
    continued power of, 3, 12, 17,
        22, 59, 207, 212, 231,
        255–57
    dating and historicity of, 15–23,
        32–33, 58–59, 93–98,
        107–10, 116–17, 134,
        138–39, 153–55, 159–62,
        171–73, 175–77, 254,
        255–57, 264–81
    divine favor in, 7–9, 10, 141,
        148
    European adaptation of,
        250–52
    evolution of, 3, 6, 119–207
    exorcisms and, 241–44
    first written version of, 144
    historical minimalism and,
        261–63, 265
    history shaped by, 209–57
    in Islamic tradition, 10, 254
    Judeo-Christian tradition and,
        5–23, 186, 251–52, 256–57
    later sources for, 233–34
    messianic visions and, 237–41
    political uses of, 7, 11–12,
        15–16, 23, 32, 94, 106–10,
        138, 141–44, 149, 162, 171,
        180–82, 189, 191–94, 199,
        203–6, 211, 220, 225, 237,
        256, 292
    rabbinic scholars and, 247–48
    reasons for composition of, 123,
        203
    recovering the history of,
        25–117
    religious uses of, 10, 141, 177,
        183–86, 211–14, 220, 225,
        228–31, 234, 241, 246–47,
        256, 262

royal Hellenistic version of,
234–37, 242
as theology, 230–31
Western Tradition and, 5–23
Davidic dynasty, 59, 101, 148, 203
Athaliah's attempted liquidation
of, 113–14
dating of, 17–20
end of, 105, 180, 207, 211,
217–20
"House of David" inscription
and, 264–66
list of, 18
messianic transformation of,
186, 206–7
Omride dynasty linked to, 103,
105, 113
prophesied revival of, 214–17
Roman extermination of
claimants to, 240–41
tombs of, 95, 271–72
Davies, Philip, 261–62
Dead Sea Scrolls, 237–38, 242
demons, 241–44
Deuteronomistic History, 12–17,
53, 74, 79, 266, 290
anachronisms found in, 193–97
Chronicles compared with,
222–25, 228
compilation of, 13–14, 157*n*,
183–86, 204
dating and historicity of, 15–20,
32–33, 193–94, 263
description of, 13–14, 183–86
earlier and later main strata of,
213–14
historical minimalism and,
261–63
moral of, 183
as political program, 203–6, 211
religious ideology of, 183–86

revision of, 213–14
see also "Acts of Solomon, The";
"Court History"; "History of
David's Rise, The"
Deuteronomy, Book of, 13,
184–85, 193, 203–5, 285
Dibon, 100
dimorphic chiefdoms, 41, 43, 52,
99
Dius, 174*n*
divine right of kings, 255, 256
Dome of the Rock, 171, 172, 268
Domitian, Emperor, 241
Donatello, 11
Dothan, Trude, 191
Dryden, John, 12
Duncan, Garrow, 269

Ecclesiastes, 234
Ecclesiasticus (Ben Sira), 235
Edom, 96, 110, 168, 169
Egypt, 17, 19, 21, 64, 82, 89, 165,
169, 188–90, 206, 216, 219,
278, 290
Assyrian conquest of, 164
biblical lands administered by,
42, 44–45, 47, 51, 69, 83,
187, 190, 197, 199, 203
as Hellenistic kingdom, 212
modern, 42
New Kingdom period of,
74–78, 251, 283
Philistines and, 83–85
Ptolemaic, 235
Sheshonq I campaign and,
71–81, 72, 75
Twenty-second Dynasty of, 72,
73
Twenty-fifth Dynasty of, 145
Twenty-sixth Dynasty of, 187,
193, 199, 292

"Egyptian, the," 239
Ekron, 191–93, 290
Elah Valley, 1
el-Aqsa mosque, 171, 172, 268
11QPsApᵃ (Dead Sea Scroll), 242
Elhanan, 57, 196, 199
Ephraim, 226
Esarhaddon, King of Assyria, 19,
    164, 191
Eucherius, 249
Europe:
    David and Solomon story in,
        250–57
    kings of, 10, 11, 254
    national identities in, 250–51
exorcisms, 241–44
Ezekiel, 171n, 212
Ezekiel, Book of, 171n, 212, 216
Ezra, 217, 219, 221, 222n, 226, 294

Fisher, Clarence, 280
Fitzgerald, Gerald M., 269
Five Books of Moses (Pentateuch),
    13, 227, 248
4Q505 (Dead Sea Scroll), 237–38
Franklin, Norma, 280

Gabriel, 245
Gath, 39–40, 48, 57, 84, 115–16,
    189, 191, 290
Gaza, 168, 169
Geary, Patrick, 250
Genesis, Book of, 167, 190
Geshur, 110
Gezer, 159–60, 275–79
Gilead, 66–67, 68, 80, 111, 162
Gitin, Sy, 191
Glueck, Nelson, 174, 282–83
God:
    commandments received from,
        13

consequences of disobedience
    toward, 183, 228
covenant between Israel and,
    185
David chosen as Saul's successor
    by, 6, 7, 15, 88, 121, 143–44,
    148
David's promise from, 143–44,
    223–25, 237–38
as giver of favor, 7–9, 10, 141,
    148
Israel promised greatness by, 7,
    9, 225, 228
kingship and, 255
Saul chosen as first king of
    Israel by, 6, 62–63, 64
Song of Solomon and, 250
Sophia and, 235
Goliath, 6, 7, 10, 12, 14, 31, 63,
    115, 189, 198
anachronistic Greek armor
    ascribed to, 1, 196–97, 199,
    291
biblical description of David's
    battle with, 1–3, 195–96, 204
Christian metaphorical view of,
    249
conflicting biblical account of
    death of, 2, 56–57, 196
historicity of, 2
name of, 199n
Greece, 21, 235
hoplites from, 197–99
Greek language, 234, 291
Hebrew Bible translated into,
    231, 235
Guy, Philip Langstaffe Orde, 276
Gyges, King of Lydia, 199n, 290

Hadadezer, 112
Haggai, 219, 221, 294

Hagia Sophia church, 11
Halpern, Baruch, 109*n*
Haram el-Sharif, 171
Har Megiddo (Armageddon), 207
Haruz of Jotbah, 170
Harvard University, 280
Hasmonean dynasty (Maccabees),
    235–36, 237, 261
Hazael, King of Aram Damascus,
    39, 101, 113, 115–16,
    264–66
Hazor, 34, 159–61, 275–79
Hebrew Bible:
    authorship of, 3, 12
    in Christian missionary teach-
        ing, 250
    as Christian Old Testament, 10
    dates of composition of, 39,
        206*n*, 231, 244*n*, 261
    Greek translation of, 231, 235
    Hellenistic knowledge of, 174*n*
    historicity and, 73–74, 80–81,
        97
    Homer's influence on, 198–99
    lands of, *34*
    as literature, 16, 22–23, 31, 167,
        261
    minimalist historians and,
        262–63
    rabbinic scholars and, 247–48
    Revised Standard Version of,
        114*n*
    see also Deuteronomistic His-
        tory; *specific books*
Hebrew language, 63, 132, 198,
    234, 263, 289, 295
Hebrews, Apiru and, 44
Hebron, 9, 19, 35, 40, 50, 58,
    91–93, 132, 295
Hegesippus, 241
Hellenistic kingdoms, 212

Hellenistic period:
    David and Solomon story in,
        234–37
    Jerusalem Temple in, 234
Herodotus, 197
Herod the Great, King of Judea,
    240, 272
    death of, 238
    Jerusalem Temple rebuilt by,
        95, 105, 172, 236, 241, 268
    reign of, 236–37
    as symbolic successor to David
        and Solomon, 236–37
Herzog, Zeev, 139, 286
Hezekiah, King of Judah, 19, 131,
    133, 138, 140–42, 144–48,
    154, 159, 162, 172, 180, 200,
    201, 212, 221, 229, 285–88
Hilkiah, 184
Hiram of Tyre, 93, 109, 153, 167,
    173–74, 175, 278
Hirummu, King of Tyre, 173
historical datelines, 26–31, 60–61,
    90–91, 120–21, 150–51,
    178–79, 210–11, 232–33
historical minimalism, 261–63, 265
"History of David's Rise, The,"
    14–16, 238–39
    dating and historicity of, 15, 17,
        37–40, 58, 122–23
    description of, 14
    storytelling tradition and,
        53–59, 82, 88–89, 121–22
Hittite empire, 51
Hobsbawm, Eric, 45
Holy Roman Empire, 11, 254
Homer, 2, 198–99
hoplites, 197–99
horses, 162, 163–67, *165*
"House of David" inscription,
    265–66

idolatry, 71, 74*n*, 181, 185, 221, 228, 285–88
Ikausu, 191–93
Iliad (Homer), 198
Index of Christian Art, The, 253
In Search of Ancient Israel (Davies), 261–62
Ioudaia, 235*n*
Iran, 163
Iron Age dates:
  Early, 35, 40, 51, 67–68
  Late, 70, 95, 135
Isaiah, 133, 155, 166*n*, 214
Isaiah, Book of, 10, 127, 133, 155, 214–15, 216
Ish-bosheth, 16, 62, 66, 81, 93, 122*n*, 142
Islam, 10, 139, 171, 254
Israel, Kingdom of:
  Assyria's control of, *124*, 125–28, 136, 164, 186–88, 200–201
  in Chronicles, 228–30
  covenant between God and, 185
  David proclaimed king of, 7, 14, 32
  Egypt and, 69, 71–81, 72, 75, 82, 83, 89
  emergence of, 21, 96–97, 101, 103
  extent of, 7, *62*, 66–67
  first royal court of, 98–101
  founding of, 3, 13, 89
  God's promise to, 7, 9, 225, 228, 237–38
  Jerusalem as capital of, 14–15, 53, 58, 84–85, 88, 97, 121, 138, 140–41
  kings of, *see* Davidic dynasty; Omride dynasty

  literacy in, 64, 71
  main biblical source for history of, 13
  in ninth century BCE, *102*
  northern highlands of, 17, 19, 62, 66–71, 98–101
  north-south conflict in, 63, 81–85, 101, 135, 180
  population of, 68, 127–28
  Samaria, as capital of, 103, 105, 116, 125, 160
  Samaria, Assyrian province of, as successor to northern kingdom of, 226–27
  Saul anointed first king of, 6, 61–63
  secession of ten northern tribes of, 8–9
  unification of Judah and, 141–44, 159, 162
Israel, modern state of:
  archaeological surveys conducted in, 20–23, 33, 37–40, 59, 67, 94–98, 100, 101, 103–4, 115, 123, 125, 129*n*, 130, 139–40, 146–47, 159–60, *160*, 163, 170, 174, 191–93, 218, 220, 227, 264, 267–74, 273, 275–84
  biblical place-names in, 36, 47, 264
Isser, Stanley, 53–54, 56

Jebusites, 51–52
Jehoahaz (Jehu's son), 115
Jehoahaz, King of Judah (Josiah's son), 207
Jehoash, King of Judah, 39, 116, 172
Jehoiachin, King of Judah, 17, 19, 207, 212, 214, 293
Jehoiada, 114

Jehoram, King of Israel, 103, 105,
265, 266
Jehoshaphat, King of Judah,
101–3, 104
Jehu, King of Israel, 113, 114–15,
125, 266
Jeremiah, 39, 171*n*, 190*n*, 199*n*,
215–16, 218, 294
Jericho, 295
Jeroboam II, King of Israel, 125,
134*n*, 161, 163, 166, 200,
228
Jerusalem, 8, 13, 19, 31, *34*, 35, 40,
67, 69, 73, 103, 105, 230,
262
    Ark of the Covenant brought
    to, 7, 107, 138, 224, 267
    as capital of Israel, 14–15, 53,
    58, 84–85, 88, 97, 121, 138,
    140–41
    as capital of Judea, 236
    City of David in, 43, 52, 93, 95,
    126, 129–31, 145, 170, 171,
    220, 236, 245, 269–71, 274
    David's conquest of, 7, 14, 32,
    51, 93, 95, 267, 269–70
    David's court in, 91–117, 122
    descriptions of, 22, 95–96,
    104–5, 126, 155, 217–21,
    274
    destruction of, 207, 211, 212,
    213, 218
    growth of, 123, 129–38, *130*
    Jesus' entry into, 244
    modern, 129*n*, 267–74
    in Persian period, 217–20, 222,
    226
    revival of, 220–22, 274
    rise of class-conscious aristoc-
    racy in, 107
    Roman destruction of, 240, 247

    Shishak campaign and, 73,
    78–81
    Solomon's construction in, 79
    Temple Mount in, 105, 139
Jerusalem Temple, 148, 200–201,
203, 205, 226
    archaeological inaccessibility of,
    139, 171–72, 268
    Babylonian destruction of, 172,
    207, 213
    "Book of the Law" discovered
    in, 184
    in Chronicles, 223–25, 230, 233
    cult worship in, 8, 185, 221,
    285–88
    first rebuilding of, 217, 219,
    220, 221, 227–28
    in Hellenistic period, 234
    Herod's rebuilding of, 95, 105,
    172, 236, 241, 268
    in independent Judea, 236, 262
    money changers cleared from,
    245
    Peter's speech in, 246
    Pompey's ransacking of, 238
    priests of, 203–4, 221, 222, 224,
    225, 233, 236, 262
    Roman destruction of, 240,
    247
    Solomon's building of, 7, 79,
    138, 141–42, 151, 153,
    171–73, 225, 242, 267
Jesse, 6, 10, 215
    Tree of, 11, 255
Jesus Christ, 249, 251
    crucifixion and resurrection of,
    245
    Davidic lineage of, 10, 11, 244,
    246–47
    entry into Jerusalem of, 244
    healing powers ascribed to, 243

Jesus Christ *(continued)*
  as messiah, 10, 244–47
Jewish Antiquities (Josephus), 243
Jewish War, The (Josephus), 236,
  239
"Jews," origin of term, 223
Joab, 108, 116, 143
  census taken by, *92*, 110–11
Jonathan, 63
Joram, King of Israel, 103, 105,
  113
Jordan River, 13
Joseph, 227, 244
Josephus, Flavius, 174*n*, 227, 236,
  239, 240, 243
Joshua, 221, 225, 227
Joshua, Book of, 13, 39, 183, 193,
  289, 290
Josiah, King of Judah, 13, 157*n*,
  182, *184*, 185–89, 194, 199,
  200–203, 206–7, 211,
  213–14, 229, 285, 286
Judah, 2, 3, 17, *30*, 63, 73, *184*
  as Assyrian vassal state, 123–28,
  124, 144–49, 154–56, 186–89
  Assyria's yearly tribute owed by,
  155–56, 172
  author's use of term, 35*n*
  Babylonian exile and, 13, 212,
  293–94
  Bethel conquered by, 200–203
  David proclaimed king of, 7,
  32, 50
  David's bandit period in, 7, *30*,
  31–32, 35–36, 46–50
  destruction of, 9, 35*n*, 207, 212,
  213, 218
  economic and social revolution
  in, 129–34
  Egyptian administration of, 42,
  44–45, 47, 51

  in eighth century BCE, *124*
  extent of, 42
  in failed rebellion against
  Assyria, 144–49
  Hebrew form of name of, 235*n*
  historical sequence of names of,
  235*n*
  imperial expansion by, 188–89,
  193–94, 203, 231
  King Manasseh's reign in,
  155–62, *158*
  kings of, *see* Davidic dynasty
  literacy in, 53, 64, 86, 94, 123,
  126, 132–34, 153, 263
  in ninth century BCE, *102*
  as Persian province, *see* Yehud
  in realm of Abdi-Heba, 40–44
  refugees from northern highlands in, 134–38, 141,
  142–43, 162
  rise of, 44, 58, 101–6, 128,
  154–59
  Roman period of, *see* Judea
  settlement patterns and population in, 37–40, 41, 52, 68, 80,
  96, 97, 123
  Shishak campaign and, 73,
  79–81
  social banditry in, 44–46, 50,
  51, 52
  split between Israel and, 180
  unification of Israel and,
  141–44, 159, 162
Judaism:
  folk traditions in, 241–42
  Rabbinic, 231, 247–48
  variations of, 234
Judas, 249
Judea, 235–44, 261–62
  exorcisms held in, 241–44
  independence of, 235–36

Jerusalem as capital of, 236
  kings of, 235–37
  messianism in, 237–41
  political upheavals in, 238–41
  Roman rule in, 236–37, 239–41
  Temple's role in, 236
Judean highlands, 35
  location of, *34*
Judeo-Christian tradition, 2–3
  birth of, 207
  David and Solomon story in,
    5–23, 186, 251–52, 256–57
judges, 6, 68
Judges, Book of, 13, 193
Justinian, Emperor, 11

Karnak, 73, 75, 81, 84, 278
Keilah, 47–48, 58
Kenyon, Kathleen, 104, 269, 270
kingdoms, creation of, 99
Kings, First Book of, 6, 8, 9, 13,
    17, 19, 65, 71, 78, 79, 100,
    101, 104, 121, 140, 174, 183,
    193, 200, 222, 229, 230, 245,
    264, 267
  "The Acts of Solomon" in,
    14–16
  "Court (Succession) History"
    in, 14–16, 91, 113–17
  Jerusalem Temple in, 172
  Solomon's reign in, 151–67,
    176, 179–82, 204, 275, 276,
    278
Kings, Second Book of, 13, 17, 39,
    126–28, 133, 137, 138,
    147–48, 170, 181, 183, 185,
    188, 193, 200–201, 206, 214,
    218, 222, 229, 266, 279, 285,
    293–94
kingship, 235, 255, 256
kittim, 198

Knauf, Axel, 106, 107
Koran (Quran), 254
Kush, 164

Labayu, 51, 69, 80
Lachish, 131, 140, 147, 188, 262,
    285
Latin, 234
law code, in Deuteronomy,
    184–85, 205, 285
Lebanon, 154, 173
Lederman, Zvi, 104
Leviticus Rabbah, 248
Lipschits, Oded, 218
literacy, 53, 64, 71, 86, 94, 123,
    126, 132–34, 153, 263
Luke, Gospel of, 245
Luli, King of Sidon, 145

Macalister, Robert Alexander
    Stewart, 269, 276
Maccabees (Hasmonean dynasty),
    235–36, 237, 261
Maccabeus, Judah, 235
McCarter, Kyle, 15–16
Maeir, Aren, 115
Magen, Yitzhak, 228
Manasseh, King of Judah, 19,
    155–62, *158*, 166, 169, 175,
    180–82, 184, 212, 214, 226
Mark, Gospel of, 243
Mary, 244, 245
Masada, 240
Matthew, Gospel of, 244–45
Mazar, Amihai, 96
Mazar, Benjamin, 272
Medes empire, 216
Megiddo, *34*, 96–97, 126, 127,
    154, 159–61, *160*, 163–65,
    165, 187, 206*n*, 211, 262,
    275–80

Menachem, 240
Menahem, King of Israel, 173
Menander of Ephesus, 174n
Mendels, Doron, 174n
Mephibosheth, 110
Mesha inscription, 100–101, 113, 279
Meshullemeth, 170
Mesopotamia, 17, 21, 64, 123, 127, 136, 145, 187
"messiah" (*mashiach*), original meaning of term, 7, 63, 207
messianism:
    Davidic, 186, 206–7
    Jesus and, 10, 244–47
    modernity and, 256
    in Roman period, 237–41
Michal, Queen of Israel, 106, 107
Michelangelo Buonarroti, 11, 255
midrashim, 247–48
Millo, 95, 270
mines, of Solomon, 173–75, 282–84
minimalism, historical, 261–63, 265
Mishnah, 247
missionaries, 250, 251, 254
Mizpah, 218, 295
Moab, 100–101, 111, 113
Moses, 9, 225
    Five Books of (Pentateuch), 13, 227, 248
Mount Gerizim temple, 68, 227–28
Mount of Olives, 239
Mount Zion, 268, 272
Mythic Past, The (Thompson), 262

Na'aman, Nadav, 112, 286–87
Nabal, 49

Nathan, 108
Nations, table of, 167, 190
Naveh, Joseph, 264–65
Near East, *192*
    before the Bible, 262
    empires of, 211–12, 216
    spread of Islam through, 254
Nebuchadnezzar, 19, 254
Necho II, Pharaoh, 197n, 206
Nehemiah, 219, 220, 222, 226, 294
New Testament, 3, 243
Nimrod, 254
Nimrud, 115
Nineveh, 147, 164
North Africa, 254
Noth, Martin, 16

Old Testament, *see* Hebrew Bible
Omri, King of Israel, 100
Omride dynasty, 100–106, 122, 125, 161, 172
    Baal worship by, 228
    as basis of stories about David, 101, 105–6, 112, 281
    dates of, 100
    Davidic dynasty linked to, 103, 105, 113
    end of, 113–14, 116, 279
    historicity of, 100
    kingdom of, 100–101, 103, 111
"Ophel," 269
Ottomans, 11, 268

pagan worship, 8
Palestine Exploration Fund, 268
Peleset people, 189–90, 196
Pelethites, 290–92
pelte, 291
Pentateuch, 13, 248
    Samaritan, 227

Persian empire, 212, 216, 222
  Judah as province of, *see* Yehud
  Samaria as province of, 225–30,
    226
Peter, 246
Philistia, 145, 146, 165, 167, 194
"Philistine Pentapolis," 289, 290
Philistines, 1–2, 6–7, 14, 21, 31,
    32, 39–40, 47, 54, 58, 63, 65,
    76, 80, 89, 96, 186–87, 188,
    189–93, 196
  Ark of the Covenant captured
    by, 61–62
  David's collaboration with, 8,
    36, 46, 48–49, 82, 84, 87,
    122, 142, 193, 223
  Egypt and, 83–85
  end of, 97, 107
  Josiah and, 191–93
  Pelethites and, 291
  Saul defeated by, 82–83, 84
  seranim of, 289–90
  sources of knowledge about,
    189–90
philosopher kings, 235, 242
Phoenicia, 21, 76, 93, 125, 146,
    174
Pompey, 238
pottery types, 135–36, 279–80
Pratico, Garry, 284
Prism of Sennacherib, 146, 148
Proverbs, Book of, 230–31, 234
Psalms, Book of, 249
  ascribed to David, 230–31, 234,
    245
  Jesus as subject of, 249–50
  Psalm 16, 245–46
  Psalm 91, 242
Psalms of Solomon, The, 238
Psammetichus I, Pharaoh, 197–98,
    206

Qarqar, battle of, 19, 100, 112
Qoheleth, 234–35
Quran (Koran), 254

Rabbah, 108
Rabbinic Judaism, 231, 247–48
Rad, Gerhard von, 16
radiocarbon dating, 280–81
Ramesses III, Pharaoh, 189–90, 196
Ramesses IV, Pharaoh, 190
razia, 74
Rehoboam, King of Judah, 19, 71,
    73–74, 101, 278
Reich, Ronnie, 129*n*, 271
Rembrandt van Rijn, 11–12, 66,
    255
Renaissance, 11, 255
resurrection, 245–46
Rezin, King of Damascus, 173
Roman Empire:
  Christianization of, 11
  disintegration of, 250
  see also Judea
Rost, Leonhard, 15–16
Rothenberg, Beno, 282–83
Ruth, Book of, 231

Samaria, city of, *34,* 98–99, 100,
    127, 128*n*, 225–30, 262,
    279–80
  Assyrian destruction of, 127
  as capital of Israel, 103, 105,
    116, 125, 160
Samaria, Persian province of, 136,
    145, 225–30, 226
  papyri found in, 227
Samaritan Pentateuch, 227
"Samaritans," origin of term, 226
Samerina, 127–28
Samuel, Saul anointed by, 6,
    62–63, 66

Samuel, First Book of, 6, 13, 84,
    107*n*, 143, 183, 189, 191,
    193–94, 202, 222, 230, 241,
    289, 290
  Augustine's commentary on, 249
  David's bandit period in, 31–32,
    35–36, 46–50
  David's battle with Goliath in,
    1–3, 57, 195–96, 199, 204
  "The History of David's Rise"
    in, 14, 15, 39, 58, 63, 121
  midrash on, 248
  Saul's story in, 61–66, 83, 85–87
Samuel, Second book of, 8, 13, 14,
    65, 66, 82*n*, 84, 88, 95, 138,
    193, 222, 224, 267, 270, 290
  "Court (Succession) History"
    in, 14–16, 91, 94, 96, 107–12
  Elhanan's killing of Goliath
    mentioned in, 57, 196
  God's promise to David in,
    143–44
  "The History of David's Rise"
    in, 14–16, 54–56
Sanhedrin, 248
Sargon II, King of Assyria, 127–28,
    144, 145, 164, 169, 170
Satan, 249
Saul, 12, 14, 19–20, 61–89, 98, 106,
    107, 134, 137, 142, 143, 191,
    204, 228, 230, 241, 247, 255
  anointed first king of Israelites,
    6, 61–63, 66
  contradictory biblical portrayals
    of, 85–89
  death of, 7, 8, 16, 32, 63, 66,
    82–83, 88, 91, 117, 122, 183
  as enemy of David, 7, 31–32,
    36, 39, 63, 67, 82, 85, 87,
    121, 122, 156
  historicity of, 64–67, 80–81

  kingdom of, 62, 66–70
  madness of, 6, 63, 82
Sea Peoples, 76, 83, 190, 290–91
Sennacherib, King of Assyria, 145,
    146–49, 154, 155, 170, 188,
    286, 288
Sennacherib, Annals of, 19
Septuagint, 235
seranim, 289–90
Shalmaneser III, King of Assyria,
    100, 112, 115, 125
Shalmaneser V, King of Assyria,
    127
Sheba, 167
  location of, 170
  queen of, 7–8, 11, 152–53, 170,
    171, 175, 254
Shebna, 133
Shechem, 51, 69, 136
Shechem temple (Mount Ger-
    izim), 68, 227–28
Shema seal, 125–26
Shephelah, *30, 34*, 35–36, 39,
    42–43, 47, 103, 115, 131,
    135, 140, 147–48, 149, 155,
    162, 188, 191, 193, 194, 199,
    285, 295
Sherdani people, 190*n*
Shield of Solomon (Star of David),
    242
Shiloh, 68, 70, 107*n*
Shiloh, Yigal, 269, 270
Shishak (Pharaoh Sheshonq I), 19,
    71–81, 72, 75, 84, 85, 278,
    280
Shosu, 42, 44
Shukron, Eli, 129*n*, 271
Shuwardata, King of Gath, 43, 48
Sikila people, 190*n*
Siloam water tunnel, 131, 133,
    145, 267, 269

Simon bar Giora, 240
Simon the Hasmonean, 236
Solomon:
 birth of, 108
 character flaws of, 8–9
 in Chronicles, 225
 contradictory biblical portrayals
  of, 179–82
 creation of myth of, 175–77
 David succeeded by, 7, 15, 16,
  79, 94, 109, 121, 142, 179
 death of, 8, 200
 decline of, 183
 esoteric powers ascribed to,
  241–43, 248, 254
 harem of, 8
 historicity of, 65, 153–54,
  159–62, 171–73, 275–81
 horses and, 162, 163–67
 Jerusalem Temple built by, 7,
  79, 138, 141–42, 151, 153,
  171–73, 225, 242, 267
 kingdom of, *152*, 154–55, 159,
  176
 legendary wisdom and riches of,
  7–8, 79, 151–53, 205, 225,
  230, 235, 242–43, 254
 magic ring and Shield of, 242
 mines of, 173–75, 282–84
 rabbinic scholars and, 248
 see also David and Solomon story
Song of Solomon (Song of Songs),
  230–31, 234, 250
Sophia, 235
Star of David (Shield of Solomon),
  242
states, creation of, 99
Steiner, Margreet, 104
Stepped Stone Structure, 269–71
storytelling, 53–59, 82, 88–89,
  106, 121–22, 137, 142

"Succession History," *see* "Court
  History"
*Succession to the Throne of David,
  The* (Rost), 15
Suleiman the Magnificent, 11,
  268
Syria, 100–101, 103, 187, 212
Syriac language, 234

Talmud, 247, 248
Tamar, 109
Tel Aviv, 96
Tel Aviv University, 103–4
Tel Dan inscription, 101, 113, 263,
  264–66, 279
"tell," meaning of term, 269
Tell el-Kheleifeh, 283–84
Tell en-Nasbeh, 218
Tell Qasile, 96–97
Tel Masos, 76–77
Temple Mount, 105, 139, 171,
  236, 268, 272, 273
temples:
 Amun, 73, 75, 81, 84, 278
 Shechem (Mount Gerizim), 68,
  227–28
 see also Jerusalem Temple
"Ten Lost Tribes," 128n
Testament of Solomon, 242
Theudas, 239
Thompson, Thomas, 262
Thucydides, 291
Tiglath-pileser III, King of
  Assyria, 19, 126–27, 128n,
  164, 169, 170, 173
Tigris and Euphrates Valleys, 216
Titus, 240
Tomb of David, 268, 272
Torah (Pentateuch), 13, 227, 248
Torijanos, Pablo, 242
"to this day," 193–94

Tower of David, 268
trade, 77, 83, 99, 104, 124, 125–26,
    131, 154, 162, 167–71, 175,
    180, 193, 205
Transjordan, *34*, 100–101, 103,
    104, 110, 111, 131, 170, 282
Tree of Jesse, 11, 255
Tripoli, 51
Trojan War, 198
"tyrant," derivation of word,
    289–90
Tyre, 173–74

Urartu, 163
Uriah, 8, 10, 93, 108
Ussishkin, David, 103, 105, 147,
    220, 279, 287
Uzziah, King of Judah, 134*n*

Verrocchio, 11
Vespasian, Emperor, 240, 241

Wadi Feinan, 174
Warren, Charles, 268, 271
Warren's shaft, 95, 271
Weill, Raymond, 269, 272

Western (Wailing) Wall, 172
Williamson, Hugh, 222*n*
wisdom literature, 234
Wisdom of Solomon, 235
Wojcik, Jan, 249
Woodhead, John, 279

Yadin, Yigael, 97, 276, 277–80
Yehud, 226, 235*n*, 262, 263
    borders of, 294–95
    description of, 217–20
    dual system of rule in, 221,
        225–26
    exiles' return to, 217, 293–95
    hostility between Samaria and,
        226–30
Yehudim, 223
Yemen, 170

Zadokite priests, 236, 237
Zechariah, 219–20, 244–45, 294
Zephaniah, 39
Zertal, Adam, 136*n*
Zerubbabel, 219, 220, 221
Ziklag, 194
Zion, Mount, 268, 272

ABOUT THE AUTHORS

Israel Finkelstein is a professor of archaeology at Tel Aviv University. He is a leading figure in the archaeology of the Levant and the laureate of the 2005 Dan David Prize in the Past Dimension—Archaeology. Finkelstein served for many years as the Director of the Institute of Archaeology at Tel Aviv University and is the co-Director of the Megiddo Expedition.

Neil Asher Silberman is an author and historian who has published widely on the archaeology of the Near East. He also serves as the director of the Ename Center for Public Archaeology and Heritage Presentation in Belgium, consulting and working on international projects in public interpretation and heritage policy.